Perspectives on Substance Use, Disorders, and Addiction

Second Edition

For Nikolaos Ritsonis
Mon homme

SAGE was founded in 1965 by Sara Miller McCune to support the dissemination of usable knowledge by publishing innovative and high-quality research and teaching content. Today, we publish more than 850 journals, including those of more than 300 learned societies, more than 800 new books per year, and a growing range of library products including archives, data, case studies, reports, and video. SAGE remains majority-owned by our founder, and after Sara's lifetime will become owned by a charitable trust that secures our continued independence.

Los Angeles | London | New Delhi | Singapore | Washington DC

Perspectives on Substance Use, Disorders, and Addiction

With Clinical Cases

Second Edition

Margaret Fetting

University of Southern California

Los Angeles | London | New Delhi
Singapore | Washington DC

Los Angeles | London | New Delhi
Singapore | Washington DC

FOR INFORMATION:

SAGE Publications, Inc.
2455 Teller Road
Thousand Oaks, California 91320
E-mail: order@sagepub.com

SAGE Publications Ltd.
1 Oliver's Yard
55 City Road
London, EC1Y 1SP
United Kingdom

SAGE Publications India Pvt. Ltd.
B 1/I 1 Mohan Cooperative Industrial Area
Mathura Road, New Delhi 110 044
India

SAGE Publications Asia-Pacific Pte. Ltd.
3 Church Street
#10–04 Samsung Hub
Singapore 049483

Acquisitions Editor: Kassie Graves
eLearning Editor: Lucy Berbeo
Editorial Assistant: Carrie Montoya
Production Editor: Bennie Clark Allen
Copy Editor: Talia Greenberg
Typesetter: C&M Digitals (P) Ltd.
Proofreader: Kristin Bergstad
Indexer: Julie Grayson
Cover Designer: Rose Storey
Marketing Manager: Shari Countryman

Printed in the United States of America

Library of Congress Cataloging-in-Publication Data

Fetting, Margaret.
[Perspectives on addiction]
Perspectives on substance use, disorders, and addiction: with clinical cases / Margaret Fetting, University of Southern California.—Second edition.

pages cm
Revision of: Perspectives on addiction / Margaret Fetting. 2012.
Includes bibliographical references and index.

ISBN 978-1-4833-7775-9 (pbk. : alk. paper)

1. Substance abuse. 2. Addicts—Family relationships. 3. Ethnopsychology. I. Title.

HV4998.F48 2016
616.86'06—dc23   2015024098

This book is printed on acid-free paper.

15 16 17 18 19 10 9 8 7 6 5 4 3 2 1

BRIEF CONTENTS

DETAILED CONTENTS

LIST OF FIGURES AND TABLES

PREFACE TO THE SECOND EDITION

I have been teaching, writing, and clinically practicing in the substance use disorders (SUDs) field for nearly 3 decades. I remain endlessly fascinated and intrigued by our individual relationships with alcohol and drugs, including during pleasurable states of intoxication, during destructive states of excess, or during lifetimes of refrain.

My first text, *Perspectives on Addiction* (2012), presented readers with the knowledge base that I developed during my years of teaching graduate students in the School of Social Work at the University of Southern California, as well as other Los Angeles and European universities. Course content included many of the professionally agreed-upon areas of study in the substance use disorders field including sociocultural influences, psychoactives and the brain, models of treatment with brief and long-term interventions, evidence-based treatments, psychopharmacology, and the use of support groups.

My 2012 text emphasized the importance of addressing, assessing, and exploring our unique relationship with substances of pleasure with the help of 12 clinical sketches. I also combined a psychoanalytic attitude and sensibility with the more traditional mindset of the substance use disorders field. Substance use disorders treatment is deepened when a nondirective, reflective analytic perspective and attitude are coupled with the sometimes inflexible and confrontational approaches of traditional recovery treatments. *Perspectives* suggests that the combination of these two clinical styles promotes more engaging treatment.

This second edition of *Perspectives on Substance Use, Disorders, and Addiction* is a philosophical, sociocultural, and clinical text that presents a refreshing blend of ancient and contemporary ideas on the natural pleasures and potential powers of alcohol and drugs in our everyday individual and collective lives. This edition of *Perspectives* emphasizes each person's unique ego syntonic or dystonic relationship with both substances and non-substance-related behaviors of pleasure. Hopefully, these perspectives will help the reader detangle some of the sentimental, overvalued, and misguided ideas that currently muddle the substance use disorders field.

Readers of both books will notice that I have undergone an energetic evolution in my philosophical approach to substance use and its disorders since writing my first edition 6 years ago. At that time, I began living and working in Europe, and this resulted in my developing a broader conceptualization of the place of drinking and drugging in our lives, including more flexible responses to problematic or excessive use.

Other forces influencing my evolution in thinking include the following developing perceptions: that we have overvalued the prevalence of true addiction in this country and undervalued the universal desire to escape reality with alcohol and other drugs (AOD); that we have underappreciated the fact that people will naturally have problems managing something so pleasurable and have oversold the universal prescription of abstinence for all nature of problems; that the DSM-5 spectrum approach to diagnosis introduced a radical shift in our conceptualization of problems with AOD; that, as a culture, we seem to have compulsively adopted the disease model of thinking and are having a hard time accepting and integrating more wide-reaching, inclusive, and flexible approaches; that we have neglected to integrate the thinking and experiences of other parts of the world that have a decidedly different orientation toward alcohol, drugs, pleasure, and excess; and finally, that we have not yet linked the rising rates of addiction with our individual and cultural attempt to self-medicate the disorienting anxieties generated from the impact of our 24-hour globalized world.

Europeans' approach to drinking piqued my curiosity, which led me to study the place of alcohol in ancient Greek culture. What I discovered was enlightening and seemed a particularly useful perspective for challenging some of the rigidity that exists in the field today. In the rough-and-tumble of polemics and politics, we have lost an appreciation of the basic fact that human beings like to escape consciousness and reality with the help of alcohol and other drugs. This desire is benign, not sinister or sinful; nor are its excesses necessarily pathological. Help or assistance with problems can be convivial and, at the same time, exact responsibility for our countenance. A symposium approach to treatment, developed from ancient philosophies as well as the current DSM-5 spectrum, is presented that is based on the "fourth drive," psychoanalytic concepts for deepening the therapeutic relationship, harm reduction, and self-medication.

The impact of globalization on rising addiction rates worldwide has also captured my attention. I began to study the dislocation theory of addiction that proposes that more and more individuals self-medicate to soothe the anxieties, confusions, and frustrations of trying to survive in an interconnected, overstimulating, ever-changing, technology-driven, and global free-market economy. We live in a state of vague ambiguity and seek out compulsive and addictive behaviors to quiet our fears and worries.

The content, tone, and spirit of *Perspectives* invite the reader on an expedition in the substance use and substance disorders field that is exploratory-based, not pathology-based; its focus is philosophical, sociocultural, and clinical, not scientific; it is preventative, not reactive; it is educational, not formulaic; it encourages individual discovery, not predetermined solutions; it leads to well-being, not necessarily to abstinence.

Hopefully, *Perspectives* will serve as a passionate contribution to our contemporary conversations on the philosophically and clinically complex field of substance use, disorders, and addiction.

ACKNOWLEDGMENTS

The solitary nature of writing is dependent on the support of many. Mike Eigen, a psychoanalyst and inspiration, imagines this support as the background presence of an unknown boundless other. Many thanks to these others. What follows are some supporters I know.

I cannot imagine this book being undertaken or completed without the intelligence, work ethic, spirit, participation, and patience of Angie Harwood, my creative assistant and frontline editor. We began working together at USC 6 years ago. We are a formidable team, living in different countries and different time zones, and also with competing needs and interests. Angie has gifted me with her creativity in conceptualization, elaboration, and editing. She is the kind of person we all need: one who is there from day one and there at the end, and by her sheer presence helping to keep all afloat the days in between.

I also deeply appreciate Ed Khantzian for his original and courageous contributions to the substance use disorders field. He is a dedicated leader and a very generous and kind professional. His gracious support of my work continues to inspire and humble me at the same time. The field is forever indebted to his body of work.

I am continually moved and inspired by the creative thinking and original capturing of human experience in the work of psychoanalyst Mike Eigen. I thank him for his generous support of my efforts in bringing a psychoanalytic attitude to the substance use disorders field.

I am also deeply appreciative of the kind support of Andrew Tatarsky. His contribution to our field is truly groundbreaking.

I also deeply value the courageous and spirited work and support of journalist and author Gabrielle Glaser and the creative clinical work of Carrie Wilkens.

I deeply appreciate the Los Angeles Institute and Society for Psychoanalytic Studies and Deree College in Athens, Greece, for inviting me to serve on their faculty and also supporting my efforts to bring psychoanalytic concepts into addiction treatment.

Linda Sobelman has kept my mind and heart afloat. Dominique Robertson, my dear friend, stayed close and once again provided encouraging comments on my manuscript. I'm deeply grateful for the ongoing support of my esteemed USC colleagues Doni Whitsett and Wendy Smith.

Once again, I am blessed with the editorial grace and wisdom of Kassie Graves, associate director and publisher, College Editorial, SAGE Publications. She is a joy.

The support of my sister-in-law, Alexandra Ritsonis, is deeply meaningful. She is the reader all writers dream of—she read every word of the first edition of *Perspectives*, and she also graced me with many warm and enlivening conversations.

I am grateful for the support of my family on the East Coast, including Mark Fetting, Lacy Fetting, Ann Lacy Bollinger, Brandon Bollinger, and Joseph J. Lacy, Sr.

I am profoundly moved by the courage of each of my patients.

My husband, Nikolaos Ritsonis, has been in my court and by my side like no other person in my life.

SAGE Publications gratefully acknowledges the following reviewers: Christopher K. Budnick, North Carolina State University; Jo Cohen Hamilton, Kutztown University; Dov B. Finman, Adelphi University; Jason D. Florin, College of DuPage; Dian Jordan, University of Texas of the Permian Basin; Todd F. Lewis, University of North Carolina; Sue Burdett Robinson, Hardin-Simmons University; Chris Rybak, Bradley University; and Robert Scholz, Pepperdine University.

ABOUT THE AUTHOR

Margaret Fetting, PhD, has been teaching substance use disorders in southern California for over 25 years. She currently lives and works in Europe and the United States, and studies and observes drinking attitudes and behavioral patterns from a global perspective. Fetting has been primarily affiliated with the School of Social Work at the University of Southern California, and is a regular guest lecturer at the Los Angeles Institute and Society for Psychoanalytic Studies and visiting faculty for the American College of Greece in Athens.

Fetting has created and conducted hundreds of local, national, and international workshops on addictions of all natures. She has been a keynote speaker at national conferences, including the Harvard Addiction Conference and in Learning from the Masters at Deree College in Athens, Greece. She has consulted with USC's men's and women's athletic teams in the area of addiction, both with substances and eating disorders. She speaks at high schools and colleges as well.

Fetting has been in clinical private practice for over 25 years in Santa Monica, where she specializes in the treatment of addiction for individuals, couples, and families. She is affiliated with Clearview Treatment Programs and Milestones Ranch, both nationally respected and multileveled treatment facilities in Southern California. She regularly writes in the field and published the first edition of her text *Perspectives on Addiction* in 2012 with SAGE Publications.

Fetting attended Rosemont College and received her baccalaureate degree from George Washington University and her master's and doctorate from the University of Pennsylvania.

INTRODUCTION

Many of us like the experience of being intoxicated, and that desire creates enjoyments for most, problems for some, and devastation for a few. *Perspectives on Substance Use, Disorders, and Addiction* philosophically and clinically explores these ancient desires and proposes a treatment approach for these human troubles.

Perspectives also covers the key content necessary for developing a comprehensive grasp of a complex body of knowledge that is filled with certainties and uncertainties, science and speculation, dogma and theory, as well as opinion and silence. *Perspectives* provides students and clinicians, individuals with a substance use disorder, and their families with a reflective understanding of a confusing body of knowledge and invites a probing and curious mindset. It provides some passionate perspectives for you to consider.

Substance use, disorders, and addiction touch us all. *Perspectives* is written and designed to have a personal, professional, educational, and treatment impact. Content is delivered with discipline and rigor, creativity and imagination, brevity as well as elaboration. Hopefully the reader will develop a novel appreciation for a human desire that pleasures, confounds, and destroys.

OUTLINE OF THE BOOK

This book is divided into four progressive parts composed of 14 chapters that were developed from 25 years of teaching semester-long graduate courses in substance dependence and abuse in the School of Social Work at the University of Southern California and other universities in Los Angeles and in Europe. These chapters build on each other and are designed to become the building blocks of your own knowledge base. The content area covered, moving from bottom to top, is diagrammed in Figure I.1.

The preface, this introduction, and the chapters in Part I ask the reader to participate in a journey of learning and reflection. The personal and professional knowledge base developed in Part I becomes your philosophical and cultural anchor for future learning and also for future professional development in this field.

Part I presents the philosophies of *Perspectives*, first highlighting those that have been informed by ancient ideas and globalized stresses. Readers are then invited to consider the influences of their own cultures. Key concepts and ideas are also presented. A reflective investment seems a necessary prerequisite for mastery of a sometimes complex, contradictory, and complicated field. A personally involved reader grasps, challenges, and retains knowledge from a deep and meaningful perspective.

Figure I.1 Progressive Knowledge Base

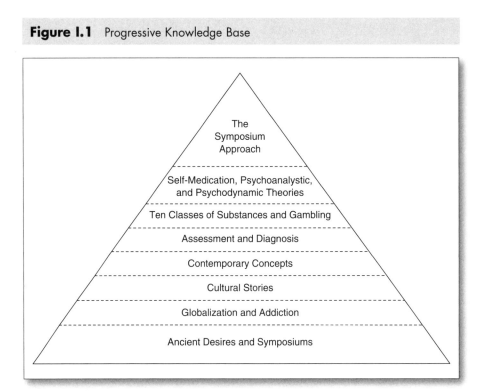

Part II and Part III present a cogent yet comprehensive overview of most of the essential elements of the substance use disorders field. One of the most important contributions of *Perspectives* is Chapter 6, which is on assessment and diagnosis. Coupling the new *Diagnostic and Statistical Manual of Mental Disorders* (DSM-5) spectrum with unique clinical sketches prepares the reader to creatively and thoughtfully engage in collaborative discussions with patients or clients about the nature of their relationship with the substance, as well as their concerns and treatment ideas. Ten classes of substances and the non-substance-related addiction, gambling, are presented with 11 easy-to-access reference charts. Part III looks at the suffering behind substance use, disorders, and addiction and presents the reader with nine self-medication theories.

Part IV includes another key feature of *Perspectives*, the adoption and integration of the ancient Greek symposium as a convivial and exacting learning environment for better management of drinking and its excesses. Five chapters present detailed case studies, organized by combining the DSM-5 spectrum with clinical sketches, and utilizing the application of the four guiding principles of the symposium as analytic treatment concepts for these cases.

CHAPTERS

Chapter 1 is a very short but important chapter for the reader. It clearly presents my orientation in writing this book for the substance use disorders field. Most importantly, it provides the reader with the seven unifying themes of *Perspectives*.

Chapter 2 explores our ancient and natural desire to seek "spirited release" with alcohol or drugs, as well as the necessity for education about the management of these sometimes potent pleasures. The philosophies and practices of the ancient Greek symposiums are presented as an approach to engage the individual in a convivial educational atmosphere that invites participants to learn to drink better or decide to abstain.

Chapter 3 presents the new dislocation theory of addiction that passionately stresses that we link increased alcohol or other drug use with the increasing isolation, confusion, stress, and overwhelming pressure from living in a globalized world. The phrase "global weightlessness" is introduced. This chapter identifies and highlights some of these insidious global impacts and provides case examples of how we sadly soothe ourselves with addictive and compulsive processes.

Chapter 4 considers the importance of our cultural influences in our thinking about substance use. The depth of these influences is often overlooked. Our identified cultural backgrounds, including extended families, parents, siblings, and the surrounding communities, are likely to influence our relationships with alcohol and drugs, starting at a very young age. Readers are asked to reflect on the influences of their own cultural identity with the help of the stories from many of my students from all over the world who pondered the same.

Chapter 5 provides the reader with concepts rather than definitions of some key ideas in the substance use disorders field. Philosophical questions are posed about this international pastime, and the frequency of our participations and indulgences. The concepts presented are designed for thinking, questioning, and conversing between students and teachers, clinicians and patients, families and friends.

Chapter 6 is designed to provide a useful, engaging, creative, and lively understanding and application of the new DSM-5 substance use disorders spectrum during assessment and treatment. This chapter is designed to help the reader transition from the decades-long use of the terms *abuse* and *dependence*, which are now deleted, to the adoption of the DSM-5 substance use disorders spectrum. Gambling as a non-substance-related disorder is included in DSM-5. The key feature of this chapter is its emphasis on individuals and their relationship with the desire for pleasure through intoxication. Fifteen clinical sketches are included for adults and youth as a way to help individuals determine their own unique patterns of desire, use, and problems, as well as their inclinations and preferences for treatment. Brief case studies are explored to enhance application of these sketches.

Chapter 7 provides the reader with an overview of 10 classes of substances, known and unknown, as well as the newly included non-substance-related disorder, gambling. Basic neuroscience, research chemicals, medication in substance use disorder treatment, gambling, and 11 easy-to-use reference charts are included. Ongoing further study is recommended.

Chapter 8 presents nine unique, yet overlapping, self-medication theories that propose that untreated human psychological suffering drives some people to self-medicate their pain or discomfort with alcohol and other drugs. Each theory presented provides the reader with an insightful and useful perspective on what might cause this suffering. Brief clinical applications are included.

Chapter 9 presents a use, prevention, education, and treatment approach adapted from the ancient Greek symposium. This ancient gymnasium provided early Greeks with a forum for learning to "tipple wisely" with wine, which the Greeks considered a gift to humanity, or decide to abstain if one's "heavy mind" leads to uncontrollable excess. The four guiding principles of the symposium approach include the unstoppable fourth drive, registering impacts, harm reduction, and self-medication. These are presented as clinical concepts to be used during treatment.

Chapters 10 through 14 provide an application of the four guiding principles of the symposium approach to clinical case studies from my private practice. The new DSM-5 spectrum coupled with 15 descriptive sketches will help provide a full clinical picture for the practitioner. Using both will provide the reader with a rich perspective for establishing and working in a collaborative therapeutic relationship.

VOCABULARY CLARIFICATIONS FOR READING

The addiction field struggles with language and precision. Therefore, I have included this section to ensure that readers understand the vocabulary choices of *Perspectives*. Please bear in mind that I have made every effort to abide by these vocabulary decisions in *Perspectives*, and please excuse any mishaps.

- The words *abuse* and *dependence* have been deleted from DSM-5. Every effort has been made to ensure that these words will only appear in *Perspectives* when citing someone's work.
- DSM-5 advises individual discretion on the adoption of the word *addiction*. The word *addiction* is used in this book. I have adopted it to refer to the approximately 3% of the U.S. population that the 2014 Centers for Disease Control study identifies as truly psychologically and physically dependent individuals. *Perspectives* considers that addiction follows severe substance use disorder on the DSM-5 spectrum.
- *AOD* stands for alcohol and other drugs.
- *SUD(s)* stands for substance use disorder(s).
- *P/SUD* identifies a person with a mild, moderate, or severe substance use disorder. *P/SUD* is often used to include a person with an addiction as well.
- *Person with an addiction* is the term I have used to identify individuals who suffer from true addiction. This expression replaces the formerly used terms *alcoholic* and *addict*.
- Readers, students, and individuals in general are referred to as "he."
- A patient, P/SUD, or person with an addiction is referred to as "he."
- Treatment providers, clinicians, and sponsors are referred to as "she."
- An italicized word in the text emphasizes the importance of the content.

CHAPTER 1

PHILOSOPHICAL CORE

INTRODUCTION

Perspectives on Substance Use, Disorders, and Addiction, Second Edition, is a philosophical, sociocultural, and clinical text that suggests innovative ideas, replacing some overused ideas with some fresh ones. While *Perspectives* will cover the key content of the traditional substance use disorders (SUDs) knowledge base, it is a primary or secondary text meant to open your heart and jostle your mind about some new ways to think about relationships, enjoyments, and troubles with substances of pleasure.

Perspectives departs from much of the 80 years of conventional and sometimes mandatory ideology that has shaped the addiction field, including many of its philosophies, interventions, and treatment suggestions. *Perspectives* joins hands with leaders in the fields who have contributed ideas that also challenge the mainstream consensus. Many core concepts of this text build upon the work of Ed Khantzian and his self-medication hypothesis, Andrew Tatarsky and harm reduction, Bruce Alexander and dislocation theory, Ron Siegel and the *fourth drive*, Herb Fingarette and his ideas about heavy drinking, Karen Walant and her work on attachment, Lance Dodes and his work on the nature of true addiction, Marc Kern, Iain Gately, Fritz Allhoff, and Tom Hovarth, and, of course, the influences of the seminal work of Stephanie Brown. Also very helpful in communicating the messages to the masses are print journalists and authors Anne Fletcher and Gabrielle Glaser. I am deeply committed to a psychoanalytic attitude, and have also included the work of Mike Eigen, John Steiner, Adam Phillips, Christopher Bollas, and Nina Coltart. Their analytic eyes help us see the deeper dimensions of the human being who tries to survive in the symptomatic world of addiction and compulsion.

Perspectives has passionately blended these contributions together in hopes that the reader will feel stimulated, energized, and encouraged, both personally and professionally.

PHILOSOPHICAL CORE

Perspectives is thematically united around seven philosophical and clinical ideas that are further developed in each of the 14 chapters in this book. These include:

- **The desire for enjoyment and relief through alcohol and drugs is an ancient and natural part of the human experience.** The ancient philosophers considered wine to be a gift to humanity, and contemporary theorists refer to our need for intoxication as the "fourth drive" behind hunger, thirst, and sex. *See Chapters 2, 9–14*

- **A nonpathological framework for the exploration and assessment of an individual's healthy and unhealthy relationships with the intoxicants is advised.** Fifteen clinical sketches matched with the *Diagnostic and Statistical Manual of Mental Disorders'* (DSM-5's) spectrum are presented as a discovery tool for the patient to explore who he is, rather than defend who he is not. *See Chapters 6, 9–14*

- **An ever-awake globalized world with its increased communications and demands for mastery of technology has destabilized our individual and societal equilibrium and contributes to rising worldwide addiction rates. A sense of not being anchored in the familiar produces the disorienting feeling of "global weightlessness."** The biggest risk factors in addiction today are societal and cultural, not genetic or biological. *See Chapters 3, 9–14*

- **Approximately 30% of the U.S. population meets the definition of excessive drinking. However, a very small number (approximately 3%) of the total U.S. population suffers with true physical and psychological addiction (Esser et al., 2014). Problem users deserve modern-day preventative and educational symposiums. Those who suffer with addiction deserve more extensive outpatient or inpatient care.** Using the symposium approach presented, the individual learns to "tipple wisely," or accept the advice of Hippocrates, the father of Western medicine: "Should a patient be suffering from an overpowering heaviness of the brain [mind], then there must be total abstinence from wine" (Gately, 2008, p. 13). *See Chapters 6, 9–14*

- **Harm reduction is the collaborative treatment approach that rejects abstinence as the best or only acceptable goal for alcohol and drug users.** This dynamic, behavioral, and cognitive approach encourages users to discover their own ideal plan toward health, whether it be moderation or discontinued use. *See Chapters 6, 9–14*

- Self-medication theories identify the psychological suffering that seeks relief in a mild, moderate, or severe substance use disorder (SUD) or addiction. Treatment with these clinical theories encourages self-reflection and self-care as a way to avoid self-medication. *See Chapters 8, 9–14*
- **Contemporary psychoanalytic concepts deepen the therapeutic relationship.** Registering impacts, awareness of psychic retreats, and waiting in faith helps contain relational anxieties, open up psychic space for the individual, and deepen the bond between patient and clinician. *See Chapters 8–14*

CHAPTER 2

ANCIENT DESIRES AND SYMPOSIUMS

INTRODUCTION

This chapter explores in greater detail one of the philosophical cores found in Chapter 1, specifically, "the desire for enjoyment and relief through alcohol and drugs is an ancient and natural part of the human experience." This ancient and benign orientation toward drinking has confirmed and supported my developing perceptions that, in America particularly, we have exaggerated the nature and the prevalence of true addiction. We have much to learn from these early attitudes about the natural place of alcohol and other drugs (AOD) in our lives. These attitudes may help us develop more realistic responses for individuals concerned about their drinking and drugging habits.

ANCIENT DESIRES AND SYMPOSIUMS

As long as I can remember, I have been passionately curious about our ancient desire for relief, relaxation, as well as escape from human discomfort with alcohol and other drugs. During the last 2.5 decades of clinically practicing, teaching, and writing in the substance use disorders field, I have become equally intrigued by our disregard of history, specifically our ancient civilizations' appreciation of the human necessity for a "spirited" release, as well as the human necessity for education on the management of these potent pleasures. Reconnecting to our earliest appreciations and concerns about the elixirs may make room for a perspective that allows us to step away from our obsession with searching for pathology in our AOD habits.

Perspectives first asks readers to return to the ancient Greek days of the fifth and fourth centuries BCE, when Greek philosophers such as Socrates, Plato, and Aristotle laid the foundations for what would become Western culture, and where the young and inexperienced learned about the pleasures and disciplines of drinking in the convivial and educational environment called the *symposium*. This word means "drinking together," but also implies a specific form of communal drinking that forges bonds around drinking's shared pleasures and escapades, and allows neighbors to discover each other's opinions on subjects from the serious to the banal (Lynch, 2007, p. 247). Plato said that the proper forum for young adults to learn to "tipple wisely" was in this gymnasium, a formal but hospitable drinking party with precise etiquette and an abundance of strict rules about the number of guests, the ratio of water to wine, and how to set a limit on the quantity to be consumed (Gately, 2008, p. 14).

Drinking alcohol was seen as ordinary, natural, safer than water, and a right belonging to each individual. The Greeks considered wine to be a gift to humanity, having great potential powers including pleasure, chaos, and madness (Allhoff, 2007, p. 25). The symposium was considered the appropriate place for exploiting the pleasures of wine while minimizing the risks. Philosophers in the symposium led discussions designed for exploring the individual's "felt sense" of his values, ethics, and responsibilities about his drinking patterns and habits. A major topic of Greek ethics was pleasure, and early Greeks were careful to separate enjoyment from indulgence (Gately, 2008, pp. 15–25).

Let us take a stroll through more of the ancient vocabulary used in and around the symposiums. *Ordinary passions* were referred to as healthy devotions, habits, or preoccupations that took place in ordinary societies, families, or communities of people. The Greek word for the drinker, *philopotes*—literally, a "lover of drinking sessions"—bore no stigma. As drinking was an inherently pleasurable activity, it was understandable that people would want to indulge in it as much as possible, and those who succumbed too often did not do so out of dependency, but rather from an inability to resist an entirely natural impulse. They were considered weak, not wrong (Gately, 2008, p. 15).

Philopotes—or, likely, today's conceptualization of misusing or problem drinkers—were encouraged to harness this natural power through gentle drinking, always mixing their nectar with water; taking a break or temporary temperance; adhering to the rules of moderation; using wine to facilitate one's goals, not hinder them; and avoiding intoxication, particularly when suffering from yesterday's hangover! The symposiums considered that the consumption of unmixed wine was not only uncivilized, but also perilous (Gately, 2008, pp. 14–15).

Philosophers of the symposiums believed that the philosophical doctrine of temperance promoted healthy drinking habits. These ancient philosophers bequeath an important caveat to our contemporary treatment providers:

"Deciding what constitutes temperate or moderate drinking for any particular individual, however, is a fact-intensive and individualized inquiry that depends on a number of complex factors" (Allhoff, 2007, pp. 76–77). For Plato, temperance meant subordinating the desire for pleasure to the dictates of reason, using will and discipline to avoid overindulgence and indiscriminate drinking. The doctrine of temperance is closely related to the concept of balance. Balance occurs naturally when an individual is interested in other things besides intoxication. It is the stable state between the extremes of overindulgence and abstinence (Allhoff, 2007, pp. 1–65). *No wars were waged during these early drinking days—neither a war on drugs nor a war on human desire.*

Early philosophers and playwrights concluded that wine should never be something that is thrown out unthinkingly because of its dangers; rather, it should be used for the better, like any other power (Euripides, 1960). "Using anything for the better requires expertise, both a general grasp of social ethics and a more technical expertise relating to the thing being used" (Allhoff, 2007, pp. 27–28).

Socrates used the term *master passions* to refer to unhealthy devotions that involved ongoing and destructive use in excess. A person under the tyranny of his passions is one who is consumed with wine and its abundance. The loss of dignity, respect, and love; the loss of work and income; and the loss of psychological and physical health are some of the devastating repercussions that follow. The life of a person ruled by a master passion is a life in ruins. These descriptions are likely similar to the 2014 Centers for Disease Control and Prevention study that found that 30% of the population were excessive drinkers, and approximately 3% of the population were truly dependent on alcohol (CDC, 2014).

People of master passions seemed unable to benefit from the ancient symposiums' cautions, behavioral suggestions, and wisdoms. These lovers of drinking were not able to achieve temperance. Were they slaves of impulsivity, characterologically weak, captured by a lifestyle, or devoted to sensual pleasures? As we recall, Hippocrates, the father of Western medicine, decisively responded to this question: "Should a patient be suffering from an overpowering heaviness of the brain [mind], then 'there must be total abstinence from wine'" (Gately, 2008, p. 13).

Hippocrates's early and simple admonition for abstinence for the small number of heavy-minded drinkers has much to teach us today about the unique, distinctive, and highly idiosyncratic selection of abstinence as a way of life. His words suggest that some of us may need abstinence, not because of an uncontrollable disease or brain disorder, but because of unbearable, nameless suffering in a human mind that will never be satisfactorily soothed by drink. These individuals live with an unquenchable thirst in search of relief. Once the elixirs touch their tongues, their thirst can only uncontrollably demand more.

Just a handful of "symposiums" (treatment centers) currently exist across the country that embrace the philosophies, concepts, and vocabularies of these early symposium days. They educate with temperance tools for drink, and leave the decision about moderate drinking or abstinence to the individual. We need more than a handful of symposiums to get closer to our nature and also support our intuitive desire to regulate ourselves if helped.

CHAPTER SUMMARY AND REFLECTIONS

Summary

This chapter introduced readers to the ancient appreciations of alcohol and excess. Symposiums encouraged individuals to develop a sound ethic and sense of responsibility for this pleasure, to learn to tipple wisely, or to follow Hippocrates's advice on abstinence for those ruled by master passions.

Reflections

Consider the following questions in a classroom discussion or paper:

- Do you think the notion of symposiums could be utilized today?
- Have you encountered a symposium approach in your community?
- If not, how could a symposium be used in your community?
- How could the term *tipple wisely* be applicable for treating SUDs?
- What are your comments on Hippocrates's considerations of abstinence?

CHAPTER 3

GLOBALIZATION AND ADDICTION

INTRODUCTION

As early as 9000 BCE, it seems that humans have always made a special place for alcohol and drugs in their culture, whether as a food, an intoxicant, a medicine, or a status symbol. In addition, it appears that the use of alcohol was regulated by social norms and the customs of ritual, whether used for nutrition or celebration. Iain Gately, in his exhaustive historical study from ancient times to the modern day, *Drink* (2008), paints a picture of more temperate and moderate drinking habits occurring in stable families, communities, and societies. Turbulent times and more excessive drinking patterns seem to go hand in hand. Simply put, cultures of balance and cultures of intoxication have existed throughout history (Gately, 2008, pp. 1–25). This chapter looks at some of the social forces from ancient times to modern globalization that have shaped the way we think, imbibe, wonder, and worry about our uses of AOD.

For decades, my semester courses have always included a section about sociocultural influences on our relationships with AOD, but have primarily focused on American culture. In the last 6 years, I have lived, clinically practiced, and taught in Europe as well as in America. I have been impressed with the variances in substance use attitudes and patterns in these two continents, as well as over the world. As a result, my perspectives on use and addiction have become more global. I have searched for a sociocultural theory on addiction that takes into account the impact of the increase in connectivity in our e-civilized economy and world, and its contribution to rising addiction rates (Technology Management, 1998, p. 1).

The concept of *globalization* is often not really understood. The media use the word regularly, despite the fact that many of us are not quite sure what it means or how it really influences our emotional state throughout our day. It signals unlimited opportunity for many; confusion for some; hopelessness, fear for survival, and destruction for others. Here is one conceptualization of globalization that can help you get started:

> The concept of globalization challenges all of us, whether it knowingly touches our lives or whether we have not given it any thought at all. It generally stands for increased communication and interconnectedness; something on a bigger scope than local; accomplishing things easier, cheaper and quicker; reducing trade barriers and growth; many different ways to do things, all of which are valid in their own right; and ultimately, its meaning depends on your point of view. (Technology Management, 1998, p. 1)

Canadian psychologist Bruce Alexander's work on the dislocation theory of addiction is unique largely because he takes into account our globalized world and economy, its demanding pace and technological frustrations. The globalization or mixing of so many diverse economies, histories, and unique cultures is potentially stimulating and exciting, but it is also confusing and destabilizing. We feel overwhelmed, frustrated, rushed, and out of balance; a sense of not feeling anchored becomes the norm. We often seek pseudo-relief and equilibrium with the excessive use of substances or compulsive processes to soothe this feeling of "global weightlessness" (Ed. Ireland & Proulx, 2004). We may seek comfort in AOD, binging or starving, shopping, gaming, texting, sexting exercising, working, traveling, accumulating wealth and power, and innumerable other habits and pursuits. Alexander refers to excessive and compulsive use of any substance or process as an "addiction."

For example, as a USC professor, I have taught classes in a virtual academic environment, inviting students in my classrooms from different states, cultures, and countries, all in different time zones and speaking different languages. While the technology inspires awe, it was not constructed by me or even the IT personnel in my department, but rather by an international corporation specializing in educational technology. Consequently, it took me a couple of years to grasp and also become skillful and appreciative of all its technological resources. It took trial, error, and time to create cohesion in the classroom.

The anticipatory anxieties, the ongoing stresses of technology glitches, and the struggles to maintain virtual eye-to-eye contact seem to have rather regularly worn out both myself and my students. A student shared with me, "It is great to learn online while being at home, but I have noticed that it has increased, not decreased, my stress level. There are so many frustrations, including being dropped from the classroom, losing audio, and not being able to open and view videos required for classroom preparation. We have less holidays than students 'on the ground,' and we miss so much of the campus experience. I've gained 15 pounds, drink too much, and smoke too much weed. Being at home, around the kitchen, my home bar, and my dealer has not helped me."

The remainder of this chapter will present the key concepts of Alexander's historical and global perspective on addiction. This theory considers the biggest risk factors in addiction as societal and cultural, not genetic or biological. This school of thought provides a societal framework for looking at the impact of globalization with its ruptures on everyday familiarities, routines, and rituals, as well as the expectation that one must master all of technology's advances for fear of being left behind. My intention is to encourage readers to open their minds to the emotional toll of these impacts and notice our attempts to seek relief with an increasing reliance on addictive behaviors for soothing our disorientations and frustrations. I have included sections on daily impacts, everyday stories, and clinical case studies as examples of different types of dislocation and different types of self-medication with AOD. The essence of Alexander's theory is described below:

> Dislocation theory does not view addiction as either a medical disease or moral failure. Rather, it depicts widespread addiction as a way of adapting to the increasingly dominant and onerous aspects of the modern world [the urgent adaptations required to survive in new and foreign locations, the barrage of media communications, and demands for technological mastery]. (Alexander, 2011, p. 125)

KEY WORDS: *DIKAIOSUNÊ*, PSYCHOSOCIAL INTEGRATION, AND DISLOCATION

But first, let us stroll through some ancient vocabulary as we become accustomed to this theory and its origin in ancient times. The Greek word *dikaiosunê,* as Socrates defines it in Plato's *The Republic,* is captured in the everyday English term *psychosocial integration*—or, as I say, living with a sense of belonging to a family or group and feeling a sense of significance or importance in life. *Dikaiosunê* is considered the essential outcome of living within a relatively cohesive family, community, or society. This provides feelings of human contentment and also offers a shield against domination by master passions or addictions (Alexander, 2014).

Living with a sense of belonging and significance fosters emotional stability in relationships and work, a healthy reliance on others, feelings of being part of something greater than the self, and a life of moderation and balance. People exude a sense of vitality when they live with a sense of belonging and feelings of significance. They feel emotionally cradled by their families, social network, community, and surroundings. This welling of connectivity binds us. People who feel deeply connected to others seem to drink well.

A lack of belonging and significance brings feelings of despair. Feelings of being excluded, with a pervading internal sense that something is wrong, create a sense of being shamefully separate from others. Our overconsumption of food, drink, and other compulsions are attempts to soothe what is lacking. People who feel alone and alienated from others do not seem to drink well.

Dislocation refers to the rupture of enduring and sustaining connections between individuals and their families, friends, cultures and societies, livelihoods, rituals, nations, and deities (Alexander, 2014, p. 20). *Dislocated individuals* struggle valiantly to establish or restore psychosocial peace of mind—to carve out a life for themselves amidst this chaos. Socrates stresses that if large numbers of people lack a sense of belonging and significance, they are likely to be overcome by master passions. Dislocation theory considers addiction to be a narrowly focused lifestyle that functions as a meager substitute for people who desperately lack a sense of psychosocial cohesion (Alexander, 2011, p. 62).

This school of thought provides a sociocultural framework for understanding addiction from a global impact perspective. Alexander's theory suggests that the current free-market competitive global economy based on Western civilization has become the center of human existence. We desperately compete in the job market, aggressively pursue advancement, manically master technology, and frantically consume for the best prices. In the process, social needs are subordinated to the needs of surviving in a free-market economy. Trusting relationships, directly addressing each other, mutual support, and genuine caring are in direct opposition to a marketplace that thrives on competition, greed, irony, sarcasm, superficiality, and playing people off each other for a greater gain. These cutthroat methods of survival are in direct opposition to the cultivation of dignity in human relations, and instead produce alienated, and later addicted, individuals. Addiction in any form is seen as an adaption to these new pressures and has become excessive in recent decades. *Perspectives* brings awareness of these impacts so that people can begin to consider healthier responses to the anxieties of dislocation and feel more grounded amidst this global excitement, as well as its chaos.

DAILY IMPACTS AND EVERYDAY STORIES

Daily Impacts

Alexander's theory captured my mind quickly; it took longer to study and sit with his work and make it my own, to make his theoretical jargon real for myself and real for my readers. I began to understand what this globalization

was all about when I applied it to my own life. As I lived and worked domestically and internationally, I became absorbed with noticing the demands and
daily frustrations of globalization. Suddenly, every feeling and gesture was seen
through the eyes of dislocation. I strongly encourage readers to consider these
impacts on their own lives as well.

The bullets listed below are an attempt to identify some of the frustrations
of our hypercommunicative world. These globalized pressures drive the need
to self-medicate with AOD as a soothing mechanism for our sense of disorganization. Globalization impacts each of us all day long, from cultural diversity in our environments, to worldwide media coverage, to the availability of
technology use 24 hours a day. Below are some questions meant to encourage
reflection about the way a globalized world impacts you every day:

- What does this word *globalization* mean to you, and how does it impact
  you?
- How are you personally impacted by the demise of the nuclear family,
  extended families being scattered throughout the world, and cultures and
  ethnic groups losing cohesion?
- How do you experience listening to 24-hour worldwide news and com-
  mentary about so many people and places around the world? Is it experienced as stimulating and relatively easy to digest; overstimulating, difficult
  to bear, and a strain to comprehend and digest; or background noise in
  your living room that is neither taken in nor comprehended?
- What is your everyday reaction to the glitches and frustrations of our
  technology-driven world? In our everyday e-mail, most of us have struggled with attachments that we cannot open, sites that are incompatible
  with our devices, and drafts that are inexplicably lost to the abyss before
  we get the chance to hit "send." Many of us experience a sense of technological helplessness before we have finished our first cup of coffee in the
  morning.
- How do you manage the frustration of regularly being dropped from
  mobile calls both domestically and internationally?
- How do presidents, teachers, and corporate presenters tolerate the all-
  too-familiar, failed media experience? What is to become of professors,
  teachers, and students nervously facing ongoing technology challenges in
  a virtual environment?
- Most physicians and nurses report the experience of digitizing hospital
  and office records as disruptive, demoralizing, disturbing to the patient
  relationship, and ethically offensive. Why are these reports of deterioration
  in medical care ignored?

- How do you deal with this paradox? We are technologically equipped for 24-hour communication; we work in different countries as efficiently as possible, but are forced to slow down and wait because the people we are connected to often live in different time zones.
- What is your reaction to increasing numbers of people leaving their home and country for better opportunities or, tragically, for asylum?
- How are you impacted by the ever-present Tower of Babel, whether shopping at a mall; ordering online; or in our classrooms, neighborhoods, places of worship, and universities?

These impacts are often not recognized and are repressed instead with, "It's a part of these modern times—what are you going to do? If you don't accept and adapt, then for sure you will not succeed." These ongoing daily psychological stressors likely seek soothing in SUDs and behavioral compulsions, and are likely responsible for the rise in worldwide addiction rates. For decades, we have seen addiction as a disease, or it has been viewed as a cognitive-behavioral disorder. *Perspectives* suggests that we need to take a harder look at the social impact of our current globalized daily living stressors and its relationship with widespread addiction.

Everyday Stories: Baby Boomers and Gen Y

Let us consider a few more of technology's dislocating and disorienting impacts. Generationally, we speak to each other with wildly divergent levels of technology expertise. Baby boomers or older adults, who comprise 40.2% of the labor force (Toossi, 2012), often give up learning and resign themselves to their mediocre skills, make do with the best that they can, but ultimately walk away feeling diminished or ill-equipped to confidently use the dominant form of communication in today's world. Again, a sense of vague helplessness pervades their human spirit. Some baby boomers may have a different reaction. I spoke briefly with a 64-year old professor as he attempted to print out his two-page airline ticket on a computer in the hotel business center. Only one page appeared after five attempts. His daughter, sitting across from him playing on her smartphone, ignored his sighs of frustration. He went to the front desk and discovered, indeed, his ticket was printed on one page, but on both sides. I asked him about his perceived sense of frustration and helplessness. He responded, "Computers are going to kill us. However, that being said, my blood pressure has actually lowered since computers have entered my life because I find them much less frustrating than people." Along the same lines, my 24-year-old editor responded as she read this, "I can relate to him. We'd rather order dinner online from our computer than have to call in and interact with people."

Young adults and teens often take on these glitches as a personal challenge and compulsively search for answers. Enthusiastic IT support staff appear excited about solving yet another problem to help their clients use technology better, but the vast majority of those in tech support are burnt out or weary of long days of dealing with the endless parade of "idiots who can't even figure out how to add an attachment or reboot a computer."

The ongoing daily stress of these feelings of frustration and inadequacy often finds relief in increased marijuana usage, the evening cocktail or glass of wine, cruising for a sexual experience online, or binging on food in the privacy of one's own home.

The Global Traveler

Another impact of globalization is increased business and leisure travel. Let us walk through a travel-day scenario for the domestic or international citizen. Again, my intention is to bring to the forefront the minute impacts or "costs" that the traveler endures, and the solutions that might be found in alcohol, drugs, or food.

We begin our 24-hour day with the dreaded anticipation of the airport experience. There is so much that will likely go wrong. A friend of mine, anticipating an international flight for work, wished that she would get bumped up to first class. Her boss advised her, "Just get drunk at the terminal bar before the flight—it will make your coach experience bearable."

We head to the airport bar or restaurant while waiting for a delayed flight. More food and alcohol help pass the time as we finally begin our journey. Our international flight from L.A. to Munich, staffed by stressed and unpleasant flight attendants, is scheduled to land before the standard 3:00 p.m. hotel check-in time. What to do with the weariness of waiting again with no ability to shower and freshen up? Once inside the hotel room, we face the dreaded ritual of getting our technology hooked up. Do we have the right outlets? Will our computer, tablet, and smartphone find WiFi service? Will these startup efforts be successful or unsuccessful? What is Plan B? As we munch on some snacks from the mini bar, we begin to wonder how much time it will take before we can reach our work colleagues.

After a pleasant-enough cocktail reception and dinner of meat dumplings and wine, we are ready to sleep. Preparations begin with checking the air-conditioning or heating accommodations. Are they easy to figure out? How do these foreign showers work? Where are the hair dryers? Is there compatible electricity for the water pick or electric toothbrush?

Now for the most delicious time of the day: lying in bed with a good book or magazine, surfing the internet with our tablet, watching our favorite reruns or TV show. How do we find the comforts of home—the fresh glass of water or tea on the night table, our favorite bowl of yogurt or ice cream, our special treats of candy, our sleeping aids, and extra blankets?

When we wake up, the first thing that many of us ask is, "How hung over do I feel from the mandatory reception, business dinner, and bar visit from the night before? How will I handle feeling so out of sorts for the rest of the day?" After our emotional self-assessment is complete, it's time to move on to the "real" issues. Where are the light switches? Will the coffeemaker in the room work, and will the coffee taste refreshing? Will we get to the meeting on time? How is the family back home? Do they need our help, and do we feel like giving it?

Now to our workday ahead—will we be able and ready to listen, engage, contribute, impress, and be a productive team member for the four scheduled meetings today? Will we lunch alone, catch our breath, or join the team lunch of starchy food and endless refills of wine? After these meetings, it's time to re-pack, check out of the hotel, and begin the airport experience again, either to home or to another business meeting or conference.

My hunch is that most of these detailed, minute measures of dislocation will be ignored, dismissed, or downplayed with a cynical acknowledgment: "Ah, it just goes with the territory. No big deal." Instead, I hope the reader can see that many of these fragmentary experiences were soothed with food, liquor, or the transitional object of a tablet or smartphone—the adult version of a stuffed animal, binky, or favorite blanket.

Dislocation theory suggests these contemporary day-to-day disruptions throw us off balance and assault our sense of self-order. Each new situation brings its frustration. We feel edgy and disjointed, like bits and pieces of a person reacting to all these impacts. A portion or fragment of ourselves is available to engage in the next activity; the other parts of ourselves are overwhelmed, shut down, distracted, or preoccupied. We attempt to seek forms of comfort with drink or other compulsions to quiet and soothe our ongoing sense of floaty ambiguity and agitation. We might consider these questions: "Is all this travel actually working for me?" "Where do I really belong, at home or on the road?" "What am I gaining and what am I losing?" "Are there other ways to achieve a sense of balance with the realities of my work schedule besides food, alcohol, pills, and drugs?"

The Partner at Home

Let us not overlook the partners, husbands, or wives left at home. They are likely to feel exhausted but also relieved that the traveler is gone and the chaos of once again planning and organizing for another trip is over. The partner at home also feels the solo weight of the responsibility for the children, whether attending a local soccer or basketball game or picking up a child from the swim team or band practice, working through homework, or preparing children and animals for bed.

The challenges of mixing our personal needs with our professional lives seem an exhausting trend that is likely to continue. More than ever, we are constantly and jarringly asked to shift our psychological mindsets—now a professional, now a parent. Gone are the luxuries of the stay-at-home mom or the 9-to-5 workday experience at the same location: "I don't know what I would do without my 5 p.m. cocktail or wine before, during, and after dinner. When my wife is gone, my marijuana maintenance program becomes less sneaky and increases in her absence." A rushed, intoxicated, and fragmented mother is distracted at her child's bedtime as she only dreams of a chance to get to her room and take her sleeping pill: "No way could I get to sleep without an Ambien."

ADDICTION SYMPTOMS AS SOCIAL ADAPTATION, NOT INDIVIDUAL PATHOLOGY

Dislocation theory has influenced and broadened my clinical thinking significantly. As I have suggested, this social theory is for a new generation of treatment thinkers and providers, regardless of their age. Its clinical adoption depends on the openness and willingness of addiction counselors and professionals to consider the possibility that the daily frustrations of living in a worldwide, interconnected economy are major etiological factors in the development of an addiction.

It is helpful to pinpoint all the social disturbances in everyday living that are directly connected to globalization, with its technology glitches, language barriers, ambivalence about immigration and asylums, and frustrations in communicating with various cultures in neighborhoods, shops, or stores, or on the phone with worldwide operators. Our reliance on a communication world that we neither fully grasp nor are able to keep up with likely creates pervasive anxieties of helplessness in most of us: "How will I get what I need with so many technological challenges and foreign voices?"

Many welcome the challenges and opportunities of a more globalized network: "The internet has really broken down cultural barriers. We are all exposed to the same media and responding to them in a giant forum of people from all over the world. They have made the thoughts and feelings from the far reaches of the world instantly accessible, creating a venue for a live global discussion unlike any we have ever seen before." Students responding to class presentations on this theory offer the following: "Some of us like all the demands. Some of us like all the challenges and aren't really confused by it." Many others respond to the frustrations and confusions of these ongoing impacts and disorientations with "I'm so pissed that people can find me anywhere. I never feel caught up, I never feel like I'm off the clock, I live in chaos, and I'm increasingly misplacing everything." They either ignore these impacts or "swallow" them, and often devote themselves to the narrow lifestyle of addiction that functions as a substitute for the yearned-for sense of calm that comes with belonging and feeling significant.

The kinds of social changes needed to avert this rising tide of addiction will not occur until an underlying philosophy changes in the minds of a great many people (Alexander, 2011, p. 392). This change in philosophy only occurs when we acknowledge and connect the stresses of our everyday, globalized lives with the rise of addiction. Natural recovery from addictions is likely to occur when people establish stronger relations with their family and community, or find a strong sense of meaning elsewhere (Alexander, 2011, p. 13). Some believe that the field of addiction is overfocused on neuroscientific, genetic, and biological forces. *Perspectives* asks us to consider the social influences in addictive practices as well.

CLINICAL CASES

Maria and Juan

Maria and Juan are a Philippine couple working in the home and office of a Greek family. They have been employed by the family for 15 years, and they had a son while living in Greece. The family speaks English, Greek, and of course, Filipino. They have left their entire extended family in the Philippines. As long as they can remember, they knew that they would travel and live in a land that provided much more opportunity than their home country. They did their research and decided to seek out the blue sky and friendly environment of Athens, Greece. They discovered that a small percentage of wealthy individuals owned multiple properties in the lush suburbs of Athens and that they often became very stable employers for many of their Philippine friends.

Years later, Juan's brother went missing for 2 weeks after the floods of late 2013. Juan and Maria became depressed, lost weight, drank more at night, occasionally smoked weed during the day, could not sleep, and were constantly tending to their son's new bouts of asthma. They took off time at work and lost income. They lived in a constant state of fear and frustration because of the lack of available communication on the mainland. There were neither extended family nor native friends close by, and their sense of disorganization and fragmentation was visible. The family they worked for did as much as they possibly could to respond to their sense of helplessness and terror. Maria and Juan had relocated, settled in, found work, had a baby, and found a good school for their son. However, during this time of physical disaster, geographical distance, and technology impairment, they both remarked, "These are the times we think we have made a big mistake in leaving our homeland just for more opportunity. Family and love is all that counts and we sacrificed this to get ahead in our lives and provide more opportunity for our son. During times like this, we want to return to our home, culture, and traditions. Unfortunately, the opportunities and rewards we have discovered in Greece will not allow that." It took about 4 months for Maria, Juan, and their son to adjust to this crisis in their lives. After 9 months, they "felt more like normal" and reported that the asthma, anxiety, and drinking had stopped. They determinedly saved money, and during the Christmas holidays of 2014 returned to "our homeland for 2 and a half months to visit brothers, sisters, parents, and cousins."

When they returned, they were more disturbed than ever about Greece's political and economic ongoing crisis. They told me, "We've made some bad decisions. We picked the wrong country, and we need to move for our son's education and future. We're planning to leave Greece in 5 years, but we're not sure where we're going to live in the future. The uncertainty and confusion of all this change is becoming unbearable."

Felipe

Felipe managed the daily operations of an equestrian barn called Sporthorse International. He did a magnificent job in all areas of his barn management, including mucking stalls and feeding, tacking, and untacking horses for their daily rides. Most importantly, he knew the horses—their moods, their states of mind, their health, and their "issues." Felipe often said, "These horses live better than my friends back at home." Felipe worked in San Diego, California, and was born in Mexico. Upon arrival in the United States, he quickly learned English and seemed to easily adapt to Southern California culture. He had a stellar work ethic and earned the trust of the barn owners, local commerce, the surrounding community, the barn trainer, and the 40 barn members. His oldest son, Romero, was born in America, but returned with his mother to be raised in his home culture. Felipe returned to America and left behind his wife and now three children in Mexico: "I left my country for more opportunity, more respectable work for my own sense of self, and for higher wages." He sent money back home to his family each week. He went home to Mexico for a month each year. When he returned, he went back to work and was as diligent as ever. Felipe had found a way to "belong in America" and feel a sense of significance.

Very occasionally, his wife and children would visit him in his one-room trailer on the ranch. Eventually, he invited his oldest son, now age 10, to stay with him in America. Romero, a shy and kind boy, wanted to go to school in America but had a very difficult and painful adjustment to his school environment. He struggled with English, made poor grades, and had a hard time making friends. The other Spanish-speaking students in his class had been in America since birth. He was a lost and lonely global child, unable to feel that he belonged in his own country, and surely did not feel any importance in his school environment.

One or two of the barn members, also parents of young children, got involved and spoke to his teacher, requested extra help, and checked in with Romero as often as they could. One could see in his held-back tears that he was in pain, and also that he really appreciated the help. He belonged to his "barn family." They gave him some respite and relief, but he knew that he needed more attention and care. Romero did the best he could, but he knew he needed his mother.

Felipe, a sober individual, got arrested one night "for an unpaid ticket." He was thrown in jail, and details were sketchy. When he was sent back to Mexico, the barn family realized that he did not have papers and that he had illegally been living in the United States for 15 years. The barn family had been led to believe that he had been sponsored by the barn owners. Romero, now 15, took over his father's job. He cried often and quit school, but he said, "There is nothing else I can do. I have no other option. I have to work and send money back to my mother, sister, and brothers." The first thing his barn family did was get him a cell phone with a good international plan, and a computer so that he could e-mail his mother, play games, and keep up with the international news that affected him. About 3 months later his father, Felipe, returned, but not surprisingly, he was arrested and forced to return to Mexico. He remains in a Mexican jail to this day.

This example is not presented as a case study on the legal complexities of immigration. Instead, it focuses on the wrenching aspects of living, working, and adjusting to a different culture initially without language familiarity, and leaving loved ones at home. As is often the case, one family member arrives first and encourages children in the family to move to, live, and be educated in America. We see the feelings of dislocation and lack of belonging that Romero suffered, and his sense of being caught between countries and cultures. Romero had caught the American bug, yearned to return home, but financial realities forced him to stay.

In preparation for writing this case vignette, I contacted Romero. It was hard to find him, and when I did, I discovered that he had moved around in jobs and was still trying to make his life in America. He relied to some degree on his father's brothers and their families, also living and working in America. He lived with them for a while and then felt "uncomfortable" and sought out new housing. He told me he was using marijuana daily and drinking more often than he wanted: "Being nowhere is scary. This is how I survive." He went home once per year and was still searching for a life and family here in America. He had a Mexican girlfriend here and thought he would probably end up marrying her. "When I do that, I know I will stop all the alcohol and all the marijuana. She will force me to."

Margarita

Margarita was born into a financially comfortable southern European family that communicated through fashion, sarcasm, irony, and hostility, and with the use of three languages at home: Italian, French, and English. Margarita felt something was wrong at home at an early age, an example of domestic dislocation. Her father was a kind, well-meaning provider who was quickly marginalized by Margarita's ill-meaning, controlling mother. Early on, the message to Margarita was, "Stick to your mother, who knows how to take care of you the best, and don't listen to your father." Margarita at an early age displayed tics and odd movements. By the time she finished high school, she had a well-established habit of trichotillomania—the excessive picking on parts of her body, usually her face—and suffered from body dysmorphic disorder. She spent hours and hours alone in her room, examining her naked body in the mirror and performing "surgical procedures" such as placing a very tight clothespin on her nose, spending hours on her makeup, and later retreating to restaurant bathrooms to reestablish cosmetic order.

She neither belonged to her home, her friends, nor her country. It is no surprise that she chose a U.S. west coast graduate school and remains there to this day, collecting degrees.

She brought her fragmented and weightless sense of self to America without feeling supported by either her parents or her brother. She cut herself off from family and friends, devoted herself to study, and spent the majority of her time alone. Different languages, different cultures, a different educational system, and a diverse student body—it was all overwhelming; and sadly, Margarita was one of those people Alexander describes as being too prideful and frightened to articulate their feelings of dislocation. Doing so would display weakness and failure (Alexander, 2014, p. 21). She refused her parents' suggestion to seek therapy and adapts with anorexia, body dysmorphia, psychic retreating, (Steiner, 1993) trichotillomania, and experimentation with psychedelics and hallucinogens. Eventually, her parents chose to cast a blind eye to her compulsions, as the success of making it in a globalized world was more important to them than figuring out a way to address her suffering.

Jeff and Amy

Jeff and Amy have been married for 10 years and have two children. As a family they reside in Southern California, but Jeff was born and raised in Europe and Amy was born and raised in Mexico and Canada. Before marriage, they decided to live in the United States. Amy recalls the difficult early times of being wrenched away from her country, parents, friends, and comforts of familiarity. It was quite a difficult adjustment for her. She was vocal about her distress. Shortly thereafter, sexual relations between them became tense, and Jeff began to develop difficulties maintaining an erection. They began drifting apart, and they increased their intake of alcohol and pot from weekend use to 7 nights a week. It was also at this time that Jeff began taking on projects in Europe that provided bountiful pay but kept him away from his wife and family for 5 to 9 months of the year.

They came to see me in great distress, bitterly resentful of each other, wanting something from the other, and wanting to control the way that they get it. Michael Vincent Miller in his book *Intimate Terrorism* (1995) says, "And therein lies the grounds for war." Their relationship had become a war zone; too much hurt and intimate diplomacy had failed.

They fought and struggled their way through our early sessions until they were able to share with each other the feelings of loss, fear, and confusion as a result of their disrupted and dislocated lives. "We're so happy that our kids speak multiple languages, have visited our countries of origin, and have a global perspective. It was our dream, but we had no idea as to how disorienting and disrupting it would be in our lives and negatively dominate our emotional landscape. We now have a language to talk about our dreams and what went wrong."

CHAPTER SUMMARY AND REFLECTIONS

Summary

This chapter introduced the reader to the dislocation theory of addiction that stresses the global factors in increasing addiction rates. It presented the key components of this theory and explored them with clinical cases and everyday examples.

Reflections

Consider the following questions in a classroom discussion or paper:

- What is your working definition for dislocation theory?
- What are the impacts of globalization in your everyday life?
- Have you or someone you've known ever experienced the vague ambiguity of global weightlessness?
- What are some arguments for the adoption of dislocation theory in the treatment of substance use disorders? What are some arguments against it?
- How would you integrate this theory in your everyday life or clinical practice with persons with SUDs?

CHAPTER 4

CULTURAL STORIES

This chapter encourages exploration of the influences of our individual cultural histories on the seemingly universal human desire to escape and expand consciousness with the help of drugs and alcohol. It also further delves into the impacts of globalization discussed in Chapter 3. Our cultural backgrounds, almost more than our globalized social context, shape our feelings, behaviors, and viewpoints. Our thinking about the adaptive uses, misuses, and addictions to these substances, as well as our denials and judgments about them, runs deep. It is important to identify the historical and generational forces that drive our current drinking and drugging behaviors. It is clinically useful and personally helpful to recognize these covert and overt influences in our patients and in ourselves.

A recent report by *The Lancet* (Napier et al., 2014) suggested that the word *culture* is a dynamic yet vague concept that is not merely defined as national, ethnic, or racial affiliations. Culture can be thought of as a set of conventional practices and behaviors defined by customs, habits, language, and geography that groups of individuals share in a particular setting over time. *Perspectives* has adopted this viewpoint.

The desire for health and well-being is highly susceptible to cultural variation, particularly in today's globalized world. In all cultural settings—local, national, and worldwide—the need to understand the cultural factors that affect health-improving (or health-deteriorating) behaviors is now imperative. This chapter invites you to ponder the short stories of many of my former students from around the world and use them as you reflect on the influences of your own cultural history on your AOD thinking and behavior.

My teaching style and the sequence of my content coverage have evolved over time. It took me years to realize that cultivating students' investment in exploring their own cultural history and current social context is the best prerequisite for the development of a clinically relevant knowledge base in substance use and its disorders. Students connected to their own familial and cultural approvals, taboos, and sanctions are then ready to invite their patients to explore these influences on their own thinking and behavior.

The School of Social Work at USC, as well as the other graduate departments I'm affiliated with, embraces the diversity in cultures and makes sure it is present in our classrooms. These rooms are populated with students from all corners of the world. I teach students of all sexual orientations, many ethnicities, and varied cultural styles.

Our classroom conversations on the influences of our cultural heritage begin early in the semester. We explore specific questions:

- How do you identify yourself culturally?
- In what ways does this identity shape your thinking about AOD?
- What are the meanings of AOD in your culture?
- How have you internalized these meanings, and how have they shaped your own relationship with AOD?
- Who partakes in the pleasures of AOD? In what ways? Who does not, and why?
- What if problems develop? How are they defined? How do people address them?
- How do your cultural prejudices and biases shape your notions about treatment?

Over the semester, students ponder the relationship between historical cultural forces and their outlook on AOD, with consideration of degrees of acculturation, experiences of oppression and discrimination, language and communication skills, education level, socioeconomic class, religion, age, and family structure.

Students tentatively open up and begin to share how their identified backgrounds shape their attitudes and values, as well as their prejudices and biases. They seem to relish understanding how these are expressed in AOD individual and cultural habits, norms, and expectations. We hear how their cultures define substance using and its disorders, as well as the ways they sanction or discourage getting help or treatment. A rich and mutually informative class discussion begins here and continues throughout the semester.

Below are individual cultural stories shared by students during our early-semester classroom conversations. *Perspectives* has chosen stories rather than statistics in order to invite personal identification, induce a rich classroom discussion, and increase participation. The stories presented capture many cultural complexities not often revealed by an overreliance on statistical numbers and percentage points. It is essential for clinicians to bring these conversations in the treatment setting as well. Recognizing the cultural influences on substance use disorders empowers the patient by reducing his sense of individual pathology. These stories, while richly unique, seem to repeatedly cluster around two over-arching themes: those that reflect cultural ideas about approvals, disapprovals, and treatments, and those that reflect the seemingly universal tendency to avoid the topic, including discussions of any problems. For decades, this class activity has been a valuable ice breaker and brings classroom cohesion.

CULTURAL PROHIBITIONS, APPROVALS, DISAPPROVALS, AND TREATMENTS

African American Women, Mid-20s

"Drinking is everywhere. It starts with shots of cognac for colicky stomachs in infancy. Our only form of treatment comes from elders. They counsel us, 'We will help you learn to drink. Watch us and the way we drink. If you can't drink, then don't drink.'"

Saudi Arabian Man, Age 26

"Alcohol and drugs are available in Saudi Arabia, and the punishments are harsh. Usually a three-strikes law is used. First strike is public flogging and a fine. Second strike is public flogging, a fine, and jail time. Third strike, pre-2005 death penalty (beheading, which is now less frequent), is extended jail time and possible death sentence later. The penalties by law enforcement are carried out by mosques, and sentences can be lenient if the amount of usage is fairly small and not frequent. These laws are strict because there is a great concern about shaming the family."

Korean Women, Mid-20s

"It seems there is a collectivist mentality going on around drinking." These women described the extraordinary stress experienced in the workplace. The country seems to sanction evening drinking and socializing four times a week. "It's okay to get drunk. It's a social stress reliever." One of the young women described being forced to learn how to drink beer. She felt group pressure.

"People gave me a drink and stared me down; I had no choice." A very popular drink for both men and women is a shot of tequila added to beer. "Still, it's a stigma for girls to get too drunk."

Armenian American Woman, First Generation

"There is a lot of drinking. The worst thing you can do is not handle your alcohol. It is a public embarrassment. Alcohol flows freely in all occasions. It is insulting not to abundantly replenish alcohol at a wedding." Her father had pancreatitis twice due to alcohol and almost died. He did not get treatment; he just stopped. People think he just doesn't drink. "I wonder if he does today and always look for signs."

Homosexual, Secular, Jewish American Man

He never saw his parents drink or smoke. The message was, "'Don't do either, especially in the house.' As a gay man, I live in a culture with a big alcohol and drug presence. It would really take a lot to get anybody into treatment. The biggest addiction in my community is cruising for sex, which includes use of methamphetamines."

Italian/Irish Woman

"My mom drank wine at dinner. My dad smoked weed every night. My grandmother needed her medicine, which was White Zinfandel wine, with a shot of Dewar's [Scotch]. Our family is relatively open about this drug and alcohol use." It helped her come to the decision to drink and smoke marijuana in moderation.

Mexican American Man, Early 20s

Both parents were born in Mexico. "There is more alcohol than kids at birthday parties." Drinking is connected with gender. If girls drink, they get in trouble with their father. The best decision for girls is to avoid "the situation completely."

Military, Conservative, Catholic, American Man

He was raised to fear drinking and preached to about the dangers of alcohol. He did not drink until junior year abroad. "I learned about drinking from being in Rome. Don't drink in front of family."

Greek Man, Late 20s

"All my friends, both men and women, drink. We like to. Our pattern is to eat dinner with our parents and other family members at home, then go to a club around 11 or 12 midnight. We stay out until 3 or 4 a.m. We have a lot of fun with drinking, but do not drink in excess. We have to go home to our parents, and we have to work the next morning. People have fun in Athens, but I don't think people get drunk like they do in London, where I went to college, or in America, where I visited."

Irish/Italian Woman

"Grew up with the joke of the seven-course meal—a six-pack and a baked potato." People who have problems with hard alcohol are stigmatized. Most won't get treatment.

Asian Woman, Mid-20s

"I think there's a stigma attached to people who are addicts, a very negative stigma. The complexity of addiction is not taken into consideration, and instead people are judged for being weak and the issues of why they are using are overlooked or ignored. I've changed—if someone important in my life becomes addicted, I don't think I would be able to stand and watch them destroy their lives. I'd ultimately have to confront or find ways to help them."

Caucasian, Christian, American Woman

"I grew up in a strict, rigid, and conservative Christian home. My father is a pastor, and we were taught that drinking is a sin. I was taught that addicts or users are sinners. Sin is bad; therefore, they were bad and deserved to go to hell. When I got to college, I went through a partying phase where I abused alcohol. Believe me, I was quite aware I was sinning, and if God came, I'd go to hell."

African American Woman, Age 45

She grew up in the South. There was no alcohol in her family house. The family looked at drinking problems as deviant. Her brother-in-law had a drinking problem, including multiple relapses. He is now in a nursing home at age 48 as a result of his alcoholism. The family said, "Just let him go." "It was progress that the family moved from viewing it as deviancy to viewing it as a disease."

U.S. Marine Veteran Woman, Age 35

"Drinking is promoted in the military, regardless of age, sex, race, or rank. Alcohol is served at formal and informal social gatherings. Alcohol is everywhere in military culture. You can purchase alcohol at every local store on the installation. When used in moderation, alcohol is culturally acceptable; however, the aftermath of alcohol can lead to sexual assault, domestic violence, career challenges, and other legal actions."

Iranian/Italian American Woman, First Generation

Parents born in Italy and Iran. Prior to the revolution in Iran there was a lot of drinking, drugs, and prostitution among the population. In her family, the men drink and do drugs freely in America. It is a rite of passage for cultural approval. "If you drink too much, it is not a problem. You get help only if mandated as a result of a DUI or assault charge." Women should not be seen drinking.

Mexican American Woman, First Generation, Mid-20s

Learning to drink is a male thing. Women aren't supposed to, although her mother hid a bottle in the closet and drank throughout the day. Her brother has a drinking problem and has been in Alcoholics Anonymous. He relapses and the men humorously call him "poor little drunky."

Korean American Woman

Parties are in different rooms in a house; the boys are with the men, the girls are with the women. The men teach the boys to drink so that their faces do not get red. They are taught first to have a beer, then take an antacid, then move to hard liquor. The boys are told to pace their drinking. "You whisper if there is a problem." Women are told not to drink. Initially they don't, but eventually some do in private.

Affluent Second-, Third-, and Fourth-Generation American Young Adults

"I grew up in an affluent community with the means to buy drugs and alcohol, and large unsupervised homes to abuse them in." She describes many Ecstasy and cocaine parties. Pill parties were stocked from parents' medicine cabinets. "Throw pills in a bowl and ingest them. Most of the kids have been in multiple rehabs. Young adults are successful, yet still party. Some died, some are seriously psychologically disabled."

Retired U.S. Naval Chief, Man, Age 55

"Alcohol has been a part of my military culture, and I have consumed alcohol throughout my entire career, even at age 17. I have myself struggled with alcohol addiction. I have turned to alcohol to help deal with my stresses, frustrations, depressions, and as a coping tool. I have witnessed numerous service members being drunk on duty, getting arrested due to alcohol charges, and even being discharged from the military."

Caucasian American Woman, Age 35

"My family's thoughts about addiction were distorted. Looking back, I see that much of the alcohol use was in the misuse and abuse range, but that was what was normal in our household. I began drinking at an early age. It became normal to binge drink on the weekends. Today, our culture approves of binge drinking, and seems to say that to enjoy alcohol we must be drunk and totally wasted to consider it a good time. Basically, I think the culture that I am a part of sends a message that alcohol problems follow the disease model, and I think they don't pay attention to the in-between problems. These also tremendously impact our lives."

Homosexual, Jewish American Man, Mid-20s

"My culture has transmitted to me the following idea—it's okay if you use or become a drug addict as long as you are successful. Or you're not really an alcoholic or drug addict if you're successful. Or maybe you're an alcoholic or drug addict, but success makes it okay. In other words, we can treat your alcohol or drug addiction (like rehab), but there is no treatment for not being successful in the way we deem success (doctor, lawyer, money . . .)."

Caucasian American Woman

"American culture is one of overindulgence, which reinforces a gluttony that encourages people to shamelessly consume or pursue excessive pleasures/highs. This imprint lends itself to a level of use where many feel okay or even quite great about overindulgence. In Europe it's different. Many see a glass of wine at dinner as a ritual, whereas in the U.S. it is an event in and of itself."

Persian/Armenian Woman, Age 45

"Both cultures, in my experience, allow alcohol but do not tolerate drug use and shun friends and family members who become addicts or users. Referrals to support groups or treatment programs are usually after the individual has been kicked out of the house or shunned by the community. Oftentimes, the person is labeled as an addict, even after sobriety. It's unacceptable for women to develop addictions."

Christian Korean Woman

"I grew up in a very strict Christian family background where my parents never drank except on occasion. In church, I learned not to get drunk, because it was not a 'holy' thing to do. My religious view of not getting drunk still holds. It is still a struggle and dilemma that I haven't figured out."

African American Woman, 20s

"It's okay to drink with other people." She described a family that viewed drinking as social and relaxing but never acceptable when alone. Someone will ask at a party, "Can you take Mike home if he drinks too much?" No one will bring up a serious conversation about his excessive drinking. "Drinking is everywhere; even if you are sick, the family will prepare a hot toddy."

Catholic/White Anglo-Saxon Protestant Woman, 20s

A woman in her 20s lost her brother to suicide. He had problems with drugs and alcohol. He committed suicide while sober. The family was devastated and still has not recovered. She got different messages from each generation of her family. Her grandparents drank martinis—it was okay to be tipsy after putting in a hard day's work. Her parents preached, "It's something to be afraid of, particularly after the loss of your brother." She's been in therapy and watches with alarm as her friends work hard and then get obliterated on weekends. She's cautious and scared.

Korean Woman, Late 20s

"In Korean culture, addiction is defined as mental illness. I used to perceive addicts as 'such a pity; sick people who cannot be cured or saved.' My church views addiction as a terrible sin that violates God's will. When I began to drink, I was terrified that my parents would blame and judge me, not love me, and then leave me."

Latina Woman, Mid-30s

She lives between the second and third generation. "Drinking is different at different levels of immigration." She shares that drinking is part of people coming together. It's accepted by both generations, but there's a big gender difference. Girls have to hide their drinks, while men can get drunk. Her father did a lot of drugs, and it was kept quiet for years. When she returned from college, he was sober. "Somehow, he got clean; it was never talked about. I think losing his job forced my mom and dad to deal with it." She describes parents who now actually enjoy a sober life together.

Mexican American Couple, Late 20s

"We like beer, all kinds of beer. We started drinking at around age 13. Our elders said to 'watch it, and shame on you if you can't drink.' We listened. We're getting married in a brewery garden."

African American Woman, Mid-20s

"My family and extended family is cool with using drugs and alcohol. We celebrate holidays and birthday parties together. Each home or apartment has what is called 'the room.' That's where the drugs are used. When I'm ready to smoke pot, I just ask, 'Where is the room?'"

Jewish American Woman, Age 45

"My family tends to use wine for many rituals, so drinking has always been an accepted part of the culture. On some occasions, you only need to take a sip of wine. On others, you are required to drink several cups of wine. And on some celebratory holidays, we are commanded to get completely drunk. On one particular holiday, the teaching is to become so drunk that 'you cannot tell the difference between good and evil.'"

Eastern European Woman, Mid-30s

She grew up watching everyone drink straight vodka. There was no age restriction for the purchase of alcohol. Since age 5, she recalls daily walking to the grocery store to pick up her grandfather's vodka. She grew up believing drinking makes you more social. "Everyone does it, all the time." She believes, as a future clinician, she might normalize all drinking, even if it is a problem.

AVOIDANCE OF COMMUNICATION ON THE TOPIC OF AOD AND ITS PROBLEMS

Salvadorian American Woman, Mother of Two, Age 35

Young children start doing inhalants at age 7 or 8, and teenagers start drinking at 14 or 15. "Drinking is ingrained in everybody. We drink to avoid feelings and sharing emotions. I know my husband has a problem with alcohol. He drinks every night. He never talks or expresses emotions. I just let him be."

Jewish American Woman, Age 37

Addiction, if it exists, is downplayed and considered dangerous. "There are nice Jewish boys, and girls will raise babies. If a problem is observed in a family, it is minimized or overlooked. It is even overlooked during the Jewish holiday of Purim. If someone gets repeatedly intoxicated, it is best not to bring attention and disgrace to the family. Hopefully, it will quietly work itself out."

Latina Woman, Age 30

Drinking occurred every weekend. "I grew up in a family where you couldn't get enough Coors and Bud Light through the back door. We never talked about all the drinking in our family, even the serious problems." Her grandfather spent a month sweating it out in the back house, and her uncle moved to Atlanta and got sober. The family considers these two "cautionary tales."

Haitian Man, Age 37

"My culture tends to withdraw from discussing or even acknowledging alcohol and drugs, despite the fact that it is a phenomenon prevalent in my culture. Drugs and alcohol are prohibited. Additional awareness and discussion of the topic is off limits. We only hope that people do not drink or use drugs, and this is an unrealistic notion."

Swiss Woman, Age 35

"Nobody really talks that much about drinking around here because everybody does it. It's deeply a part of our daily rituals. It's normal to drink at breakfast, lunch, and dinner. We all know people with red faces who drink too much, but nobody says anything."

Husband of U.S. Army Private, Age 41

"I belong to this culture because of my wife. I have come to understand the rituals and celebrations where alcohol is required. I have also heard about the staff sergeant who gets into trouble with alcohol and loses everything. They turn their backs on service members after one alcohol-related incident, even after they have spent months/years teaching them that you have to drink alcohol to be a good army soldier."

Brazilian Woman, Age 35

"I believe my culture discounts and ignores the use of alcohol and drugs. The problem is left untouched and unspoken about. This may be done to maintain the dignity of the family's name. On the first day of class, I was surprised when classmates disclosed their family history and past use and abuse. It has been modeled to me to never air out your dirty laundry, especially to strangers."

Vietnamese Woman

Parents were refugees. There was no alcohol in the household. The focus was on food. "You drink when you are of age. It's a rite of passage. If there's a problem, my culture says, 'Don't let anyone know. If others have a problem, that's their private family business.'"

Hispanic Woman, Third Generation, Age 26

She is the youngest of six children. Her father and all her siblings are either alcoholics or addicted to drugs. Her mother has tended to them all, quietly and alone. "She approached me when I was young and said, 'I want you to go to church.' Church is what saved me from addiction."

Salvadorian American Woman, First Generation, Age 33

The message: Alcohol is wrong, and just don't do it. There was a grandfather who was alcoholic and a "funny uncle." Drinking brings with it a negative stigma. The whole issue of drinking is burdensome to her. "Should I drink?" "Is it negative?" "How much is too much?" "Who can I talk to, as nobody is talking about this?"

Armenian Man, Age 35

"Our culture is very private about our personal lives. If someone has a problem with drugs or alcohol, it would not be addressed to that person. If it was addressed, there is likely denial. In our culture, we do not believe in getting help, nor do we believe in AA or counseling. Do not hang your dirty laundry out to dry."

African American/Belizean American Woman

"I drank with my mom at age 12." Her mother did crack, alcohol, and prescription drugs. There was no talk of treatment. "This is what she was doing with her life." Her father is homeless, an alcoholic, and a drug addict. She says he is not interested in treatment.

Mexican/Guatemalan Catholic Woman

"Being Catholic and from a Latino culture, I was told that drugs were evil. Only bad people like criminals use drugs. However, alcohol was not spoken about. My nonimmediate family members drank heavily during the holidays, and my parents would remind me of their irresponsibility. I believed what I was told and was embarrassed by my drinking family members."

Traditional Mexican Family

"My personal experience with my culture has led me to believe that alcohol is normal and a part of life. It is always looked forward to in social gatherings because it means we are going to have a good time. When it comes to addictions, I realize that no one talks about it openly. We see it as, 'Oh, your uncle, he is just an old drunk.' There is no emphasis on helping the individual with an addiction—you have to fix your own problems."

Indian/Malaysian Woman, Age 38

"If any family notices that someone has a problem with any kind of addiction, we call them out on it and let them know what the consequences will be. However, most of them do not want to admit they have a problem. They never get help for their problem. They may stop for a while and pick their habit back up again."

Biracial Ivy League Student, Woman, Age 38

"As a woman of color, I felt shameful and secretive about my father's drug use. I connected this to the racism and classism in society's attitudes—people of color are deviant and dangerous and should be locked up. So the lesson I learned was to keep using a secret. When I went away to college and interacted with the elite upper class, I was floored to hear many of them laugh or even boast about their parents' drug use. It is clear [that] culture forms our beliefs and behaviors about drugs and addiction."

CHAPTER SUMMARY AND REFLECTIONS

Summary

This chapter invited readers to think about how they culturally identify themselves and also consider how their cultural identity influences their thinking and behavior about the pleasurable and problematic uses of alcohol and drugs. It is hoped that readers will consider the impact of these influences on future clinical work. The future clinician is encouraged to include these explorations in the practice setting.

Reflections

Consider the following questions in a classroom discussion or paper:

- What is your cultural identity, and how does it influence your relationship with AOD?
- What is the role of your culture in defining SUDs and addiction, recovery, and treatment?
- What are some biases or prejudices you may bring to your approach to treatment?

CHAPTER 5

CONTEMPORARY CONCEPTS

INTRODUCTION

By now readers have started to develop a more grounded sense of how globalization and its disorientations and their own cultural history have influenced the direction of their relationship with alcohol and other drugs, as well as their thinking about substance use, its disorders, addiction, and treatment in general. Readers are now ready to consider the often conflicting range of conceptual and definitional ideas about substance use, its disorders, and addiction. This chapter provides an opportunity to ponder and philosophize about what imbibing, intoxication, excess, refrain, and treatment mean to you. Far too often, others have provided conceptual or definitional frameworks for you; now is your chance to think about and confirm some of your own.

Everyone has ideas about what substance use, its disorders, and addiction mean to them. They have developed them from their own experiences and observations, their families, their friends, and the media. These experiences leave impressions, and most of the time they are not neutral. The use and misuse of intoxicants arouse conflicting emotions that cloud our thinking. People develop judgments and values, fears and blind spots, expectations and entitlements.

It is helpful to briefly review the evolution of the meaning and use of the word *addiction* in more recent history. *Addiction* first appeared in the 1600s, and was used to "assert that a person was doing something regularly and predictably." This traditional English meaning was neither medical nor moral in character. In fact, it carried a benign tone. However, if we move to the late 19th century, the word starts to evoke images of sickness and moral failure, and it begins exclusively to be referred to as the most extreme form of drug and alcohol misuse. It now carries a sinister tone.

How did this shift from benign to sinful occur? In the late 19th and early 20th centuries, modern scientific medicine subdued illnesses that had long plagued the human race, including smallpox, cholera, typhus, and influenza.

The status of medicine was elevated as a result of these breakthroughs. Quite independently, during this same time period there was an extended moral panic over increases in excessive drinking of distilled spirits and, later, excessive use of opium, morphine, chloral hydrate, cocaine, heroin, and other drugs. In the loose confluence of these two historical movements involving doctors and moralists, the meaning of the word *addiction* was gradually medicalized, moralized, and again restricted to alcohol and drug use (Alexander, 2014, p. 5).

With these historical events in mind, take the time to explore the following questions:

- What is your reaction to the historical transformation of the tone of the word *addiction*, from benign to sinful?
- What is your current attitude toward the desire for intoxication?
- Why are so many of us interested in getting high?
- Is it a national pastime?
- Why does a pleasure turn into excess?
- What's behind the sizeable number of people salivating at 5 p.m. each day, knowing that the day is over and a beer, glass of wine, martini, or more will soon follow?
- Why do we start earlier than 5 p.m. on vacations and often continue drinking and drugging throughout the rest of the supposed "stress-free" days and evenings?
- Why are most social occasions and holiday celebrations organized around drinking/drug use?
- Why do we search for the bar as soon as we arrive at a party?
- Why do we look for seconds and hope we don't have to ask?
- Why are parties, charities, and sporting events saturated with booze?
- Why are children's birthday parties filled with drunken parents?
- Why does drinking and drug use begin during lunch on many Saturdays and continue with brunch on Sundays?
- Why do we notice nondrinkers? Why are some of us uncomfortable around them?
- Finally, and most importantly, how do I define my own relationship with AOD?

This chapter introduces various concepts, definitions, and ways of thinking about substance use, its disorders, and addiction. These come from a variety of reference points, including our ancient desire for intoxication, cultural influences, a medical model approach, social sciences, neuroscience and biology, psychological suffering, a psychoanalytic attitude, attachment, spirituality, philosophy, family, recovery and treatment, support groups including Alcoholics Anonymous, Moderation Management, religious organizations, and various websites, online communities, and message boards.

You might be confused or frustrated by the lack of definitional or conceptual consensus in the field, but hopefully you will learn to embrace the uncertainty and value the diversity of thinking. Most importantly, my hope is that you will energetically endure all the confusion and mythology, and find your own way of thinking.

The list below is divided into five sections organized around both a DSM-5 substance use disorder and its equivalent ancient passion. For example, the term *nonpathological use* (NPU) of the DSM is paired with the ancient term *ordinary passion*. Alexander has postulated that there is a surprising similarity between the lives of today's most notorious addicts and those of the young Athenians whom Socrates described as "overwhelmed by master passions" (Alexander, 2011, p. 317).

The concepts presented are designed for thinking, questioning, and conversing between students and teachers, clinicians and patients, families and friends. Included are direct quotes; amalgamation quotes from myself, students, patients, and colleagues; and quotes modified or further developed from the original sources. Citations are included when available.

CONTEMPORARY CONCEPTS

Nonpathological Use/Ordinary Passion

- A natural human right.
- A necessity.
- Since humankind began, we have always looked for ways to escape, expand, heighten, or avoid consciousness.
- There is a need for a loss of consciousness (Eigen, 2014, p. 45).
- Humankind cannot bear very much reality (Eliot, 1936).
- AOD can give people a sense of magical oneness with the world.
- Is a conscious or unconscious choice to remove oneself from reality in order to relax the mind and enhance experiences.
- A way to fill space and a way to fill time (Phillips, 2013, p. 121).

Mild Substance Use Disorder/Minor Passion

- An adaptive compromise.
- Is a predictable response to social conditions that destroy self-esteem, hope, solidarity, stability, and a sense of purpose (quoted in *Rolling Stone* magazine).

Moderate Substance Use Disorder/Moderate Passion

- Is a substitute employed by those who cannot wait for time's unfolding (Bion, 1992, p. 299).
- Always represents an effort to bring about an internal change (Director, 2005, p. 567).
- Exists when a person's attachment to a sensational object is exclusive and the person is increasingly dependent on this experience as the only source of gratification (Peele & Brodsky, 1991, p. 43).
- Is a passive activity. Individuals take pills, powders, or liquids and wait for the desired effect—an alteration of their consciousness. The individual passively changes what he or she feels by using alcohol/drugs instead of facing and working through feelings of boredom, sadness, stress, and loneliness. Changing one's mood by more active approaches involves more effort and motivation (Fields, 2010, p. 28).
- "The peculiar charm of alcohol lies in the sense of careless well-being and bodily comfort which it creates. It unburdens the individual of his cares and fears. Under such conditions, it is easy to laugh or to weep, to love or to hate, not wisely but too well" (Emerson, 1932, p. 263).
- "Involves conditions in which problems with regulating emotions, self-love, relationships, and self-care interact in varying degrees with each other and also with genetic vulnerability and the environment" (Khantzian & Albanese, 2008, p. 19).
- Is seen as a way to clutter up the empty canvas of one's life and then become unable to do anything with it (Phillips, 2013, p. 121).
- An emptiness and spiritual void that requires spiritual healing (Vaillant, 1983).
- Is a radical escape from freedom (Levin, 2001, p. 3).
- Is consistent use despite negative consequences (Alcoholics Anonymous member).
- Has *nothing* to do with alcohol and *everything* to do with alcohol.

Severe Substance Use Disorder/Severe Passion

- Is an adaption to the overwhelming stimulation of the modern world, which produces individuals who feel fragmented and disoriented (Alexander, 2011, p. 18).
- Is a form of adaption that can become excessive under certain conditions, causing harm to individuals and populations (Alexander, 2011).
- To say that an addiction is adaptive is not to imply that it is desirable, either for the addicted person or for society, but only that, as a lesser evil, it may buffer a person against the unbearable evil of dislocation (Alexander, 2011, p. 63).
- Is a dramatic conflict that avoids real conflict.
- Even the most harmful addictions serve as a vital, adaptive function for dislocated individuals (Alexander, 2011).
- Functions to put a buffer between ourselves and our awareness or feelings. Use of AOD serves to numb us so that we are out of touch with what we know and feel (Schaeff, 1987, pp. 18–19).
- Is characterized by a person's marked impairment in his ability to control his alcohol or drug use (Hyman, 1995).
- Saturates the lives of those it touches—their families, friends, and work associates; their decisions and plans; their aspirations and dreams; their identities and self-concepts; their very assumptions about what is real and possible (Denzin, 1987).
- Is not just defined by symptomatic using, but also defined by who is watching the user (Vaillant, 1983).
- Perversion of social drinking into solitary excess (Rotskoff, 2002, p. 74).
- Is a disorder of intimacy. The alcoholic is extremely anxious over matters of interpersonal closeness, involvement, and intimacy. He wants closeness, but it is safest to keep others at a distance. Preconsciously and unconsciously, the addicted individual equates interpersonal intimacy and closeness with annihilation, rejection, and potential destruction of one's self. By drinking alcohol, and through the medium of intoxication, the alcoholic achieves a distorted or neurotic ability to be intimate (student).

Addiction/Master Passion

- Addiction is neither a disease nor a moral failure, but a narrowly focused lifestyle that functions as a meager substitute for people who deeply lack psychosocial integration (Alexander, 2011, p. 62).

- Addiction as a symptom is a talent, if only to ensure survival.
- The addict's attachment to chemicals serves both as an obstacle to, and a substitute for, interpersonal relationships (Flores, 2001, p. 64).
- Addicts crave being high. Being high is the opposite of being deep. Being high is a substitute for being spiritually deep. Being high prevents one from going to the deeper places where the human heart resides (Zoja, 2000).
- The drug addict is today's scapegoat (Alexander, 2014, p. 26).
- Addiction is the individual's behavioral and cognitive preoccupation with a substance, and an overwhelming compulsion to have the substance (Brown, 1985, p. 71).
- "Over the course of nearly a half-century of clinical work with addicted individuals, I have yet to meet a person who became or remained addicted to drugs because of the pleasurable aspect of their use, or whose motives in initiating and using drugs was suicidal in nature" (Khantzian, 2011, p. 3).
- Addictions do not have the breadth or depth to produce wholeness, and so addicted people do not find the contentment they are seeking.
- The problem with intoxication and excess is that the drugs wear off; the feeling is only temporary. Addicted individuals are driven to search for more. This hyperfocus severely disturbs one's sense of self, as well as intimate relationships with others. Sexual relationships are not needed anymore. The ego tragically surrenders itself to all that the drug world promises (Loose, 2002, p. 105).
- Addiction is defined as a primary, chronic disease with genetic, psychosocial, and environmental factors influencing its development and manifestations. The disease is often progressive and fatal. It is characterized by periodic or continuous impaired control over drinking, preoccupation with the drug alcohol, use of alcohol despite adverse consequences and distortions of thinking, most notably denial. Each of these symptoms may be continuous or periodic (American Society of Addiction Medicine).

CHAPTER SUMMARY AND REFLECTIONS

Summary

This chapter has encouraged the reader to develop a more personal and thoughtful perspective on the meanings behind substance use and addiction. Carefully selected concepts and definitions from multiple sources were presented. Personal reflection was encouraged. Readers were asked to consider the application of these in their personal and professional worlds.

Reflections

Consider the following questions in a classroom discussion or paper:

- What is your interpretation of the range and number of differing concepts presented?
- How will you utilize these differing concepts in your own practice?
- What are some concepts that feel intuitively and clinically useful for you in your work?

CHAPTER 6

DSM-5 AND 15 CLINICAL SKETCHES OF USING, MISUSING, AND ADDICTION

INTRODUCTION

Gone are the days of thinking you're addicted or you're not—enter a future that asks the question, "Are you a healthy user of substances, or do you have a mild, moderate, or severe Substance Use Disorder (SUD), or an addiction?"

The newest version of the diagnostic bible of the American Psychiatric Association (APA), the *Diagnostic and Statistical Manual of Mental Disorders* (DSM), was released in May 2013 and is still being actively studied for progressive implementation. It will be a time of confusion for clinicians, doctors, students, mental health facilities, patients, families, and insurance companies until these revisions are ready for everyday implementation. This chapter proposes a clinical framework to address some of these confusions.

DSM-5, replacing DSM-IV-R, identifies significant revisions in the area of addiction diagnosis. It presents a spectrum of substance use disorders, replacing the decades-old binary diagnostic choice between substance abuse and substance dependence. These new disorders range from mild, to moderate, and severe. In addition, nonproblematic use (NPU), nondisordered, and nonpathological use are newly discussed. These spectrum diagnostic revisions, possibly inadvertently, have also opened up an explosive opportunity for all of us to get more real about our relationship with the fourth drive, the ancient human desire to escape and expand consciousness through the use of AOD.

The word *addiction* is omitted from the official DSM-5 substance use disorders diagnostic terminology. However, continuation of its use appears to be at the discretion of the individual. "Some clinicians will choose to use the word *addiction* to describe more extreme presentations, but the word is omitted from the official DSM-5 substance use disorder diagnostic terminology because of its uncertain definition, and its potential negative connotation" (American Psychiatric Association, 2013, p. 485). I have adopted both the SUDs spectrum and the word *addiction.*

The new dimensional approach encourages the patient *to explore who he is, not defend who he is not.* The emotional focus is likely to shift from "How can I defend and continue my AOD usage?" to "How can I explore my relationship with AOD and consider healthier options?" A diagnostic reconsideration along a spectrum of behaviors breathes fresh air into a stifling paradigm.

This chapter proposes an assessment and diagnostic framework as a lens for exploring the contemporary expressions of this ancient drive, reducing decades of overdiagnosing and overpathologizing these human desires. It begins with a brief history of DSM diagnosis and also summarizes the diagnostic revisions to which we need to adapt as we wean ourselves from DSM-IV-R and gradually adopt DSM-5. There is a section on overdiagnosing and underdiagnosing. An exploratory framework of clinical sketches is introduced.

Clinicians and students are strongly encouraged to engage in a collaborative exploration of the patient's relationships with a substance with the help of 15 clinical sketches for adults and youth, which include short case vignettes. This step is often overlooked as clinicians attempt to divert a potential disaster, require 12-step participation, propose inpatient or outpatient treatment, prescribe medication, or impose a solution through a manualized treatment protocol. In our haste to be helpful, we have jumped to solutions before providing the patient "a relational home" (Stolorow, 2007, p. 26) to explore the meanings and the matters of his own personal AOD relationships. A section on DSM-5 revision implications for everyday practice ends the chapter.

RECENT DSM HISTORY

Before the release of DSM-5 in the spring of 2013, treatment providers had been instructed to assess whether someone's maladaptive use of a substance was one of abuse or dependence. These two *Diagnostic and Statistical Manual of Mental Disorders* terms framed our thinking and directed our choices for decades. Individuals, families, and clinicians became discouraged and frustrated by the limitations of these two categories (American Psychiatric Association, 2000). The ritualized and repetitive use of these terms diminished our clinical acumen and prevented us from being open and receptive to all the complexity that was sitting across from us. This restriction in choices contributed to the field's tendency to overdiagnose, see too much, and prematurely ascribe a label. Or to underdiagnose, see too little, and look the other way. Nobody benefited from this parochial vision. The DSM-5 addiction work group assigned to construct the 2013 revisions seemed to agree. The shift from a binary choice of abuse and dependence to a spectrum of SUDs is a radical change indeed. The revisions are listed below (American Psychiatric Association, 2013, pp. 483–589).

Diagnostic Symptoms

Substance-Related

In DSM-5, the presence of at least two of 10 or 11 symptoms indicates a substance use disorder (the hallucinogens and the inhalants eliminate the withdrawal symptom category as the evidence of withdrawal is undetermined for these two classes). Substance-related legal problems have been dropped; craving has been added. The four symptoms of abuse and the seven symptoms of dependence from the DSM-IV-R have been combined. The 11 symptoms are:

- Tolerance*
- Withdrawal*
- More use than intended
- Craving for substance
- Unsuccessful attempt to cut down
- Spending excessive time in acquisition
- Activities given up because of use
- Use despite negative effects
- Failure to fulfill major role obligations
- Recurrent use in hazardous situations
- Continued use despite social or interpersonal problems

*Not counted if prescribed by a physician.

Severity Index

A severity index has been added to determine one's place on the spectrum of SUDs:

- Nonproblematic use (NPU)*: Presence of 0–1 symptoms
- Mild: Presence of 2–3 symptoms
- Moderate: Presence of 4–5 symptoms
- Severe: Presence of 6 or more symptoms

* The words *nonproblematic use, nondisordered use,* and *nonpathological use* are referred to in the text of the DSM-5 for most of the 10 classes of substances. I have included it in the severity index for all classes. I anticipate that future DSM revisions will include discussions of nonproblematic use for all 10.

Some therapists may take these revisions with a grain of salt. These clinicians may comply with a 2013 SUD diagnosis, but continue practicing within their own treatment paradigm. Other therapists may very much value the range of AOD experiences to consider; many counselors and clinicians may need to rely on these new diagnostic directions while treating in either an inpatient or outpatient setting. Insurance reimbursement will eventually require adherence to the SUDs spectrum, matching the number of symptomatic criteria to severity. An initial clinician response from a Los Angeles therapist: "There is too much spectrum uncertainty, a confusing leeway about the use of the word addiction, and much anxiety about determining how to diagnose and, more importantly, treat these disorders."

Non-Substance-Related

In DSM-5, the presence of four or more of the following nine symptoms occurring in a 12-month period indicates a gambling disorder. These nine symptoms are:

(A)
- Spends increasing amounts of money
- Becomes restless or irritable when trying to reduce or stop
- Makes unsuccessful attempts to control, cut back, or stop
- Is preoccupied with gambling
- Gambles when distressed
- Chases one's losses
- Lies to conceal involvement
- Jeopardizes or loses a significant relationship, job, educational, or career opportunity
- Relies on others for bailout

(B) The gambling behavior is not better explained by a manic episode.

Severity Index

- Nondisordered use: Presence of 0–3 symptoms
- Mild: Presence of 4–5 symptoms
- Moderate: Presence of 6–7 symptoms
- Severe: Presence of 8–9 symptoms

FROM OVER- AND UNDERDIAGNOSING
TO EXPLORING CLINICAL SKETCHES

Over the last 2.5 decades, I have also found it helpful and useful to think expansively about diagnosis, not just limit assessment to abuse and dependence. I have both conceptualized and developed clinical sketches of using, nonusing, misusing, and addiction. I have observed human behaviors, organized my impressions, and developed 15 profiles or clinical sketches that describe some of the idiosyncratic stories of our attachments and involvements with alcohol and drugs. The number of profiles has expanded over the years as a result of my own clinical observations, as well as collegial and student input. To a certain degree, we are bound by the DSM, and I hope these clinical descriptors are of service to your thinking as you adjust to the DSM-5 dimensional approach.

A common reaction to problems with AOD is to panic about what is going on around us—how bad things are becoming, how hopeless we feel, and how incapable of really reaching out and helping we have become. We feel confused, scared, and useless. During these moments of fear, worry, and helplessness, we seem to do one of two things in an effort to get relief.

First, we overdiagnose. We intervene in dramatic ways and prematurely label. We are sure people are "alcoholics," are "addicts," or have a drug problem or alcohol issue. If we are able to identify them, we can tell them what to do. We can get control. We insist on treatment or arrange an intervention. George Vaillant reminds us that addiction is not just defined by symptomatic using, but also by who is watching the user (1983). Overdiagnosing has a strange effect—it calms family members and incites the user. This effect cancels out any real progress. It doesn't help.

Second, we underdiagnose or imagine that the problem is not that bad. We excuse it away and thus avoid the labels altogether. For complex and tragic reasons, many seem unable to clearly and convincingly tell those they love that they are in trouble with drugs and alcohol. One of my patients who has struggled with facing a family member's AOD problems has said, "My husband's drinking is out of control, but I guess this is what I have to accept with someone who is so intense with everything he does. You know, I just have to take the good with the bad." A couple discussing his overreliance on Vicodin and her daily ritual of compulsively pulling her eyelashes out, commented, "You know, in this day and age everybody has something. And what we do doesn't interfere with our jobs and our lives." Finally, a repeated marital or partnership refrain about daily disturbing AOD dependence, "There is already so much going on with the children, her work, and her illness. You know, we all do the best we can."

I have seen this pattern time and time again over the years—frantically label or helplessly resign. Neither helps. The following sketches of substance use, disorder, and addiction begin to address the problems of seeing too much or seeing too little. These profiles are *guidelines* to help us understand what we are witnessing and experiencing, and to help to make sense of what is overwhelming, confusing, or frightening. These are guidelines designed to encourage reflection. These are profiles for everyday conversation about our relationship with substances and compulsive processes (including gambling), and for assessment and clinical treatment. These clinical sketches are designed to help us embrace a pleasurable and complex human drive, and the ways it can confuse us and get us in trouble.

READING THE CLINICAL SKETCHES

This chapter is written in an informational and informal tone. Again, the DSM-5 diagnostic spectrum terminology of nonpathological use and mild, moderate, and severe substance use disorders are included alongside the 15 clinical sketches. These sketches were designed during and after my own observations of many idiosyncratic clinical cases over many years. The presentation, style, and length are unique for each category. The informational tone delivers clear-cut content for your consideration; the informal tone invites your engagement and reflection.

This framework is noteworthy for its inclusion of 10 healthy relationships for both adults and young adults. We have become too accustomed to defining our uses of AOD as pathological and have often overlooked the more pleasurable and responsible ones. Again, I have chosen at my discretion, as DSM-5 advised, to include use of the word *addiction* to indicate the approximately 3% of the population who are truly physically and psychologically addicted (CDC, 2014).

Hopefully, readers will extrapolate what is useful, add to what is missing, and consider alternative descriptions. Class discussions on this topic are usually very energized and exciting; conversations are meant to further explore the process of assessment thinking. Most students feel comfortable talking about their own relationship with AOD and discovering "my profile." They discuss the clinical sketches with family members and friends. The sketches also open up a new opportunity to explore their patients' unique relationships with other compulsive processes.

These sketches are designed to bridge the gap between assessment and treatment. They encourage patients and individuals to consider and explore the meaning behind a mild, moderate, or severe SUD before deciding on a response to their problem. Use of the 15 sketches is intended to depathologize our desire for intoxication, foster an exploratory conversation around the "drive" to escape and expand consciousness, deepen our individual and cultural understanding of our relationship with AOD, enhance diagnostic and assessment skills, expand clinical imagination, and assist in managing the new complex process of assessment. The more nuanced our vision, the more thoughtful our treatment.

The two clinical sketch tables that follow (see Figures 6.1 and 6.2) provide a visual overview of 15 different clinical sketches with AOD. Again, they are designed to begin a conversation with a patient or a loved one. The 15 profile descriptions or sketches that follow each figure briefly illustrate the nature of the relationship users may have with their substance of choice or other substances they struggle with or enjoy. Adults and young people *can move in and out of these categories, visit or dwell in them during periods of stress. They can also get stuck in one of them for decades or a lifetime.* Regardless, all are encouraged to continuously explore, maintain, or repair their relationships with these substances.

Just a reminder—each clinical sketch description includes a spectrum diagnosis in parentheses. DSM-5 uses the term *nonpathological use* (NPU) to identify

Figure 6.1   Clinical Sketches—Adults

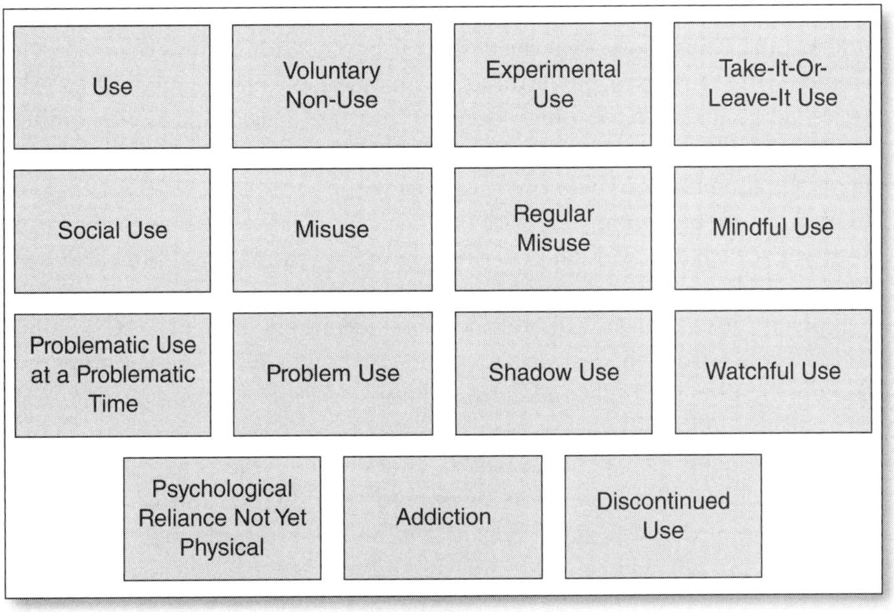

use that is not harmful; my preference is to use the word *healthy* instead for each clinical description that is nonpathological. These sketches can stand on their own, are not necessarily progressive, nor necessarily linear. These are suggestions for the clinician to assimilate within her own treatment approach and style. Remember, this framework is noteworthy for its inclusion of 10 healthy relationships with our ancient desire, as well as five problematic ones.

CLINICAL SKETCHES (DSM-5)

For Adults

Use (Healthy)

Since humankind began, we have always looked for a way to escape or expand consciousness. Sometimes this is done for spiritual ecstasy and other times for fun. We now know the special place that alcohol assumed in early civilizations. Wine was being made as early as 5400 BCE. Ancient Romans had their god of drink, Bacchus, and the Greeks their Dionysus. In ancient Egypt, both beer and wine were deified and offered to the gods (D. J. Hanson, 1995; van Wormer & Davis, 2008, p. 38).

As has been mentioned, Ronald K. Siegel (2005) at UCLA proposes that this ancient desire is actually another human drive, similar to our need for food, water, and sex. He suggests that the urge to get high is among our basic motivations; he proposes that the desire for intoxication is the *fourth drive*, an acquired drive that is as powerful as an innate one. And like all drives, desire varies. Some people have a high desire to escape consciousness, while others have medium or low drives. Thomas Szasz (1988), psychiatrist and academic, likens the contemporary war on drugs to a war on this human desire, suggesting that we are uncomfortable with our need for pleasure, escape, or oblivion. Both suggest that a war on our own nature is ultimately doomed (Siegel, 2005, p. 208).

A lively discussion always follows these remarks. Students' AOD habits are explored—from the last drink, to the last hangover, to the last time they said no. We discuss family and cultural habits. We look at people's emotional relationships with AOD.

I pose a question to students each semester, and the response is telling. "Would you be willing to explore or give up your own troubled AOD use for the duration of this semester?" A gasp and an embarrassed laugh usually follow. Many are not willing at first blush, and quickly they are struck by their protective and defensive response. Eventually, a sizable number of courageous students agree to examine or forgo a bothersome pleasure and write a chapter about the experience in their final paper.

Voluntary Nonuse (Healthy)

This is a profile of people who early on and voluntarily make a decision not to include alcohol or drugs in their lives. They respond to this drive of human desire with a no, either emphatically from bad experiences, indifferently, or derived from a value. Some are influenced to make this choice as a result of what they have seen in their upbringing. These experiences range from a grandfather who drank himself to death to a mother who hid pills in the closet, thinking no one saw her take them throughout the day. Others lived in an alcohol-fueled household or with a sibling who repeatedly got himself in trouble. One who was scarred by an alcoholic parent said, "I'd rather play it safe and not drink than live on the slippery slope of a possibility." Another volunteered, "I'm a pretty intense guy, and I'm worried that I wouldn't be able to control it."

Sometimes there is no negative influence at all, just a sense of "I don't need it to relax, and actually, it gets in the way of getting close to people." A college student with a father she has only known sober, because his addictive drinking took place before her birth, chooses not to drink. She struggles with her judgmental attitudes; she considers the choice to drink a moral weakness, as giving into something and a waste of time. Others say they feel they don't need it: "I get enjoyment and satisfaction from sitting around a board game with friends; others get that pleasure from sitting around a bong pipe." One woman in her 30s who does not drink proudly announces, "It distinguishes me."

Many nonusers acknowledge the pressures they experience from drinkers who want them to join in their partying. "Drinkers seem to feel guilty about their overdrinking and don't want someone sober watching them." As one nonuser observed, "It's sad to see someone who is drunk reduced to a form of amusement, rather than a person."

Many report not liking the taste of alcohol from that first drink. These are often a category of people who are not affected in any way by others' responses to their nondrinking. They are self-assured instead. "I don't feel that I am missing anything and always have a good time with drinkers or nondrinkers. When I'm having fun, drinkers usually think I'm drunk anyway."

Informal surveys conducted in my classes over the years show that nonusers make up about 5% of the student population. Approximately 95% of students report using drugs or alcohol. Most of these student users report an increase in AOD use during their graduate studies. They are upset and somewhat alarmed by this tendency. It is part of our semester-long conversation on the profiles of using, nonusing, misusing, and addiction in our own lives.

Experimental Use (Healthy, Mild, Moderate, or Severe)

"To experiment is to undertake, to discover something not yet known; to try out something to find out whether or not it will be effective. To experiment is to test something out; to tentatively explore" (Guralnik & Friend, 1968, p. 512).

A young adolescent girl has grown up in a family of glamorous-looking evening parental cocktails. She watches her parents drink at dinners and cocktail parties. They look stylish, happy, and relaxed. It seems to her that drinking brings comfort, ease, and fun. She feels pressured by schoolwork and parental expectations. She remembers where her parents keep their gin. She runs down the backstairs to the kitchen and takes a gulping swig. She has begun experimenting.

Parents are gone all day, and their children's curiosity is left unnurtured. These boys and girls roam the neighborhood and the streets, hang around malls all day, looking for something. They run into other kids from different parts of town whose pockets are filled with solvents, drugs, and alcohol. These are passed around. This group of children has started experimenting.

Other kids feel anxious and unhappy in their home situation. There is poverty, neglect, violence, anxiety and depression, drugs, and alcohol. It helps to stay away from home as much as possible. These boys and girls are not sure what they feel, but they know they want to feel differently. Before they leave the house, they empty their parents' medicine cabinets of pills or find household liquids that might give them a buzz. AOD provides an immediate sense of relief and comfort. These kids are experimenting.

Some graduate students share their fears of losing control; they prefer not to explore the world of drugs and alcohol. Many test out experiences with one drug and not another. Other students like the thrill of experimenting with all of them.

After several conversations, a sober man and his wife in their mid-50s decide to start drinking again. They both feel they have benefited from regular participation in AA, as well as ongoing psychotherapy, and now believe that they have the ability to pace their alcohol use. Are they in denial, are they relapsing, or are they experimenting?

Many individuals explore, experiment, or tentatively test what getting high feels like and what results it brings. For some, it's an unsatisfactory experience and usage comes to a halt rather quickly. Others have a mixed experience and return to it periodically. Still others are immediately taken by the pleasure, excitement, and danger, and begin an ongoing search for more.

We have made experimentation into something dreadful and foreboding. A mother called me a month ago and said she is very alarmed by her son's increasing preoccupation with marijuana, and said, "I think I'm going to put him in a rehabilitation boot camp." I listened and cautioned, "Testing an unknown is not a bad thing." She scheduled an appointment, cancelled it, and said, "I will call you in the future." I have not heard from her since.

Sharing our response to our experimentation is a good thing. Conversations encourage ongoing monitoring of the pleasures and dangers involved in our desires to escape and expand consciousness.

Over the years, I have asked students in my semester classes and participants in my workshops the following question: How many of you have experimented with any or all of the 10 classes of substances that we use to get high? More often than not, nearly all of the students raise their hands.

Take-It-or-Leave-It Use (Healthy)

Most drinkers are planners. They know when they are going to drink, how much, and if they will stop, slow down, or keep going. A number of people have a take-it-or-leave-it attitude toward AOD. It is not a pocket of meaning in their lives. That is, it is not a habit or activity that they invest with importance and repetition. They do not pay attention to AOD; it is not a big interest in their lives and, therefore, it is not part of their planning.

A party either has alcohol or it doesn't—if it's there, fine, and if it's not, 7-Up is fine too. These people are not preoccupied with the place of alcohol in their lives; they barely give it any thought. There is no anticipation about the presence of alcohol, as there is for many who drink. There are also no regrets about one's experience with alcohol. Life feels full enough without drugs and alcohol, and life is enjoyed without the desire to get high. That being said, these folks are certainly capable of enjoying a glass of wine or a beer.

Take-it-or-leave-it people baffle many regular users of AOD. They generate envy in most problematic drinkers or users. "I watch people at a party or at a dinner and can't understand how they leave a glass of wine half full, not drink as much as they can get their hands on, or voluntarily refuse a glass of wine and choose an ice tea instead. I really can't fathom that." The drive to get high is so preoccupying to some and so incidental to others.

I conducted an informal survey while teaching a recent workshop. I asked the 50 students, "How many of you feel you belong in this profile?" One person raised his hand.

Social Use (Healthy)

Social drinkers are people who enjoy a drink or two in the company of others. They look forward to a night out with friends and anticipate a relaxing glass of wine, beer, or spirits during an intimate dinner or at a festive gathering. They enjoy getting high with other people; they relish the relaxing effects. Social drinkers occasionally drink alone; they just don't make a habit of it.

Social drinkers imbibe to enhance a social event. They plan for a good time and gauge for any overindulgence. They usually do not want to lose control, ruin an evening, embarrass themselves, or feel any ill effects. They are gifted with an intuitive sense of moderation. They are fun-loving and responsible. They enjoy sharing a buzz, know when to stop, and can also drive home. They are blessed with the capacity to learn from experience after that rare occasion of exceeding their limit. Their problems in life are not distorted by the effects of drugs and alcohol.

Social users like alcohol. Katie remembered, "This was a really tough week. My children and work were both too demanding. There was no time for me. All week I kept dreaming about my friend's 50th birthday party on Friday. I wanted to dress up and let go. Just thinking about the freedom and relaxation got me through the heartache of the week." Katie later described a really fun evening with laughter, friends, and acting silly. She had a glass of wine as soon as she arrived and switched to water before dinner.

All drinkers want to believe they belong in this profile. They may, or they may not. Katie seemed to.

Misuse (Healthy or Mild)

Sometimes we overindulge at a birthday lunch. We can later attend an evening event that same day and also drink too much. And we can do that on several occasions. Does that mean that we are on the road to severe SUDs or addiction? Not necessarily. Check family history, as well as the meaning behind the misuse of alcohol. Mishandling an attempt to satisfy a human desire does not justify hysterical and controlling responses.

Sally, a patient of mine, called one morning in an agitated and slightly panicky mood. When asked about recent activities, she described an unusual day of heavy drinking. It started with a farewell luncheon for a colleague at work. A designated driver allowed many, including herself, to overdrink. She continued drinking at a social event with her husband that same night.

Sally's day and evening of drinking were noteworthy. She is not a regular drinker, nor does she have any family history with addiction. Her agitation was probably a result of a hangover from double-event drinking the day before.

Some misusers like Sally are "too inexperienced" to connect edgy apprehension with the withdrawal symptoms of overusing alcohol, which is a central nervous system depressant. I shared this with Sally, and she felt relieved that she was able to identify the source of her physiological panic and psychological discomfort. She could now wait it out until her symptoms disappeared.

Another student shared with the class, "I've made up this word—it's called 'time traveling.' It sounds like a symptom of misuse. Here's how it goes: I time travel when I drink too much. I wake up the next morning and remember how I started the evening, but can't remember how I got to the end of the evening. I remember the beginning and the end, but not much in between. That's time traveling." Another student added, "I do that too. I plan for a party night and I start out pounding drinks, and then I let these carry me through the evening. I feel some sense of control because I know I'm not going to drink anymore. I think that's why I remember only the beginning and end of the night." Both commented, "I hope it is only misuse. I better watch this." Many in the class smiled with recognition. More seemed alarmed by the universal frequency of this experience. There appears to be an element of choice in time traveling, which seems to distinguish it from a blackout (full amnesia) or a brownout (partial amnesia).

A young graduate student and social drinker feels a nice buzz, desires more, and regrets it later. A troubling pattern starts to develop. She shared, "It's happening a little bit more than I would like." She described looking forward to a night of relaxing drinking with her friend. She liked the warm feeling of that first drink. It felt good; it calmed her down. She counseled herself, "I know I should stop and stay with this feeling of pleasure. Instead, I drink more and lose more control than I want. I am starting to get a little worried. I want to keep things at social drinking. I need to work harder at this."

Misusers are not afraid to acknowledge their mishaps and talk about their drinking anxieties. They prefer to address these, not hide them. They are not ashamed of overdoing it; it feels normal. "It's what all people do some of the time." Misusers have the ability to reverse this infrequent but bothersome behavior.

Regular Misuse (Moderate)

If you are repeatedly and recklessly misusing substances, chances are that the motivations for using are becoming more psychologically complex. Private monologues of worry begin to occupy the user's mind. Some readers may identify with this profile and likely know friends and family who predictively and repeatedly misuse a substance. These are the people who usually start drinking with gusto and desire a good time for all. They may be the life of the party: "He's a good person to invite, and we want him to help get things going."

More often than not, family and friends can "count on Jeff to start acting like the camp counselor you always wanted to punch." Unfortunately, all too often these folks do not know how to stop. They often maintain this pattern for a lifetime, and may be a part of a family that does not believe this pattern is necessarily on the road to severe SUDs or addiction but a part of Jeff's way to relax and unwind. Together, they may successfully work on behavioral agreements rather than insist on abstinence.

Other misusers sink into silence, withdraw, or fall asleep.

Mindful Use (Healthy)

The contemporary values of physical and mental health contribute to the widespread adoption of this profile. Mindful users want to drink, continue to learn from misusing episodes, and consider physical and mental health a priority.

More and more individual users are working with mindfulness as a way to moderate their drinking or drugging behaviors. Misusers first need to be willing to acknowledge that they have problems with pacing alcohol or marijuana; that they often overindulge and regret it later. After acceptance of problematic patterns, the challenge begins: to stay present and connected to your state of intoxication before giving yourself full permission to move on to a more destructive level. Many patients literally carry a drink diary in their pocketbook or pocket and remind themselves that before they have another drink or another hit they must fill in the diary entry identifying their mood and why they feel that another drink or hit of marijuana would enhance their pleasure.

A patient of mine named Sophie travels, lives, and works in several states in America. Sophie is a regular misuser who is practicing mindfulness. Before her last trip she told me of a dream she had the night before: "I was traveling by car in a dark, rainy forest on a narrow, foggy road. I remember telling myself, 'This is foggy and dangerous, but you can stop, look, and navigate through the fog. I don't have to keep going.' I got to the end of the road. It narrowed and dropped off, but somehow I miraculously found the space to turn my car around. I then began traveling back to the lighter part of the forest. I got out of my car, and as I was walking, I caught sight of a menacing man with a cougar and a lion protecting his home. My unintentional trespassing alarmed me, and I ran back to the car. The animals were now huge guard dogs, and attacked me in the car as I drove away in terror." Sophie's dream helped her grasp the extent of her extreme anxieties over traveling again to another state for 3 months. The dream was "extremely useful in depicting how the traveling and its dislocations really upset me," and she felt that it would greatly help her mindfulness while away and while drinking.

Problematic Use at a Problematic Time (Moderate or Severe)

Drinking at problematic times in one's life can mimic more severely disturbed use and seduce clinicians or family members into thinking of more extreme treatment responses. These users are typically self-medicating during a stressful time in their lives. They are often easily coached through changing their short-term destructive behaviors into healthier patterns or even discontinuing use altogether.

A mom and dad with two children under 3 years old are working, parenting, and struggling with real and self-imposed impossible tasks (Obholzer & Roberts, 1994, pp. 110–118). Their lives are feeling too pressured and unfulfilling. Norris and Ann don't think they are managing well.

They invite a parent from another part of the country to live with them. They all share the same small, two-bedroom apartment. Things become tense, and Ann, a young mother with no previous interest in AOD, discovers that alcohol has become, to quote the Rolling Stones, "mother's little helper." Occasional weekend evening drinking turns into daily habituation, beginning each evening at 5:00 p.m. Soon, Ann's drinking escalates, including hard liquor and in larger amounts. She drifts into day drinking on Saturday and Sunday. The children are vulnerable and suffering under her watch. Frightening and dangerous mishaps begin to occur. She is even missing days at work. Norris and Ann are surprised by this escalating and destructive trend, and after a discussion agree that they do not want it to continue.

This nonadversarial couple increasingly lives in a panic and seeks therapeutic help. There is no discounting the problem—not the existence, significance, or impact of the drinking on each other and the family (Lasater, 1988, pp. 30–31). At first blush, this looks and smells like a severe SUD, with six of the 11 required symptoms, including tolerance, drinking larger amounts over longer periods of time than intended, continued use despite persistent problems, and not fulfilling major role obligations. She is drinking 7 days out of the week and can't imagine her life without the help of alcohol. Yet, at the same time, she is developing a sense that the alcohol is no longer helping.

As mentioned, Ann has no history of an alcohol SUD, and there is none in her extended family. This couple works together as a team and wants to address the issue before it gets out of hand. They scare themselves and catch the problem before real habituation sets in. They both are internally motivated (Miller & Rollnick, 2002).

Using Lance Dodes's (2002) work, we explore ways that Ann and Norris both feel trapped. We identify drinking as the substitute action that she hoped would reverse her feelings of overwhelming helplessness. In five joint sessions, I help them nurture a broader perspective while thinking about their dilemma, their lifestyle, and their choices. They begin to make adjustments, and they quickly feel relief. Life soon feels more manageable, and the need to self-medicate with alcohol significantly decreases. They both become better problem-solvers (see Chapter 8, pp. 114–116).

We were able to reverse a short-lived, unhealthy drinking pattern by exploring its history and the current contextual demands, as well as by noticing the considerable motivational strengths of each person. What looked and smelled like a severe SUD or addiction was actually an example of problematic use at a problematic time. The couple felt empowered and left therapy after 4 months. They greatly appreciated a therapeutic response that neither underdiagnosed Ann's problematic behaviors nor slapped on a label that was actually inaccurate.

Problem Use (Moderate or Severe)

This profile identifies persons who are regularly drinking or drugging not just for fun or short-term stress release, but also to cope. It gives them a sense of imaginary intactness (Eigen, 1999, p. 222). Life has gotten away from them, demands are overwhelming, and over time, drinking has gotten sloppy. Physical and mental health, marital relationships and partnerships, children and work are impacted in insidious and unhealthy ways. Honest discussions about these difficulties stop working; silent, seething resentment and angry accusations abound. Despair is pervasive. A terrifying resignation permeates the household, with the growing sense that there might not be a solution for this disturbing habit. Family members begin to live with a very unhealthy compromise and a destructive fantasy: "Maybe miraculously, without help and effort, things will get better; maybe the drinking will stop, and then we will no longer live in anticipatory terror of the next bad episode."

The Centers for Disease Control and Prevention (CDC) recently reported that binge drinking is a bigger problem than was previously thought, and that a large number of people who binge drink are not alcohol dependent or addicted. Adults binge for more than 50% of their drinking time; youths for 90%. Most binge drinkers earn more than $75,000 a year. If you earn less than $25,000 a year, your frequent binges usually include the highest number of drinks among the general binging population (CDC, 2012).

Andrew Tatarsky is a leader in the field of harm reduction and a member of the board of Moderation Management (MM), an organization that maintains there are four times as many problem drinkers as alcoholics in this country. This suggests that the largest group of people having issues with alcohol are not in a state of addiction. They instead are problem drinkers who experience ongoing problems but do not have a severe physical addiction to alcohol (Institute of

Medicine). We offer very few services for their nightly or weekend heavy drinking, their blackouts or brownouts, or their periodic or regular binge episodes. We are loath to acknowledge and embrace this drinking pattern.

A recent study by the Centers for Disease Control and Prevention found that nine of 10 adult excessive drinkers did not meet the diagnostic criteria for alcohol dependence—or, as we now refer to it, a severe substance disorder or addiction (CDC, 2014).

The United Kingdom's Department of Health launched a Change4life alcohol campaign urging its country of habitual and heavy drinkers to consider 2 to 3 alcohol-free days per week. A TV advertising campaign presses this message home (Department of Health, United Kingdom, 2012).

For problem users, drinking is occupying more attention in the drinker's mind. More time is spent planning for it and doing it. More often than not, the drinking is overdone and comes with a problem, such as increased isolation, angry outbursts, or ignored children. The drinker defensively avoids any acknowledgment of drinking's destructions. All members of the household soon become discounters of what they see. Two rather lengthy case studies reflect this oft-seen profile.

Agreements With a Couple

Over the years, I have attempted thoughtful responses for this complex profile. Usually one or both problem drinkers want to keep drinking, and they are not interested in Alcoholics Anonymous (AA) or abstinence. As one partner in a marriage said to me, "My problem with my drinking is that my wife has a problem with my drinking." While he admits he overdoes it, he wants to keep drinking and is not sure that help is out there for his goal. His wife is concerned that he is becoming an alcoholic. George and Sarah show up to begin therapy.

Here is a couple that seems to truly love each other. They value their marriage and their work, love their friends and their children, protect their health, and like their booze. More frequently, George's drinking comes with problems—drinking 7 days a week instead of 3, increased sloppiness and memory lapses, their shared fear of his inability to protect and care for the children, and his increasing isolation. He acknowledges these patterns. Sarah is worried and is haunted by growing up with an alcoholic mom.

Efran, Lukens, and Lukens (1990) introduce the notion of agreements. Simply stated, life works if you keep your agreements. We have agreements with ourselves and agreements with others. At any time, agreements are being kept, breached, or are under renegotiation. Life works well if you keep your agreements; your life will not work as well if you breach them, or if you are secretly, privately, or even publicly renegotiating the terms of them. Life feels weighty, cumbersome, and edgy, and it gets messy during these times of reorganization or violation. This is a most practical mental health concept. Try it out; your life might work better (pp. 115–121).

I often use agreements with this clinical sketch. Agreements can be a useful tool with problem drinkers who want to solve their drinking problem. For starters, I want to make sure that I'm not colluding with the avoidance of the necessity for abstinence. I have developed eligibility criteria that help determine this profile's suitability. For example, I used the following while assessing this couple:

- Is the drinking truly just problem drinking, or is it true addiction?
- Is the couple willing to be educated about what we know and don't know in the fields of SUDs? Are they willing and able to appreciate the difference between excessive use and addictive drinking?
- Is the couple able to be nonadversarial? Do they want to problem-solve together?
- Do they have pockets of meaning in their lives other than alcohol? These are activities or habits that are invested with importance and nurturance (family, friends, hobbies, sports, work, religion, and so forth).
- Are they discounting (p. 61) the problem in any way?
- Do they want something so much they lose their judgment?

This couple met the suitability criteria and, with some assistance, devised agreements to address their drinking concerns. The agreements were:

- Agreement #1: Monday through Thursday—drink Calistoga water
- Agreement #2: Friday night—drink as much alcohol as desired
- Agreement #3: Saturday and Sunday night—drink two glasses of wine or beer each
- Agreement #4: Directly address infractions

The couple was internally motivated and quickly rehabituated their drinking behaviors (Miller & Rollnick, 2002). They settled into a new lifestyle. The results were steady and promising, and our therapy conversations cleared up any confusion. Then there was a mishap that needed some attention.

George went on a business trip during the week. It was supposed to be a Calistoga night. He was "away from home, children, and responsibilities," and he broke Agreement #1 and drank two glasses of wine. He chose to keep this breach and subsequent desire for agreement renegotiation from Sarah until our next session. She was not happy with the news, and he was embarrassed and remorseful. Life was not working well. Consequently, a new agreement was created about weekly business trips. Let's call it Agreement #1a: Two small glasses of wine while on a business trip.

Delightfully, the couple left after 6 months, content with their agreements. They seemed to experience therapy as a place to get down to business. George called for a session 6 months later. He noticed some agreement sloppiness, and he wanted to talk. We discussed the issue, and he has not called since. I suspect they would return if they were unable to negotiate their drinking agreements. Not all can do this, but more can if we conduct a proper assessment and provide helpful tools.

Agreements With an Individual

Daniel was 41 years old when we began therapy. He mechanically described a neglectful and violent childhood. He started smoking marijuana and drinking at age 11. He added cocaine to the mix in his late teens. He used drugs and drank heavily for decades. Daniel went to law school, passed the bar, but decided to pass on being an attorney. He became a writer. His dream was to sell a screenplay. He married and divorced. He was surviving and enduring without much feeling or meaning. He didn't know the difference between surviving and living; he just knew that he liked to drink and do drugs "as often and as much as I could."

Daniel's drinking and drugging days gradually came to an end after his girlfriend, Julie, "kept making such a big deal out of all my partying. She got on my case a lot; it bugged me. We fought; our relationship almost came to an end. And then her concerns started to make sense." Daniel took to abstinence with sincerity and passion. He came to therapy weekly. He cherished his sober mind and experiences. His writing improved, he lived with more ease with his girlfriend, and he began valuing different kinds of friends. "I've never felt this clearheaded or good about myself."

Daniel occasionally mentioned a desire to drink again after his first year of sobriety, but he repeatedly admonished himself: "I want to make it to one year. I've never been sober for that long. But, eventually, I also want to include alcohol in my life. I want to enjoy it with others, but I don't want to lose control, and I don't want to lose the mental and emotional clarity that I've gained in this last year. I've talked it over with Julie, and we both agree it's worth exploring in therapy. I want to make social drinking a part of my recovery."

Daniel talked extensively about why he wanted to drink and concluded, "It's a risk I want to responsibly take on." He seemed ready, willing, and able to explore and reexamine this option (Miller & Rollnick, 2002, p. 10).

Daniel wanted to use therapy as an accountability tool. He felt able to self-soothe anxieties that had always been silenced with alcohol. He relished his developing ability to think before impulsively acting out. He didn't want drinking to interfere with his growth. He was willing to address any mishaps and return to sobriety if needed.

He was intrigued by the idea of agreements. Daniel queried me about their use with other patients. Later, he and Julie talked for hours; they designed a plan. It would begin after a luxurious vacation to a faraway land. He did not want to drink during his travels. "I'm trying to see if I can bring drinking back into my everyday life, not my vacation life."

Daniel designed his agreements, took to heart successful and not-so-successful results, and crafted new ones. His first agreement was two drinks on one weekend night ("2 in 1"). He loved that first drink, the ease it brought, and the fun he felt. He sensed instantly that his experiment was probably going to work. He didn't want to get drunk; he wanted to enjoy the buzz with Julie. He was content with 2 in 1 for months, and then he wanted more. Daniel and Julie designed a new agreement—two drinks on 2 nights during the week (2 in 2). This also went well for months.

Toward the end of that first year of renegotiating alcohol's place in his life, Daniel went to Las Vegas. He willingly succumbed to the enticement of this extravagant partying environment. He broke his 2-in-2 agreement. He got drunk for the first time, very quickly recalled being an everyday drunk, and didn't like it. He suffered through the forgotten feelings of a hangover. It took days for his head to clear. He hated the ill health he felt. "I kept dreading talking about this to you in therapy."

The results of our Vegas postmortems brought a new agreement—one the reader might not imagine. Daniel continued to relish clearheaded moderation, but he also wanted to enjoy the pleasures of drinking a few nights out of the week. He believed he had gotten drunk in Vegas because "to tell you the truth, two drinks have never really done it for me. I'm 6 foot 4, you know." He voiced a new desire: "I want to experiment with getting a real buzz and see how I do. I really think I'm ready for this and can handle it, and I want to see how it goes." His new agreement was three drinks on 2 nights during the week (3 in 2).

Daniel developed a capacity not always seen in severe SUDs drinkers. He was excited by risk yet also valued responsibility. He successfully and comfortably abided by his 3-in-2 agreement for quite some time. We regularly tracked the relationship between his moods and his agreements. He periodically stopped drinking when it was interfering with everyday problem-solving and enjoyment in living. Daniel felt very good about his ability to make this decision and stick to it. I'm always comforted by Michael Eigen's wisdom: "We must always give our patients space to do their best or their worst" (personal communication, 2008). This applies to many of our problem-drinking patients as well.

Shadow Use (Moderate or Severe)

This profile identifies persons whose lives are going relatively well. They have jobs, pay their bills, and show up for life. They also drink or drug nearly 365 days of the year. This oftentimes destructive preoccupation casts a shadow over their lives, preventing them from enjoying love and work as they might. Many of us are shadow users, though most of us are loath to acknowledge this pervasive pattern in our lives.

Forme fruste is an unconventional medical term used to describe an incomplete expression of an illness (Ratey & Johnson, 1997, p. 33). These two doctors identify shadow syndromes as mild or subtle forms of otherwise serious mental disorders (p. 36). The more disabling symptoms of a disorder may not be present, but enough appear and cast a shadow over one's life. Again, this incapacity impairs one's enjoyment of love and work. These syndromes, as they call them, serve as incomplete expressions of some of the more serious diagnostic categories delineated in DSM-5. Ratey and Johnson's original book cover was designed with a question above a round plastic mirror: "Do you know someone with a shadow syndrome?"

Over time, some underlying tensions may emerge in the user's life. Increasingly, the shadow user is less interested in participating in family activities, or if he does, is always under the influence. Afternoons or nights of drinking or drugging are never missed, deeper conversations among family members decrease, and the distance between and among family members slowly increases. Traveling becomes problematic and cumbersome. The first stop after arrival is a liquor store or a dealer. While all seems okay on the surface, this once-benign intruder is now robbing family members of vitality and spontaneity.

The distance and lack of connectivity take their toll, and eventually someone in the family starts acting out. Help is sought, and in the mix of investigative and reparative efforts, the shadow user begins to get some attention for his nightly using. Ideally, this invites reflection into the meaning of this intoxication ritual, including its impact on the user and his family.

One of my patients, Sam, who is in his mid-40s, is attached to a substance on a daily basis and is a shadow syndrome user. He is married with three children, is ambitious and financially stable, exercises regularly, and works very hard at being a provider, husband, and father. He is also psychologically reliant on his daily relaxant. He occasionally discusses his "marijuana maintenance program" with his wife, and together they are watchful that this entrenched pattern does not get in the way of their relationship, evening duties, and the children. He wants to avoid any escalation of using, and he also doesn't want to stop his nightly ritual of 3 one-hitters (miniature smoking pipe designed for a single inhalation, or "hit," of cannabis or tobacco) over a 4-hour period.

Sam increased his use during a very stressful period of time. Graduate studies overpowered his emotions and his judgment. He felt unable to cope with multiple pressures, and convinced himself that his increased usage was only temporary. We engaged in a very focused exploration into the meaning of this escalating every-evening ritual. Sam uncomfortably, but willingly, considered the avoidance function of his shadow syndrome use. Overwhelming demands felt frustrating, expectations felt threatening, his inability to experience the pleasures of father-hood felt despairing, and his increasing secrecy with his wife felt even more so. His nightly reliance on this relaxing substance was now full of tension.

Sam begrudgingly faced the dysfunction of his increased daily reliance. He was able to be more truthful with himself, talked more with his wife, and hesitantly sought out one of his sober friends. He explored different patterns of using, was defensive and protective for a while, but then faced a habit that had become invasive and consuming, and decided to stop using. He was content with his sobriety and valued his emotional reawakening. He periodically announced during that first sober year, "One day I want to return to social using." We talked. I encouraged him to continue letting his everyday experiences build without marijuana interference. He agreed.

Sam grew tremendously during his first year of sobriety. He became more comfortable being intimate with his wife, felt noticeably more connected to his children, and advanced at work. We missed three sessions after his first-year anniversary, and on the fourth session, he informed me that he and his wife had gone away for a weekend, and he resumed experimenting. Again he reiterated, "I want to be normal. I want to relax like normal people do."

Over the next 2 years, Sam increased his using, and by the end of that first year was smoking marijuana 7 nights a week. There were fits and starts, periods of total sobriety, and periods of weekend use only. He gradually connected his extreme anxiety at work—including his lack of decisiveness as a CEO and his lack of internal motivation—as a struggle similar to his struggle with marijuana. Shortly thereafter, he decided to smoke only on Friday, Saturday, and Sunday nights. As a matter of fact, he often skips a weekend night. It's not easy for him not to use. He struggles often with the desire to escape reality. Well into 6 months with several instances of weekday use, Sam tells me, "I want my smoking to be conscious, not for self-medication, but a form of relaxation only."

Not all shadow syndrome users can evolve into watchful users (next clinical sketch), and they are not able to arrest or reverse the insidious, creeping, destructive potential of this profile of using. Sam and his wife are a nonad-versarial and nondiscounting couple. They value their passions and nurture each other and their lives. They are working together to achieve Sam's goal of "normalcy."

Watchful Use (Healthy)

Ongoing patterns of problematic use have firmly caught the attention of the user. After exploration of his relationship with AOD and oftentimes a substantial period of abstinence, the user resumes drinking with a watchful eye. It is likely his drinking and drugging will require serious scrutiny throughout his lifetime. This scrutiny is not a sign of pathology, but a part of the healthy management of a natural and pleasurable appetite.

Let's refer back to Daniel from earlier in this chapter. As you may recall, he was a severe problem user who "finally responded" to his girlfriend's concerns about his drinking and drugging patterns. They created and renegotiated agreements, but were committed to embracing both his desire to drink and her fear of his excess. I talked with Daniel in preparation for this second edition. He married Julie, has twins, and is enjoying his new work in commercial real estate. He and his wife, of course, struggle with the demands of child-rearing. He proudly told me, "The drinking is good, though. We talk all the time together about it. We still drink together and work together as a team about our drinking. It helps a lot. I drink 1 night during the week, and 1 or 2 nights over the weekends. I can't say that I don't overdo it at times, but I can say that I take seriously those nights and work hard to learn what I can do better next time." Daniel spent a great deal of his life destructively using AOD; as you may recall, he began his relationship with alcohol and marijuana when he was 11. He was abstinent for a year in his 40s, was committed to addressing his drinking problems and what drove them, worked hard in therapy, and had great support from his wife. Daniel is a watchful drinker today!

Psychological Reliance Not Yet Physical (Severe)

In this profile, physical addiction is being held at desperate bay. Just enough of the drug is used to stave off the symptoms of physical withdrawal and quiet the escalating psychological terror of one's habitual reliance on AOD. This individual is in a last-ditch effort to keep AOD in his life. Living without it feels impossible.

Alcohol, the opiates, and the sedative hypnotics have the potential to create physical and psychological addiction. Increased use disturbs, disrupts, and resets both the mind and body's homeostatic balance, or resting point. The problem user becomes obsessed with maintaining this body/mind new normal. The user senses that total loss of control is looming. Family and friends are both frantic and silenced.

The AOD use is secretly and tragically consuming more of the person's time. Life's tasks are about endurance, not meaning and fulfilment. The only hope is to complete them so that drinking and using can resume. People are desperately functioning while using increasing amounts of AOD. Pockets of meaning are discarded, isolation increases, and a sense of despair overwhelms. The possibility of not using is incomprehensible. Each night of heavy drinking is deathlike, and upon awakening, a new day of resurrection feels miraculous (Szasz, cited in Levin, 2001, pp. 213–214). This grim path is followed until it no longer can be.

The Dilaudid (opiate) user does not want to be dope-sick at work. Shira is convinced that she is cleverly avoiding physical collapse with careful strategic dosing, just enough to take care of any physical withdrawal. Her real desire is to psychologically prove she is beating addiction, as well as self-medicating away the ever-frightening realization that life with this opiate is surely coming to an end.

James, an ambitious attorney, is increasingly and frenetically focused on rearranging appointments, getting the minimum accomplished, and avoiding every other attorney at both work and social engagements. The point is to get his work done and get home to drink. By now, most of James's drinking time is alone. He drinks quickly and repeatedly functions in a blackout. His hope is that he did not use the phone during his alcohol-induced amnesia.

Eventually, both Shira and James are forced to fold into physical or psychic collapse. The final hours and days are lived in withdrawal from everyday functioning with close to round-the-clock using and passing out.

Friends or family frequently find these persons in some degree of intoxicated incoherence, often near a coma. The next step is an emergency room, likely in preparation for some sort of intensive rehabilitation treatment. After awakening in the ER, the lucky ones in this profile are overwhelmed by the terrifying realization that it is finally time to end this tortured life of isolation, secrecy, intoxication, and deep misery. Most often, this profile results in a life of discontinued use or abstinence.

Addiction (Addiction)

Addictive use results in physical and psychological reliance, tolerance, withdrawal, debilitating or life-threatening problems, and loss of a healthy sense of self. Isolative drinking or drugging round the clock or roaming the streets intoxicated often result in severe physical problems, coma, and eventually death.

The person in this profile is using AOD 24/7. His psychological and physical addiction requires this. He is often waking up, having a hit or a swig before or in his coffee. He continues nipping throughout the day and evening. This continues into weeks, months, and for some, years. Concerned pleas are ignored or angrily responded to, and friends feel alienated and exhausted. Family talks are often met with the individual's hardened desire to continue using. This person feels fated to his existence; he imagines that he will use and live this way for the rest of his life.

To avoid over- or underdiagnosing in this profile, I have designed three additional criteria to add to the DSM-5 SUDs list of 11 symptoms. These unconventional terms and concepts have sharpened my assessment capacities over the years. They warn me of upcoming psychological and/or physical addiction, or confirm their presence.

These terms are described below; a clinical question is posed and their application is demonstrated in a clinical case.

The Mess Factor (Is it high, medium, or low?): Individuals with addictions don't have problems due to using—they have messes. They live in a world of financial, health, family, physical, and work disasters. A work mess collides with a financial one. A health mess collides with a family one. Life is about dodging these messes and figuring out a way to stay high.

A high mess factor suggests that wanting and needing drugs and alcohol so much have severely incapacitated any kind of judgment. The person is tragically unable to anticipate and address life's responsibilities and difficulties. Feeding his physical and psychological addiction is paramount, staving off the consequences of withdrawal and his messes a mainstay. The user's collapse is his final mess. Discontinued use or lifelong abstinence is needed to reverse this destructive trend.

The Length of the Moratorium (Is it long, medium, or short?): Leon Wurmser (1978), a psychoanalytic addiction psychiatrist, proposes that all addiction is about a moratorium on the development of age-appropriate skills. During this developmental time-out period, the person repeatedly uses AOD to assist in problem-solving. This overreliance on an external substance results in a severe deficiency in the establishment of psychological and behavioral coping skills. Users have a constricted emotional vocabulary, are unable to face everyday distress, and are incapacitated by their incapacities.

The length of the moratorium measures the years people have used AOD to address or avoid these emotional difficulties and everyday problems. During this time, alcohol and drugs have resided in the user's back pocket, always available and ready to be pulled out and used in times of upset or stress. The constant return to this choice prevents the development of necessary life skills. A medium or long moratorium begs for some sober time. Without it, it is too tempting to rely on that back pocket again and again to repeatedly dodge facing reality. Abstinence forces the addicted person to draw on his own internal and external resources in ways never used before. Psychic capacity is then built, and new problem-solving skills are developed.

Pockets of Meaning (Are they decreasing? Is there only one left?): This lovely term, very loosely adapted from Jay Efran's work, is also diagnostic (Efran et al., 1990, p. xv). I have previously defined *pockets of meaning* as passions that are invested with importance. These are the things that are valuable in a person's life, the things people pocket and protect. They may include children, family, friends, hobbies, religion, or work. There is only one pocket of meaning in the world of the person with addiction. Life is about survival, and the substance is perceived as the only thing that can ensure that. Other pockets of meaning have long since been discarded.

This loss or lack of interest in protecting ongoing pockets of meaning or discovering new ones strongly suggests that people are paying attention to AOD too much, and for the wrong reasons. Courageously letting go of this perceived pocket of survival allows abstinence and its discoveries to become the primary pocket of meaning. Sobriety delivers time, and with it, a chance to discover new meanings and passions.

Use of these terms solidifies my clinical hunches and prepares me for the possibility of direct interventions that authoritatively propose discontinued use or abstinence (Molino, 1998, p. 128). A clinician needs this confidence to guide someone who is aggressively ambivalent about his escalating addiction. Testing positive for all three criteria authoritatively suggests that surrendering to this weary and futile battle is necessary, that discontinued use is the unavoidable and likely best course of recovery.

Messes, Moratoriums, and Meaning

A 27-year-old man calls for appointments over a 6-month period in the spring of 2011. During one brief phone conversation, he hesitantly reveals an alcohol problem that started at age 13. Dean either cancels scheduled appointments or does not return my calls. His avoidant ambivalence is obvious. Finally, gastritis, pancreatitis, elevated liver enzymes, severe pain, an emergency room visit, doctor's orders, and family pressures alarm him. He arrives at my office. He was able to stay off alcohol for 2 weeks and then began drinking again. "Nothing really changed in 2 weeks." He added, "I just don't want to be an alcoholic."

And so a relationship is forged, with him reporting that "things" are bad but not that bad, and me searching to find him in his hiding place, in order to provide the right level of care. Our relationship was both distant and intense.

Dean keeps drinking, increases his physical isolation as well as his psychic retreating (Steiner, 1993). He stops surfing, seeing friends, and talking with his family. He stops working. He has no money. His family believes he is sober while in treatment; he comes to a few sessions smelling of alcohol. Suggestions to attend AA or SMART meetings, undergo intensive outpatient care, and involve his parents in his treatment are given polite lip service and then ignored. As I begin to think and plan for an in- or outpatient treatment option that would start to reverse his physical and psychological reliance on alcohol, he is planning an exotic trip to a tropical island. What a mismatch. It has been 3 months of twice-weekly sessions, and I begin to feel uneasy. The growing attachment between us felt right; however, the level of treatment for him felt wrong.

Let's reflect on messes, moratoriums, and pockets of meaning, and use these clinical descriptors to determine the best level of treatment for Dean. Remember, testing "positive" for all three strongly suggests both physical and psychological addiction with its necessity for abstinence, at least as a start.

Dean's mess factor was high. He had overwhelming difficulties with his family, his friends, his ability to work, his finances, and his physical health. The length of his moratorium was long; almost half of his young life had been preoccupied with drinking. Very few age-appropriate skills were nurtured and developed during his years of overreliance on alcohol. Pockets of meaning were rapidly decreasing. These positive test results suggested that Dean needed a level of treatment that would protect him from his incapacities and promote the beginning days of his abstinence.

Conversations about higher levels of care are always anxiety-provoking and difficult. A clash of wills is likely to develop; things can get very messy and go very wrong. There is always the risk that a caring therapeutic relationship can get blown apart.

I consulted a Los Angeles psychoanalyst and received some sage advice: "It sounds like you are worried about Dean and feel that a higher level of care is the right thing to do." I agreed, and he offered, "Trust your gut, do what you think is right, and see what happens." This is profound wisdom for everyday life, and is very useful while making assertive treatment decisions for severe SUDs or individuals with addictions who have tragically and destructively lost their way in life. I heard my gut, listened to what it had to say, recommended my sense of the right level of care, let it go, and let Dean decide.

Dean was hostile and abusive. He also wanted to hear more about my suggestion. Our discussions took place during very emotionally intense therapy sessions or agitated phone calls afterward. I asked Dean to involve his parents, to let them know of our mismatched plans and my suggestion for a higher level of protection and care. Over two phone calls, I reflected back to him his words from his hiding place that he had shared with me in previous sessions: "I'm drinking too much and drinking too often. I'm in trouble. I'm lost and alone. Nothing is getting better. Tell me what to do. I'm scared and I know that what you are telling me is right. I'll listen to you, doc."

I simply said, "Then it's time, Dean. It's time for your parents, time for more care, and time for more protection. Let's meet with your mom and talk. Let's tell her that you're still drinking, even after your pancreatitis attack, and that you are having a really hard time listening to your physician's orders. Let's tell her that you are worried—let's ask her for her support."

I strongly urged him to call his mom, and I reminded him that for legal, medical, and ethical reasons, I might have to do so. He panicked, I was weary with frustration, we unraveled a bit, things got messy between us, and he cried out, "Don't I have any recourse?" At that moment, my agitated impulses wanted relief, and I lost my therapeutic balance and replied, "Dean, you don't have to accept my recommendation. You don't have to continue working with me. You can fire me, you know." He asked, "Can I?" I felt my relief, his relief, and our relief, and responded, "You always have that choice." He quickly shouted back, "You're fired!" and hung up.

Panic, anxiety, extreme embarrassment, and guilt, relief, regret, and second-guessing immediately flooded my mind. For days I reflected on my utter fatigue with him and my "invitation" for him to fire me or reject my treatment recommendation. Sadly, I later realized his refusal of my care left me feeling helpless and angry. I also recall that I had lost the capacity to dream or engage in reverie about Dean and had given up fighting for his healthy future. I was worried and sought out more consultation. With support and perspective, I reclaimed my gut and knew that my recommendation for a higher level of care was the right thing to do for this patient. I reaffirmed this, as well as his decision to terminate treatment, in a letter. He did not respond.

Half a year later, his parents called me, concerned about Dean's isolation and excessive drinking. I informed them that I would be willing to talk but I could not disclose anything until I received their son's permission.

Discontinued Use (Healthy)

Many times after continued debilitating problems and treatment, individuals decide to stop using AOD. They have come to the conclusion that it is not a good or healthy thing in their lives, or they acknowledge its destructiveness. This initial decision usually involves a robust commitment to abstinence. It may or may not be for a lifetime.

James had a profound recovery after decades of Psychological Reliance Not Yet Physical drinking (pp. 69–70). He does not drink. He is ever watchful about his desire to psychologically retreat. Although he would prefer hours of rock climbing alone, he makes a big effort to socialize more and has opened up in intimate relationships with others.

There are times when James longs for the opportunity to enjoy a glass of wine or a cocktail, to unwind and relax. In his sober lifestyle, he is more astounded than ever by the frequency of drinking in American society, and saddened by the amount of problem using that exists today. He also sees people enjoying a shared buzz with each other, and finding relief at the end of dislocated or fragmented days. He has talked to his new partner, Sandy, about his desires. "Sandy really accepts me and is open to hearing my interest in drinking again. Her receptivity to my ideas has allowed these conversations to linger, and currently I have a resolution for myself. At 59, I have decided that life overall is good, very good. I still struggle with my comfort around people, and for that reason alone, drinking feels too much of a risk for me now."

For Teens and Young Adults

Figure 6.2 Clinical Sketches—Teens and Young Adults

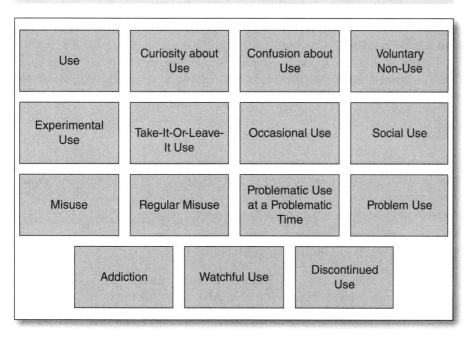

Often, I present these clinical sketches to high school and college audiences. They are very well received and engender lively and productive discussions. I do not treat young adults and teens in my private practice. This group is a specialized treatment population with unique developmental needs in the areas of individuation from their parents, peer acceptance, responses to childhood traumas, and current family and life stressors. As a result, I am unable to provide the kinds of clinical examples I did with the adult sketches.

Use (Healthy)

Since humankind began, we have always looked for a way to escape or expand consciousness. Sometimes this is done for spiritual ecstasy, rest, and relaxation, and other times for fun.

Curiosity About Use (Healthy)

These are young people who are willing and able to talk about these urges in an open and caring place, either with parents, trusted older siblings, other adults, or in school: Why do we want this, why do we not, why do we think we need it, why do we think it is good for us, and why do we get into trouble with it?

Confusion About Use (Healthy)

These are youth who are confused about what to think about getting high—is it a good thing, and why does society say it is a bad thing? They prefer to keep these questions to themselves either out of embarrassment from what they are wondering about or what they do not understand. They feel intimidated or uncomfortable talking.

Voluntary Nonuse (Healthy)

These are teens who for many reasons want to stay away from AOD. Many have seen destructive usage in their families, other families, and among friends. Others are more interested in sports, maintaining healthy bodies, the arts, religious or spiritual life, or the pure fun and comfort of relationships.

Experimental Use (Healthy, Mild, Moderate, or Severe)

These are young people who want to discover something not yet known, to try something out, to find out for themselves if it will work out okay. They may go through some troubled times while experimenting. They may decide that AOD is not for them, or they may wish to continue experimenting and exploring.

Take-It-or-Leave-It Use (Healthy)

A number of young people have a take-it-or-leave-it attitude toward AOD. It is not an activity that they pay attention to; it's not a big interest in their lives or part of their planning.

Occasional Use (Healthy)

These are youth who want to get high when there is a special event or party. They have a good time but do not feel an ongoing urge to use alcohol or drugs.

Social Use (Healthy)

These are youth who want to get high whenever they are with people in any type of social setting, from partying to "just hanging out." These are young people who are blessed with the sense of moderation or are fearful of losing control.

Misuse (Healthy or Mild)

Sometimes we are upset or embarrassed about the way we act while using AOD. Youth who misuse openly talk about this and learn for the next time.

Regular Misuse (Moderate)

These are young people who are repeatedly and recklessly misusing substances. They can act as if it is no big deal, but inside they know it is a problem to binge, blackout, and get sick. They keep their worries secret instead of confiding in others or seeking help. They believe they will do better next time.

Problematic Use at a Problematic Time (Moderate or Severe)

AOD use can get out of control during times of considerable stress either from school or sports, relationships, social worries, divorce, or death in the family. These patterns may look like severe SUDs or addiction, but they may just be occurring temporarily to cope with a particular situation.

Problem Use (Moderate or Severe)

These are young people who are using not just for fun, but to cope with confusing feelings or the difficulties in their lives. Their using is creating more and more problems with how they feel inside and also with family, parents, school, and friends. They usually think that a binge, a brownout or blackout, or getting sick is "no big deal" and that they have things under control. Anyone worried about their use "doesn't get it" and is annoying to them.

Addiction (Addiction)

These are young people who are using every day, 24/7, and need AOD to feel okay as they live their lives. They have lost choice. They may or may not binge, black out, or get sick. Deep down, they know they are in trouble, but feel this is the best way to cope in their difficult life. They ignore people's concerns, avoid people altogether, and more and more often prefer to get high alone.

Watchful Use (Healthy)

Patterns of problematic use have caught the attention of the young drinker/user, who may decide to give up AOD for a while and then may resume using with a watchful eye. This individual wants to enjoy alcohol or drugs, but also wants to continue to learn from problematic experiences and not repeat them.

Discontinued Use (Healthy)

Sometimes after continued problems or treatment, young people decide to stop using AOD. They have come to the conclusion that it is not a good or healthy thing in their lives. This decision may or may not include a lifetime of abstinence.

CHAPTER SUMMARY AND REFLECTIONS

Summary

This chapter summarized the new SUDs diagnostic criteria and introduced the reader to 15 clinical sketches designed to assist treatment providers and a therapeutic team as they prepare to assess from the new DSM-5. Ideally, these adult, teen, and young adult clinical profiles will help treatment providers organize some of their spectrum ambiguities and assist in their interpretation of leeways around the use of the word *addiction*. Hopefully, these clinical sketches will expand and deepen the patient's exploration of the complex nature of his relationship with AOD. Likely, the SUDs therapeutic dyad will experience a more collaborative, less adversarial search for a healthier lifestyle for the SUDs patient. This approach is likely to promote more self-reflection, as well as an internal sense of responsibility.

Reflections

The DSM-5 revisions and this chapter's clinical sketches and commentaries invite the student, counselor, clinician, or physician to engage in individual or group reflective thinking around the questions listed below. These revisions and suggestions have implications for the direction of your philosophies about AOD use and its problems, and your clinical practice as well. It is likely that self-reflection and discussion will assist in the integration and articulation of your likes and dislikes of these diagnostic revisions, as well as cultivate a better understanding of their widespread philosophical and treatment implications.

Consider the following questions in a classroom discussion or paper:

- Clinical decision-making will change from an either-or diagnostic approach to an exploration of using, misusing, and addiction. Are you personally and professionally able to buy into and utilize a spectrum of substance use disorders for diagnosis? If not, how will you make use of them, or work around them?
- How will the dropping of the words *abuse* and *dependency* influence your clinical thinking and treatment? Since use of the word *addiction* is at your discretion, have you decided if you will keep using this term?
- How does the traditional notion of a progressive disease fit into the diagnostic spectrum? Does it fit?
- Does a spectrum encourage a new understanding about taking responsibility for how we manage our *fourth drive* to escape consciousness, or does it invite irresponsible using?
- Will these changes promote more use of an AOD Weight Watchers mentality, support groups, and meetings rather than immediate consideration of rehab?
- Will it be difficult for you to wait for the patient's uncovering of his own understanding of his relationship with AOD? How will you manage?
- Does use of a spectrum encourage a new scrutiny and articulation of the concept of prevention? What are we in the business of preventing?

- The word *relapse* also deserves reconsideration. Are you able to embrace the notion of struggling or experimenting again, instead?
- Will more people be willing to explore a responsible resolution to a drinking problem rather than avoiding it until they "hit bottom" or are in a crisis?
- Will you still feel confident to act decisively when the patient is unable to care for himself during a life-or-death situation?
- Who decides a treatment path?
- Will you be able to tolerate exploring temperance or moderation as well as discontinued use or abstinence?

CHAPTER 7

TEN CLASSES OF
SUBSTANCES AND GAMBLING

INTRODUCTION

This chapter is designed to be clinically practical. It introduces the reader to the 10 classes of substances that we ignore or enjoy, problematically use or are psychologically reliant on, become destructively addicted to, and then, if fortunate, either learn new habits or refrain from using. A substance is meant to refer to any drug that when taken has an impact on thinking, mood, feeling, or behavior. This is accomplished through manipulation of the central nervous system. This chapter considers each individual drug that is related to a substance as identified in the DSM-5 (APA, 2013). Included in this revision is a class of substances referred to as "unknown."

DSM-5 and this chapter also include gambling disorder as the sole condition in a new category of non-substance-related disorders. DSM-III and DSM-IV listed pathological gambling as an impulse control disorder. This new term and its location in the new manual reflect research findings that gambling disorder is similar to substance-related disorders in clinical expression, brain origin, comorbidity, physiology, and treatment.

While gambling disorder is the only addictive behavioral disorder included in DSM-5 as a diagnosable condition, internet gaming disorder is included in Section III of the 2013 manual. This section includes conditions that require further study before they can be classified as formal disorders.

People repeatedly seek out 10 classes of mood-altering substances and often seek out psychotherapy for their troubles with them. These 11 (alcohol; caffeine; cannabis; hallucinogens [including phencyclidine and others]; inhalants; opioids; sedatives, hypnotics, or anxiolytics; stimulants [including amphetamine and cocaine]; tobacco; and other [or unknown] substances) are the focus of this book, as well as this chapter. While caffeine is included in the list of substances, DSM-5 does not list it as a substance use disorder.

There are more than 15,000 texts written on substance use, disorders, and addiction. All of them cover the 10 classes of substances in varying degrees of depth. Scientists, treatment providers, and academicians devote anywhere from 10 paragraphs to 10 pages to 10 chapters to these mind- and mood-altering substances. Topics for each substance may include:

- Historical, medical, and recreational uses
- Legal issues
- Methods of administration, absorption, distribution, biotransformation, and elimination
- Pharmacology and side effects
- Neuroadaption, tolerance, and addiction potential
- Brain chemistry
- Withdrawal features
- Short- and long-term impacts on the digestive, cardiovascular, endocrine, reproductive, emotional, and neurologic systems
- Pharmacological treatments
- Current and future research
- Legal highs

Our understanding of the pharmacology, neuroscience, and medical complications of each of the 10 classes of substances continues to rapidly evolve. The field is indebted to—indeed, dependent upon—the writers of scientific texts. They devote a substantial amount of time and research toward updating this body of knowledge. They provide a generous gift to treatment providers, addicts and their families, and students.

Most of us do not have the education or background to fully comprehend and keep up with the science of how the 10 classes of substances enter and leave our brains and bodies, the physical damage they cause, or the pharmacology of their treatment. Some of us are dizzied and derailed by the details and soon become disoriented and disinterested. The task of learning the science behind it all can appear daunting, and we don't know where or how to start. This chapter is designed to provide such a start—to present the basics of these drugs of pleasure or prescription in a simple and useful form.

The chapter is divided into five sections. *Basic Neuroscience* begins with a simple explanation of how and why these substances work in our brains and how naturally occurring endogenous (internally generated) highs are adulterated by substance ingestion. *Research Chemicals, Legal Highs, and WEB 2.0* provides new data and insights on the production and selling of legal highs on the internet. *Medications in SUDs Treatment* provides an overview of the most commonly used medications in the treatment of SUDs. *Gambling and DSM-5* offers a brief overview of gambling as the sole non-substance-related disorder listed in DSM. *Reference Charts* includes 11 easy-to-use charts on the different classes of substances and, new to this second edition, a reference chart for gambling. These charts provide the key points necessary to develop a foundational grasp of these mind-altering substances as well as the non-substance-related disorder of gambling, and are also useful for both clinical assessment and treatment.

Use of additional reference texts is highly recommended to further one's own knowledge about the brain and addiction, provide answers to perplexing scientific or medical questions, offer guidance during clinical emergencies, and, more importantly, assist our patients and their families in their own education process (see Further Study section at the end of this chapter).

BASIC NEUROSCIENCE

To understand how drugs and alcohol work, let's review some basic neuroscientific information about cells, neurons, and neurotransmitters. We begin with the cells of the brain called neurons and the communication signals that are passed on from one neuron to another. Neurotransmitters are the chemical messengers that carry these communication signals. They leave one cell, move across the synaptic cleft, and are introduced to another cell through receptor sites. These endogenous neurotransmitter messengers play important roles in mind-body regulation (Erickson, 2007, pp. 42–44).

Here are a few examples. Serotonin levels determine our feelings of depression or well-being; dopamine affects the experience of pleasure and pain; norepinephrine regulates many bodily functions, including growth and digestion; acetylcholine activates muscle tissue and gland activity; endorphins are involved in both pain regulation and feelings of euphoria; and endocannabinoids also influence mood and pain control. In addition, the amino acids glutamate and GABA (gamma-amino-butyric acid) act like neurotransmitters. Glutamate excites or agitates, while GABA inhibits or relaxes (Erickson, 2007, pp. 42–43).

The chemical structures of basic drug molecules are similar to endogenous neurotransmitters, again ones that originate from within an organism, tissue, or cell. Consequently, once in the brain, the drug molecules are able to join ongoing neuronal activity. They introduce a new message that impacts existing neurotransmitter communications (Erickson, 2007, p. 42). This produces a high, a low, or something in between (Inaba & Cohen, 2007).

The fundamental point here is that natural mood- and mind-altering neurochemical pathways exist in the central nervous system. Endogenous molecules travel from neuron to neuron on these pathways, attaching at a specific receptor site. They give the new cell directions that influence our physical and emotional state of being. The more salient point here is that drugs and alcohol work on these existing pathways—they do not create new ones (see Table 7.1). They work on what is already working. They modify normal neuron functioning of the brain; they strengthen or weaken, block or imitate ongoing neurotransmitter messages in the body (Doweiko, 2009, p. 46; Erickson, 2007, p. 42).

Simply put, drugs and alcohol cannot create sensations and feelings that don't have a natural counterpart. Again, this implies that human beings are naturally able to create virtually all of the sensations and feelings we try to get through alcohol and drugs. There are four big differences: (1) the drug or alcohol experience is a more intense one; (2) the timing of its impact is more predictable; (3) drug or alcohol effects weaken with repeated use; and finally, (4) drugs or alcohol can carry deleterious side effects (Inaba & Cohen, 2007, p. 61).

Table 7.1 The Relationship Between AOD and Neurotransmitter Systems

Drug	Neurotransmitter or Amino Acids (aa) Directly Affected
Alcohol	GABA (aa), glutamate (aa)
Benzodiazepines	GABA (aa)
Marijuana	Endocannabinoids
Opioids	Endorphins
Hallucinogens (LSD, PCP)	Serotonin
Cocaine and Amphetamines	Norepinephrine, acetylcholine, dopamine
Ecstasy	Serotonin, dopamine, adrenaline
Inhalants	Dopamine, GABA (aa), glutamate (aa)
Tobacco	Acetylcholine, serotonin, dopamine, norepinephrine, epinephrine
Caffeine	Dopamine, norepinephrine, GABA (aa)

SOURCES: *The Science of Addiction: From Neurobiology to Treatment* (pp. 42–45), by C. K. Erickson, 2007, New York: W. W. Norton; *Drug and Alcohol Abuse: A Clinical Guide to Diagnosing Treatment* (pp. 279–288), by M. A. Schuckit, 2010, New York, NY: Springer.

So, as examples, let's look at the natural ways our neurotransmitter messages work on the brain and how AOD molecules are able to enhance or diminish endogenous communications.

Good teaching requires a tremendous amount of energy. Many a professor, preparing for an 8 a.m. class, panics after a sleepless night. Ann gradually learns that her "fight" response will release the neurotransmitter norepinephrine, also called noradrenaline. Despite exhaustion, she will suddenly feel more aroused and alert. She will benefit from her "natural" production of speed. Her teaching will feel energized. The psychoactive stimulants work on this same neurotransmitter system.

Regular daily joggers benefit from a runner's high. Natural endorphins are released, and the runner feels euphoric. Ongoing psychological and physical pain is diminished. Consequently, the serious daily runner thrives in this altered state of well-being. This often fuels tremendous output and accomplishment. These endogenous pain relievers mitigate the psychological and physical suffering that accompanies these high levels of productivity. Heroin and other opiates also influence this endorphin neurotransmitter system.

Working the overnight shift in a psychiatric hospital or emergency room results in overwhelming and uncomfortable fatigue. This sleepiness often produces visual and auditory hallucinations. This natural trip is initiated by endogenous serotonin activity. The hallucinogens work on this neurotransmitter system as well.

Finally, relaxation exercises such as yoga and meditation calm the individual through increased release of the amino acid GABA. It takes discipline, effort, and time to achieve these natural, soothing benefits. The antianxiety medications, the benzodiazepines, also relieve stress and panic. The results are felt in 20 minutes. This speedy and predictable response, unfortunately, entices too many in the United States and others around the world.

These introductory neuroscience notes provide a rudimentary and working background for using the reference charts found later in this chapter.

RESEARCH CHEMICALS, LEGAL HIGHS, AND WEB 2.0

The concept of buying drugs online has given birth to a dream for many: the right to buy and sell natural and artificial (synthetic) chemicals that affect consciousness without interference from the State. It is a paradigm shift that cannot be easily reversed.

Like nearly every other industry, the drug market has been revolutionized by the web. Chemists, consumers, and criminals all use the internet to share copious amounts of drug information and also exploit globalized manufacturing possibilities. We live in an anarchic free-market world in which drug legislation is being outpaced by chemistry, technology, and ingenuity (Power, 2014, pp. xiv–xix).

Once upon a time, in the last 30 years, friends used to call each other to find out the name of a trusted dealer, get his phone number and address, travel to his home, walk up three flights of stairs, knock on his front door, enter, and test out drugs before departing with a "score." As one web vendor today reminisced, "Dealing in real life (IRL) is much more pleasant. Had I known from the start how much more mental torment and stress were involved with web vending, I probably would not have started" (Power, 2014, p. 223). Web vendors often deal with the tedium of 80-hour weeks packaging drugs that enable self-destructive behavior, and sometimes the alarming experience of waking up to the sound of the door being kicked down for inadvertently selling MDMA to a 12-year-old.

The second edition of Mike Power's book *Drugs 2.0* (2014) was published just 12 months after the first, indicating the consumers' desire and the ever-changing world of the online drug trade. Power's writings are among the first in the world to document the emergence of the popularization of drug substitutes. Drug substitutes are completely legal drugs that chemists create in their laboratories. These research chemicals are referred to as analogues, or chemicals that are structurally related to a banned or illegal drug. Some of the names include AB-001, UR-144, 4-AcO-BMT, AMT, DTT, MET, or MiPC (Power, 2014, p. 303).

As an example, when Ecstasy or MDMA was banned, chemists went to work, motivated by "pure science, scientific curiosity" (p. 134). Legal versions of banned drugs were created. The process of producing new drugs is called *ring substitution* (p. 30). These new drugs use ring substitutes to replace atoms on the molecular structure of a chemical. In drug chemistry, this is carried out by chemists in labs worldwide to change the drugs' effects or their legality (p. 303).

The following are recent examples of a pattern that is likely to continue: A substance is banned; a legal substitute is created; and, later, the substitute is banned.

Mephedrone

When the stimulant hallucinogen drug MDMA was banned in late 2008 and early 2009, users were crying out for either more MDMA or some new replacement. This was an unsatisfied and untapped market. This global MDMA drought inspired a chemist known as Kinetic to devise a new substitute or analogue called mephedrone. As Power says, "If one drug disappears because it is banned or becomes illegal, another will replace it" (p. 123).

Mephedrone is chemically related to khat, or *catha edulius*, a plant used for thousands of years in Arab countries, especially in Yemen and Somalia, as a social lubricant enjoyed for its stimulating qualities when chewed in a quid held between the teeth and cheek. The active ingredient, cathinone, is sold as a pure compound, a banned substance in most of the world (pp. 126–129).

The internet, the use of social media, and new commerce techniques guaranteed that the news of mephedrone would spread quickly. The way many drugs are created, sold, and bought around the world was to change forever (p. 124).

"I prefer mephedrone to MDMA," a 27-year old Londoner working in the factory told Power at the height of the craze in 2009. Power describes "Andrew" as

> sensible, intelligent, articulate, in good physical shape, dressed well. He liked to spend his weekends, from the second he left his office, getting as wasted as you could possibly imagine. He always liked taking drugs and partying, but said with the low quality of drugs available in the U.K., mephedrone is just a better option and far easier to get a hold of. "Mephedrone is more reliable, cheaper, and actually more convenient than going to a dealer. I pretty much stopped buying coke, pills, and MDMA once I found meph. I just make a bulk order, send off my bitcoin payment [bitcoin is an electronic cash system], and the package will arrive a few days later. I've been doing this for 14 months, and I have not experienced any negative effects, although I'm a little less motivated in work and training at the gym. It makes me laugh when I see people try it for the first time. Many are skeptical that something that's legal can actually work, but it does." (2014, pp. 129–130)

Andrew said he preferred mephedrone to MDMA as it gave him less of an emotionally fraught comedown after a weekend use of the drug, and it gave him greater mental sharpness. "What a drug!" he said. "No downside, no comedown or hangover to speak of, and it's far cheaper than cocaine."

Mephedrone was banned in the United Kingdom and European Union in 2010. President Barack Obama banned bath salts, synthetic marijuana, and mephedrone in 2012. The search for replacement chemicals remains constant, but the products being made contain more and more unknown stimulant, psychedelic, and depressive blends. An ever-evolving pattern of old markets, closed-down markets, and new markets exists today. It boils down to "I'd rather take a risk on an unknown substance sold over the internet than have a felony on my record" (p. 149).

Spice

At more or less the same time as mephedrone appeared, reports started to emerge on dozens of drug forums that a new synthetic marijuana product branded with the name "spice" was actually very powerful and smoked like marijuana. Bags of spice quickly began selling on the web (Power, 2014, p. 139).

A brilliant chemist named John William Huffman, now 82 years old, was one of the pioneers of spice. Between 1984 and 2011, Huffman and his colleagues at Clemson University had created over 400 synthetic cannabinoid compounds: "As it turns out, the human endocannabinoid system has profound effects on human behavior, pain, mood, nausea and appetite, and lots of other important biological functions" (p. 134). His research, funded by the National Institute on Drug Abuse (NIDA), was focused on making a drug to target endocannabinoid receptors in the body. Around 2006, somewhere, somehow, these "experimental medicines" were being sold for profit on the research chemical market. In addition to spice, more brands appeared quickly, such as Black Mamba SKUNK!, K2, and ABAMA. These compounds, legal in the United States, the United Kingdom, and Europe, were soon being exported in massive bulk from Chinese labs to the United States. Drug sites all over the world were selling Huffman's compounds or legal pot, thanks to Huffman and his team. Be assured that hundreds, if not thousands, of possible analogues remain "legal," although their impacts and effects are completely unresearched (Power, 2014, pp. 117–148).

The Synthetic Drug Abuse Intervention Act is part of the Federal Drug Administration's Safety and Innovation Act of 2012. The purpose of this act was to control synthetic cannaboids and cathinones. It was signed into law by President Obama in 2012, and included spice. At least 44 states have also taken action to control synthetic cannaboids and cathinones.

Finding Legal Highs Online

A quick search of "legal highs" will turn up countless sources of information on how to obtain and use legal substances. Some sites provide lists of the best legal highs and where to purchase them. There are also drug databases where users can find and share advice on which legal highs are the best, with detailed descriptions of their effects, recommendation of dosage, and more. When in doubt, many turn to large online forums for advice from the masses, where thousands of users can openly ask about drugs and freely share their experiences behind a shield of anonymity. With such a wealth of information available online from vendors and users alike, finding the ideal legal high has never been easier.

MEDICATIONS IN SUDS TREATMENT

This section provides a brief overview and list of some of the medications that are commonly and currently in use for the treatment of AOD. These are medications used to reduce uncomfortable withdrawal symptoms and cravings, restore neurotransmitter balance, and interfere with the pleasurable effects of AOD so that desire is inhibited or reduced. It is important to note and respect the uncertainty of science in this area. Mechanisms of action for most medications are still unclear. This is underscored by the repeated caveats and cautions that pepper the research literature on this subject: "presumably," "most likely," "research indicates," "it appears," "it seems," "it's unclear," "it's not so well known, however."

The medications include:

- Acamprosate: This drug, calcium acetyl homotaurine, has the trade name Campral. It was first shown to be effective in Europe, and is now approved by the U.S. Food and Drug Administration. The mechanism of action is thought to involve the restoration of normal receptor activity in glutamate systems. Campral has been effective in maintaining abstinence and also decreasing the desire for alcohol (Erickson, 2007, p. 169).
- Buprenorphine: Now under the trade names Subutex or Suboxone, buprenorphine is a partial agonist (activator) of the opioid receptor, unlike methadone, which is a total agonist. In other words, unlike methadone, its effects plateau. Buprenorphine has less abuse potential than methadone. The basic idea of opioid substitution therapy has been enhanced by the use of buprenorphine (Erickson, 2007, p. 170).
- Disulfiram: Now under the trade name Antabuse, disulfiram was the first medication to "treat" alcoholism, and is among the most well known. It blocks the enzyme alcohol dehydrogenase (ALDH). Consequently, acetaldehyde accumulates in the blood, causing "acetaldehyde sickness." The symptoms include flushing, rapid heart rate, nausea, vomiting, and faintness. The threat of getting sick is sufficient to keep many individuals sober (Erickson, 2007, pp. 166–167).
- Methadone: Methadone has the trade names Symoron and Methadose. Methadone is indicated for the maintenance treatment of opioid dependency. Methadone programs are designed primarily to help prescription opioid–dependent patients or heroin users detox and stabilize. Studies indicate that methadone balances the brain's reward pathway and reduces the craving for heroin. The best methadone clinics require patients to take an oral tablet under observation and require drug testing and counseling (Erickson, 2007, pp. 158–161).

- Nalmefeme: This drug is now under the trade name Selincro. Nalmefeme is a semisynthetic opiate receptor antagonist, structurally similar to naltrexone. It is a newer opioid antagonist, approved in more than two dozen countries. It is very effective for moderating the use of alcohol. It has been used to treat acute opioid overdose and the management of alcohol dependence and addictive behaviors (Glaser, 2015).
- Naltrexone: Now under the trade names Deparde, ReVia, and Vivitrol, naltrexone is a full opioid antagonist. It is used to treat opioid and alcohol dependence. Naltrexone, presumably, reduces the euphoric effects of alcohol by blocking the endorphin rush caused by alcohol and opioids for certain individuals. A new, long-acting form of naltrexone (Vivitrol) produces drug action for 30 days. Naltrexone is effective in maintaining abstinence, as well as decreasing desire (Erickson, 2007, pp. 168–169).

Please refer to the Further Studies section at the end of this chapter. I also encourage continuous research on this topic, as this is one of the most rapidly evolving aspects of the field.

GAMBLING AND DSM-5

Perspectives considers gambling in the category of our *fourth drive*, as an activity of human enjoyment and pleasure that allows us to escape consciousness as well as reality. Examination of one's relationship with gambling, exploring its meanings and adaptive functions with consideration of both its pleasures and its problems, is encouraged. Remain cautious, however, about overpathologizing its nature.

Pathological gambling (PG) was added to DSM-III in 1980. The DSM-III criteria began with a statement about the individual experiencing progressive loss of control, and then listed seven items with an emphasis on damage and disruption to the individual's family, personal or vocational pursuits, and money-related issues. DSM-III classified PG as an impulse control disorder. In DSM-IV, PG was classified under the section title "Impulse Control Disorders Not Elsewhere Classified," along with trichotillomania (compulsive hair-pulling), intermittent explosive disorder, kleptomania, and pyromania. The DSM-5 workgroup proposed that PG be moved to the category of non-substance-related disorders (Reilly & Smith, 2013).

Gambling is the "active activity" regularly enjoyed by millions of people. In the United States, this is supported by the rise of state-sponsored lotteries; around the world, with the growth of casinos, slot machines, and other gaming venues. Many countries claim that approximately 80% of adults have gambled in their lifetime and almost nine in 10 had no symptoms that would indicate problem or pathological gambling. According to these estimates, about 9% of gamblers reported some risk due to their behavior; 1.5% were classified as problem gamblers (Wolfe & Owens, 2009, p. 413). While these numbers provide an encouraging perspective, gambling problems can impact the individual's well-being, as well as that of his partner, children, and extended family, not to mention work, stress, and health.

Many factors can contribute to a gambling addiction, including desperation for money, the desire to experience thrills and highs, the social status of being a successful gambler, and the entertaining atmosphere of the mainstream gambling scene (Rickwood et al., 2010). On a philosophical level, it is deeply connected to our worship of money, our ancient fascination with luck, our desire to see chance as a possibility rather than a problem, and our longing to give up the quest to control outcomes and simply play the odds. The impulse to gamble arises from the inescapable uncertainty at the heart of the human experience. Jack Richardson, in his book *Memoir of a Gambler* (1979), states that the gambler is engaged in theodicy—an effort to glimpse some coherence in the cosmos.

Gambling cannot be separated from our economic life. Many individuals around the world risk in stock markets and horse races, and many others stand for hours in lottery lines, all the while scratching their way to "fortune." The spread of legalized lotteries and casinos suggests that gambling, like economic risk-taking in general, has become more openly condoned, even encouraged (Wolfe & Owens, 2009, p. 308).

When looking at gambling, it is valuable to reflect on the influences of two contexts: a sociocultural context, as well as one's psychological state of mind. T. J. Jackson Lears (2003) suggests it is important to consider a broader, philosophical context—specifically, how the American culture of chance parallels and overlaps the culture of control. The culture of chance, Lears says, is not a culture of losers, but a culture more at ease with randomness and irrationality, more doubtful that diligence is the only path to success, as advocated by our dominant culture of control.

The culture of chance, in short, is more willing to value the "seriousness" of play. This hero is the individual (likely male, according to Lears) who has his eye on chance rather than the moral imperative of the Protestant ethic. Lears refers to his universe as a contingent one where luck matters. This hero is sometimes referred to as a confidence man (con man).

The hero in the culture of control is disciplined and self-made; his success comes with hard work and devotion. The culture of control assumes a coherent universe where earthly endeavors are justly rewarded. He is often referred to as the self-made man. A conflict between these two cultural tendencies often exists within the individual as well (Lears, 2003).

The global theory of dislocation posits that rising addiction rates, including "gambling addicts in the casinos and other venues, and power addicts in the financial district," are a product of the disorientations and stresses of globalization. We are overwhelmed by technology, its dominance, and its demands. We are dizzied and disoriented by our global interconnectedness, and sometimes find soothing space in the hours we spend on gambling. As Liz Karter states in her book *Women and Problem Gambling* (2013), "Gambling becomes out of control, often as a response to feeling psychologically overwhelmed and emotionally out of control" (p. 3).

Karter continues that gambling, for both men and women of all ages, creates a bubble of excitement and escapism as well, an intoxicating high that produces increasing amounts of craving for more. The bubble becomes so desirable as it prevents any unwanted thoughts or unpleasant feelings from entering. The experience functions to keep one out of touch with what is really going on in one's psyche, relationships, family, and work (Karter, 2013, p. 22).

REFERENCE CHARTS

The charts on the following pages are quick, easy, and useful reference guides. They are designed to include the key content necessary for understanding the basic essentials of each of the classes of substances listed in DSM-5. The material has been gleaned from multiple sources—reading and studying technical texts on SUDs, teaching and listening to student stories over decades, and listening to and learning from my patients. The historical, factual, and medicinal materials have been gathered from the texts identified in the Further Reading section at the end of this chapter. The number of categories is intended neither to overwhelm nor underwhelm the reader with AOD facts. This selective grouping is designed to be a concise guideline for treatment.

The categories are described below:

- Introduction in italics: A factoid of historical interest
- Group: Examples of the pills, powders, or liquids in each substance class and their effects on the mind and body
- Pattern of Use: Method of administration
- Natural History: The likely number of years and patterns involved in using this substance (Vaillant, 1983, pp. 107–180)
- Potential for Addiction: Physical and psychological addiction potential—high, medium, or low

- Withdrawal: Short- and long-term physical and psychological symptoms that appear after an addicted user stops using
- Points to Ponder: Selective clinical considerations and salient features

(1) ALCOHOL

Alcohol has been a part of human culture since the beginning of recorded history. Making sense of alcohol's place in human culture engenders avoidance and conflict.

Group

- Beer, wine, liqueurs, distilled spirits
- These are central nervous system depressants.

Pattern of Use

- Oral

Natural History

- 25 years to a lifetime of addictive use
- 15 years of problematic use
- 15 years of poly, or mixed, AOD use and experimentation

Potential for Addiction

- Physical—high
- Psychological—high

Withdrawal

- Initial acute withdrawal of 24–96 hours includes the following symptoms: hyperarousal, anxiety, irritability, insomnia, tachycardia, delirium tremors, agitation, sweating, vertigo, alcohol hallucinations, muscle weakness, excessive fatigue, irritability, incontinence.
- Alcohol has a 2-year protracted withdrawal period with decreasing severity and frequency of symptoms.

Points to Ponder

- Alcohol is the most popular psychoactive pleasure in the world. It isn't easy for people to learn how to enjoy—not misuse—this central nervous system relaxant.
- The health benefits of alcohol depend on a person's age, gender, and overall medical history; used intelligently, alcohol can relieve stress (Erickson, 2007, p. 131).
- BAC (blood alcohol content) over 0.35 signals danger of overdose.
- Alcohol overdose or death results from suffocation on one's own vomit or respiratory failure.
- Treatment of overdose involves hospitalization with respiratory, hydration, and vitamin monitoring and support.
- Naltrexone was approved by the Food and Drug Administration (FDA) for the treatment of alcohol dependence in 1994.
- Alcohol releases an amino acid called GABA, which results in euphoria, slow reaction times, and impaired muscle control. The brain then releases a stimulating chemical called glutamate. When alcohol is cut off, glutamate levels remain high and cause irritability and discomfort. The brain craves another drink to relieve this irritability. Campral, a newer pharmacological treatment, helps the brain resist these cravings by checking the production of glutamate; it brings brain chemistry back into balance (Erickson, 2007, p. 69).
- Recovery of any kind usually involves working through anxieties about interpersonal closeness and intimacy.

(2) XANTHINES (CAFFEINE)

Origins of tea are traced back to China in the fourth century. Coffee was first cultivated in Yemen in the sixth century. By the 1600s, coffeehouses spread rapidly in Europe. Specialty coffee shops and cafés developed on the U.S. west coast in the 1980s and continue to be highly popular meeting places around the world today.

Group

- Coffee, tea, chocolate, soft drinks, energy drinks, over-the-counter pain relievers, stimulants, and medications
- This class of drug enhances concentration, alertness, and attention.

Pattern of Use

- Oral

Natural History

- 25 years to a lifetime of addictive use
- 25 years to a lifetime of episodic use
- 1–5 years of experimentation

Potential for Addiction

- Physical—high
- Psychological—high

Withdrawal

- Symptoms develop between 12 and 24 hours after the last dose of caffeine.
- Symptoms include headache, fatigue, yawning, and nausea.
- Nonprescription pain relievers for headaches are used during withdrawal.

Points to Ponder

- It is estimated that more than 50% of Americans drink coffee every day.
- Prenatal and postnatal effects include reduced chances for pregnancy and lower birth weights (Kuhn et al., 2008, p. 69).
- Caffeine disturbs, stresses, or interrupts functioning in the heart, eyes, kidneys, and digestive, reproductive, and respiratory systems.
- Caffeine causes constriction of blood vessels, and this is a likely reason why it is effective for migraine headaches (Kuhn et al., 2008, p. 71).
- Overall, caffeine is fairly safe if consumed by a healthy person in moderate amounts.

(3) CANNABIS

The industrial, medical, and recreational use of the cannabis plant has a long history, beginning in 8000 BCE.

Group

- Marijuana—unprocessed leaves, dried flowers, seeds, stems of the plant
- Hash—processed from the resin of the plant; cakes/lumps: hashish; oily liquid: hash oil
- THC (tetrahydrocannabinol)—the active chemical in cannabis resin, the primary mind-altering agent
- Legal highs
- Cannabis produces variable effects—stimulant, depressant, relaxant, psychedelic

Pattern of Use

- Smoked in a pipe, joint
- Inhaled from a bong
- Eaten in food
- Drunk in tea
- Ingested from a pill

Natural History

- 25 years to a lifetime of addictive use
- 15 years of a pattern of on-and-off use—on during the weekend or nighttime, off during the week or daytime
- 1–5 years of poly drug use and experimentation

Potential for Addiction

- Physical—low
- Psychological—high

Withdrawal

- Symptoms include irritability, restlessness, mental confusion, anxiety, depression, cravings, insomnia, and agitation.

Points to Ponder

- Marijuana is the most commonly consumed illicit drug, with 200 to 300 million users worldwide (Earleywine, 2002, p. 47).

- The experience of marijuana is influenced by one's mindset and one's physical and emotional setting; it is referred to as a set/setting drug.
- Strength of preparation of hemp depends on the resin content. Some strains produce a great deal of resin; others do not.
- With increased use, tolerance develops. People learn to adapt to being high—they soon can perform normal activities while under the influence. Consequently, using marijuana 24/7 is not uncommon and is an extremely difficult habit to break.
- No documented case of fatal overdose exists (Earleywine, 2002, p. 11).
- The concept of marijuana as a gateway drug is seriously questioned (Earleywine, 2002, p. 64).
- Marijuana has many established medicinal purposes—from serious medical problems to mild ailments.
- The federal government is waging what seems to be a misguided and losing fight against medical and recreational marijuana use in the United States.

(4) HALLUCINOGENS

PHENCYCLIDINE (PCP)

Phencyclidine was introduced as a surgical anesthesia for humans in 1957. Discontinued in 1965. Discontinued for veterinary use in 1975. Illegal in the United States.

Group

- PCP and ketamine
- Legal highs
- These produce dissociative states. Users feel detached from the body and from external reality.

Pattern of Use

- Oral
- IV
- IM
- Smoked
- Snorted

Natural History

- 5–8 years of mixed use, including periods of daily use interspersed with episodic or binge using.

Potential for Addiction

- Physical—low
- Psychological—low to moderate

Withdrawal

- Mixed evidence about withdrawal symptoms.

Points to Ponder

- "PeaCe Pill" is the street name for PCP.
- As a drug of abuse in the United States, its popularity waxes and wanes. PCP is considered a set/setting drug; mindset and setting greatly determine outcome.
- Levels of intoxication range from mild to induced psychosis.
- Rash of scare stories about PCP may reflect society's need to have "devil drugs."
- A toxic reaction to PCP can be one of the longest lasting produced by any drugs of abuse. Recovery progresses into a 2- to 6-week period (Schuckit, 2010, p. 226).
- PCP's structure resembles a depressant (Schuckit, 2010, p. 226).

OTHER HALLUCINOGENS

Hallucinogenic plants have been used since long before recorded history.

Group

- LSD (lysergic acid diethylamide), *Salvia divonorum*, morning glory seeds, psilocybin mushrooms, peyote, mescaline, ibogaine, Ecstasy, MDMA, DMT (dimethyltryptamine, "the businessman's LSD")
- Legal highs
- This group alters perceptions and consciousness; it is an intensifier of experience.

Pattern of Use

- Oral—pill, cubes, capsule, tablets, seed or plant, drink
- IV—rare (LSD) and legal highs
- Smoked
- (DMT)—Injected (intravenous or intramuscular), sniffed, or smoked

Natural History

- 25 years to a lifetime of episodic or ritualistic use
- 5–10 years of planned monthly hedonism
- 1–5 years of poly drug use and experimentation

Potential for Addiction

- Physical—low
- Psychological—low
- May be the substance that results in the lowest potential for addiction.

Withdrawal

- Flu-like symptoms, depression, fatigue, and anxiety

Points to Ponder

- Drug seekers search for sensual experimentation and ritualistic use.
- Hallucinogens are set/setting drugs; the mindset and one's setting greatly influence outcome. Predictability is reduced, thus long-term interest decreases.
- Many "bad trips" are related to the dose and quality of the drug.

(5) INHALANTS

Inhaled substances altering perceptions of reality can be traced to ancient Greece. Currently, inhalant abuse is a worldwide problem.

Group

- Volatile substances—glue, paint, paint thinners
- Volatile nitrites—amyl nitrite, butyl nitrite

- Anesthetic gases—nitrous oxide, ether, chloroform, halothane
- This group produces intoxicating, stimulating, and stupefying effects on the central nervous system, as well as euphoric giddiness, loss of inhibitions.

Pattern of Use

- Inhaled from a container, rag, or canister ("huffing" or "bagging")
- Boiled to inhale fumes

Natural History

- 5–8 years of mixed use—daily, episodic, or binge
- 1–5 years of poly drug use and experimentation

Potential for Addiction

- Physical—low
- Psychological—moderate to high

Withdrawal

- Symptoms include mental confusion, disorientation, ringing in the ear, headache, fatigue, and muscle weakness.

Points to Ponder

- Inhalants are breathable chemicals that were never meant to be used as recreational drugs.
- One-time use of inhalants can result in sudden sniffing death syndrome.
- Learning disability symptoms develop with increased inhalant use.
- Children who regularly sniff solvents develop tolerance to them. This sniffing habit can be difficult to break.
- Medical disorders associated with inhalants include cardiac irregularities, hepatitis and liver failure, kidney toxicity, transient impairment of lung functioning, skeletal muscle weakness, and peripheral neuropathies (Schuckit, 2010, p. 245).

(6) OPIOIDS

Opioids have been used in religious rituals, and cultivated as a crop as early as 10,000 years ago. Narkoticos *is the Greek word for numbing or deadening.*

Group

- Naturals—the opium poppy, morphine, codeine
- Semisynthetic—derived from the naturals: heroin, Vicodin, Percodan, Dilaudid, and OxyContin
- Legal highs
- Synthetic—produced in a laboratory: Demerol, Darvon, methadone, buprenorphine, and legal highs
- These drugs are analgesics and reduce physical and emotional pain. They provide a euphoric rush, lower anxiety, and increase an overall sense of well-being.

Pattern of Use

- Oral
- IV
- IM
- Subcutaneous—between the layers of the skin (skin popping)
- Snorted
- Smoked
- Mucous membranes of mouth, nose, or rectum ("booty bumping")

Natural History

- 25 years to a lifetime of addictive use
- 15 years of daily periodic or episodic use
- 1–5 years of poly drug use and experimentation

Potential for Addiction

- Physical—high
- Psychological—high

Withdrawal

- Initial acute withdrawal of 48–72 hours of withdrawal includes symptoms of nausea, vomiting, goosebumps, intestinal spasms, abdominal pain, kicking movements, diarrhea, irritability, violent yawning, sneezing, runny nose, restlessness, and increased heart rate and blood pressure.
- The opiates have a 2-year protracted withdrawal period with decreasing severity and frequency of symptoms.

- Opiate withdrawal is not usually fatal unless the person is medically compromised by a serious condition such as hypertension or heart disease.

Points to Ponder

- Prescription pain relievers all too often result in problem use or addiction.
- Beware of the opiates' daily seductions as mother's, or father's, "little helper."
- Buprenorphine (Suboxone, Subutex) has been approved by the FDA and seems to have replaced methadone as the treatment for opioid dependence. It is unique because its therapeutic effect plateaus at certain levels; addicts are less likely to get high (Erickson, 2007, p. 237).
- Naltrexone was approved by the FDA in 1984 for the treatment of opioid dependence to block the drug's euphoric effects. Chipping is the occasional use of heroin or another drug.
- A heroin high is a most pleasurable sensation, usually considered more powerful than an orgasm.
- Many opioid users become experts in finding new veins.
- Chronic use of these drugs does not produce organ pathology as with alcohol.

(7) SEDATIVES, HYPNOTICS, AND ANXIOLYTICS

In 1960 a new class of antianxiety drugs replaced reliance on barbiturates. Benzodiazepines (BZs) are the most prescribed psychiatric medications in the world.

Group

- Barbiturates—Seconal, Nembutal, Amytal, chloral hydrate
- Benzodiazepines—Librium, Xanax, Ativan, Klonopin, Restoril, Rohypnol
- Drugs that act at BZ or melatonin receptor sites—Ambien, Lunesta, Rozerem
- Other sedatives-hypnotics—quaalude, GHB (gamma hydroxybutyrate), meprobamate (Miltown)
- Legal highs
- This class of drug reduces anxiety and induces relaxation. It can also promote sleep and a sense of well-being.

Pattern of Use

- Oral
- IV

Natural History

- 25 years to a lifetime of daily addictive use
- 15 years of periods of daily use
- 1–5 years of poly drug use and experimentation

Potential for Addiction

- Physical—high
- Psychological—high

Withdrawal

- Initial acute withdrawal of 24 to 72 hours includes symptoms of apprehension, anxiety, insomnia, stomach cramps, sweating, fainting, nausea, restlessness, agitation, a sense of paranoia, depersonalization, and impaired memory. Acute withdrawal can last 15 days and into months.
- The benzodiazepines have a 2-year protracted period with decreasing severity and frequency of symptoms.

Points to Ponder

- These medications are thought to increase function of GABA and suppress unnecessary anxiety and insomnia.
- Sudden cessation will produce withdrawal symptoms. Tapering of dependent use is strongly recommended.
- Be wary of alcoholism-sedativism. The effects of daily heavy drinking are mitigated with nightly benzodiazepine use.
- Watch for increased daily usage as an antidote to our fast-paced, anxious society.
- Likely increased use with anxiety of living longer through medical hardware, multiple surgeries and treatments, and medications.
- Increasingly used as a recreational drug that may lead to problem use or addiction.
- The risk of fatal overdose with benzodiazepines is small if they are taken alone. High dosing causes prolonged sleep and memory impairment.

(8) STIMULANTS

AMPHETAMINES

Scientists have discovered ephedra plants thought to be 60,000 years old. The Chinese used ephedra for medicinal purposes 5,000 years ago. Ephedra was used for asthma in 1930. Amphetamines were synthesized as a result of ephedra's high demand.

Group

- Dexedrine, Desoxyn (meth), Ritalin, Adderall, Ephedrine, diet pills, Ecstasy, and MDMA
- Legal highs
- These are central nervous system stimulants.

Pattern of Use

- Oral
- Intravenous (IV)—into a vein
- Intramuscular (IM)—into a muscle
- Nasal inhalation
- Smoked

Natural History

- 25 years to a lifetime of addictive use
- 15 years of daily, episodic, and binge using
- 1–5 years of poly drug use and experimentation

Potential for Addiction

- Physical—debated in the literature
- Psychological—high

Withdrawal

- Withdrawal is most intense for 3 to 5 days but remains in decreasing intensity for weeks and months.
- Symptoms include craving, irritability, agitation, aggressiveness, restlessness, insomnia, fatigue, depression, and anhedonia (inability to experience pleasure).

Points to Ponder

- Amphetamines massively increase the amount of dopamine in the synaptic cleft. Amphetamines work through this release, as well as from blocking the reuptake of other neurotransmitters (Erickson, 2007, p. 41).
- It is estimated that 60% to 80% of amphetamine users simultaneously drink alcohol (Schuckit, 2010, p. 140).
- Repeated use can temporarily decrease the number of dopamine receptor sites and severely damage the brain's pleasure centers. There is some evidence of reversal after long-term abstinence.
- Amphetamine-acting substances are found in many over-the-counter products. They provide easy responses to fatigue, stress, and depression.
- Amphetamines enter the bloodstream very quickly when smoked or injected. This leads to a rapid high and to a greater likelihood of toxicity.
- When used carefully, Ritalin and Adderall can be very effective for the treatment of attention deficit hyperactivity disorder (ADHD) in children and do not necessarily predispose the child to drug dependence.

COCAINE

Derived from the pulped leaf of the South American coca plant. Cultivated by natives of South America for thousands of years. Chewed daily throughout parts of the world.

Group

- Coca leaves, coca paste, cocaine hydrochloride powder, and cocaine alkaloid
- Legal highs
- These are central nervous system (CNS) stimulants.

Pattern of Use

- Coca leaves are chewed.
- Coca paste is smoked.
- Cocaine hydrochloride powder is snorted or injected.
- Cocaine alkaloid is smoked or injected.

Natural History

- 1–5 years of daily addictive use
- 5–30 years of a mix of daily use, episodic use, and binge use
- 1–5 years of poly drug use and experimentation

Potential for Addiction

- Physical—debated in the literature
- Psychological—high

Withdrawal

- Acute withdrawal of 36 hours includes symptoms of anhedonia, craving, paranoia, agitation, fatigue, chills, nausea, headache, vomiting, and muscle tremors.
- Post–acute withdrawal of 7–10 days includes symptoms of fatigue and flu-like symptoms.

Points to Ponder

- Cocaine increases the amount of dopamine in the synaptic cleft by preventing its reuptake.
- It is estimated that 60% to 80% of cocaine users simultaneously drink alcohol (Schuckit, 2010, p. 140).
- Beware of crack cocaine's addictive potential. It can rapidly take over one's life and result in death.
- Speedball is a street name for a combination of a CNS stimulant and a CNS depressant.
- Rapid intake can result in increased heart rate, respiratory arrest, and death.
- Remember, crack and freebase cocaine are chemically the same—both are altered forms of cocaine hydrochloride powder. The smoked product is usually 40% more pure (Schuckit, 2010, p. 141).
- Crack—cocaine mixed with baking soda and water over a hot flame. The substance, which is 90% pure cocaine, is then dried. The soapy-looking substance that results can be broken up into rocks and smoked. These rocks are about five times as strong as cocaine. Crack gets its name from the popping noises it makes when it is smoked. One puff of a pebble-sized rock gives a high for about 20 minutes. The user can usually get three to four hits off the rock before it is used up (Doweiko, 2009, p. 137; G. R. Hanson, Venturelli, & Fleckenstein, 2009, pp. 268–269).
- Freebase—produces a stronger high, and the process eliminates cutting agents. It is made with cocaine hydrochloride (street market cocaine). It is dissolved in water, and a solvent (usually petroleum ether or ammonia)

is added to release cocaine alkaloid from the salt and other adulterants. A stronger base (such as baby laxatives) is then added to neutralize the acid content. The solvent rises to the top, where it can be filtered or drawn off. As the solvent evaporates, the cocaine salt oxidizes, and what is left is cocaine base. Freebase cocaine is water soluble and can be smoked or injected. These methods get rid of all possible cuts in cocaine (Doweiko, 2009, p. 137; G. R. Hanson et al., 2009, pp. 268–269).

(9) TOBACCO

References to tobacco are etched into Mayan stone carvings from 600 BCE. Tobacco was used during transcendental ceremonies to ward off evil. In the 1500s, tobacco was used to treat a number of ailments, from headache to colds. It was called the "holy plant." The psychoactive ingredient in tobacco was identified as such in 1828. Medicinal prescriptions ended in 1890.

Group

- Cigarettes, tobacco, snuff, nicotine gum, nicotine skin patches, cigars, pipe tobacco, and salves
- This class of drug decreases anxiety, calms, and decreases appetite.

Pattern of Use

- Smoked
- Chewed

Natural History

- 25 years to a lifetime of addictive use
- 25 years to a lifetime of chipping or episodic use
- 1–5 years of experimentation

Potential for Addiction

- Physical—high
- Psychological—high

Withdrawal

- Symptoms begin within hours, peak on days 2 to 4, and last up to a month.
- Symptoms include increased craving, increased appetite, irritability, anxiety, difficulty concentrating, and restlessness.

Points to Ponder

- In the 1960s, 40% of U.S. adults were smokers. This is down to 17.8% today (CDC, 2015).
- Family studies reveal a twofold to fourfold increased risk for smoking if parents or siblings are smokers (Schuckit, 2010, p. 290).
- 80% of men and women who use alcohol in excess currently smoke (Schuckit, 2010, p. 211).
- Prenatal and postnatal effects include oxygen depletion, resulting in smaller head circumference; compromises in verbal and mathematic abilities; and hyperactivity (Kuhn et al., 2008, pp. 181–182).
- Tobacco may prove helpful in the treatment of ADHD and schizophrenia.
- There are two sources of smoke from cigarette smokers: the smoke they exhale (secondhand) and the smoke rising off the lit cigarette (sidestream). Sidestream smoke has a higher concentration of carcinogens than either secondhand smoke or the smoke taken into the lungs through a cigarette filter (Kuhn et al., 2008, p. 181).
- A fatal overdose of tobacco is quite rare, but it is possible. Symptoms include nausea, abdominal pain, diarrhea, vomiting, decreased heart rate, and dizziness (Kuhn et al., 2008, p. 172).

(10) OTHER (OR UNKNOWN) SUBSTANCES

"A person's needs *are met, and his appetite subsides. A person's* wants *are met, and his thirst swells greedily without end." – Richelle E. Goodrich,* 2013

Group

- Anabolic steroids; nonsteroidal anti-inflammatory drugs; cortisol; anti-Parkinson medications; antihistamines; betel nut, kava, or cathinones

- New black market drugs not yet identified
- Familiar drugs illegally sold under false names

Pattern of Use

- Varies (dependent on the substance)

Natural History

- Varies (dependent on the substance)

Potential for Addiction

- Varies (dependent on the substance)

Withdrawal

- Varies (dependent on the substance)

Points to Ponder

- A diagnosis of other substance use disorder is indicated when the nine substances listed previously in this chapter are not involved.
- Certain cultures may be associated with other substance use disorders involving specific indigenous substances within the cultural region.
- No single pattern of development or course characterizes the other (or unknown) substance use disorders.
- Substance use disorders are generally associated with elevated risk of suicide, but there is no evidence of unique risk factors for suicide and other (or unknown) substance use disorder.

(11) GAMBLING

"Every roll of the dice is a question addressed to destiny." —Theodore Reik (Wolfe & Owens, 2009, p. 302)

Group

- Betting, lottery, slot machines, penny slot machines, online gambling, fantasy sport games, card games, blackjack, horse racing, stock market, bingo, dog racing

Natural History

- 25 years to a lifetime of addictive use
- 15 years of problematic use
- 1–5 years of experimentation

Potential for Addiction

- Physical—low
- Psychological—high

Withdrawal

- When addicted gamblers cut back, they experience withdrawal symptoms that look like stimulant withdrawal.
- Withdrawal symptoms include craving, depression, anxiety, irritability, restlessness, insomnia, headache, diarrhea, difficulty breathing, and muscle ache.

Points to Ponder

- Dopamine spikes from unpredictable events. Games of choice are events. There is an increase in dopamine activity only when winning is unexpected (AddictScience.com).
- There is no unifying theory on the etiology of gambling. Psychological, biological, cultural, and social factors are considered important. Consequently, interventions range from behavioral, cognitive, motivational enhancement therapies, psychotherapy, support groups, and pharmacological treatments.
- Gamblers may no longer be considered sinners, but they can still be considered deviant.
- Men are more likely to gamble on sports, racing, and casino card games. Both men and women participate in gaming machines and the lottery. Young people, when they gamble, are more likely to gamble in a variety of forms, but especially internet gambling.
- There are numerically more gamblers in the middle-age range of 40–60 years, but the probability of initiating gambling activity decreases during adulthood.

- The gambling behavior of family members, particularly fathers, is an important risk factor for children. The degree to which gambling is accepted as a legitimate pastime by others in the community influences the decision to begin gambling.
- The gambling industry recognizes that problems are created when consumers lose control over purchasing decisions. Consequently, they post signs and brochures warning customers about problem gambling and promote counseling support services.
- Pharmacological treatments include antidepressants, mood stabilizers, and opioid antagonists, such as Naltrexone, to reduce the number of endogenous opioids.

CHAPTER SUMMARY AND REFLECTIONS WITH FURTHER STUDY

Summary

This chapter was designed to be clinically practical. It covered five topics, including some neuroscience, legal highs, and medications used in SUDs treatment. Salient features for each class of substances, unknown substances, and gambling were included in 11 easy-to-read charts. These serve as a ready reference guide for clinical work. This chapter provides a recommended reading list for further study. These books contain additional information about each substance, more in-depth clinical applications, and current research focus and findings. Readers are strongly encouraged to read updated editions every year.

Reflections

Consider the following questions in a classroom discussion or paper:

- How is it that alcohol and other drugs work in our body?
- What are some of the differences between each of the nine classes of known substances that can result in a substance use disorder?
- What are some of your thoughts about adding gambling as a non-substance-related disorder?

Further Study

Doweiko, H. E. (2009). *Concepts of chemical dependency* (7th ed.). Belmont, CA: Brooks/Cole.

Erickson, C. K. (2007). *The science of addiction: From neurobiology to treatment.* New York, NY: W. W. Norton.

Hanson, G. R., Venturelli, P. J., & Fleckenstein, A. E. (2009). *Drugs and society* (10th ed.). Sudbury, MA: Jones and Bartlett.

Inaba, D. S., & Cohen, W. E. (2007). *Uppers, downers, all arounders* (6th ed.). Medford, OR: CNS Publications.

Kuhn, C., Swartzwelder, S., & Wilson, W. (2008). *Buzzed: The straight facts about the most used and abused drugs from alcohol to Ecstasy* (3rd ed.). New York, NY: W. W. Norton.

Schuckit, M. A. (2010). *Drug and alcohol abuse: A clinical guide to diagnosis and treatment* (6th ed.). New York, NY: Springer.

Teresi, L. (2011). *Hijacking the brain: How drug and alcohol addiction hijack our brains—The science behind twelve step recovery.* Bloomington, IN: Author House.

Von Stieff, F. (2012) *Brain and balance: Understanding the genetics behind addiction and sobriety.* Tucson, AZ: Ghost River Images.

CHAPTER 8

SELF-MEDICATION, PSYCHOANALYTIC, AND PSYCHODYNAMIC THEORIES

INTRODUCTION

During the 1970s and 1980s, Ed Khantzian did much to humanize addiction. His 1999 classic, *Treating Addiction as a Human Process,* gave the field its heart.

He and others debunked the popular and prevailing notions that addiction resulted from hedonism, sociopathy, or self-destruction. Instead, Khantzian suggested that P/SUDs suffer more intensely and with greater difficulty than most when facing life's hardships. He proposed (in his seminal paper on the self-medication theory in 1985) that they use alcohol and other drugs to self-medicate for these disturbing emotional states, as well as for a range of psychiatric problems. In many cases, this has led them to discover that the short-term effects of their drug of choice can help them cope. Continued use gets them in a lot of trouble. In these cases, psychological treatment can have a powerful impact (Khantzian, 1999, 2011; Khantzian & Albanese, 2008).

Since the mid-1980s, psychiatrists, psychologists, and social workers have been moved to understand and explain addiction from the point of view of psychological suffering. They have drawn on psychoanalytic theory; examined vulnerability, dependency, attachment, and self-soothing capacities; and have also looked at self-disturbances and emotional dysregulation. They have tried to understand the relationship between widespread contemporary addiction and psychological distress. They all suggest, and in different ways, that people self-medicate with drugs and alcohol because they are unable to self-care (Khantzian, 1999, pp. 335–356).

This chapter presents material that has been respected and valued by students, clinicians, and patients, and further developed over 20 years of teaching. The following theories are from a group of addiction and psychoanalytic writers who value connecting psychological and emotional vulnerabilities with the development of substance disorders and addiction problems. I have also included several renowned psychoanalytic thinkers and specific aspects of their work. Their contributions deepen and further our understanding of the psychological suffering driving the need to self-medicate.

This chapter provides a clear and straightforward synopsis of selected aspects of the work of each contributor. I have used discipline, imagination, and creativity in my interpretations of their contributions to the field. These theorized essentials are followed by discussion ideas, brief clinical vignettes, and suggestions for their use in clinical treatment. Each theory stands alone, yet together they provide a rich understanding of the relationship between emotional pain and the need for relief through AOD. These theories present a rich tapestry of ideas best used when coupled with your own intuition (Eigen, 1996). While some of these references may be dated, their contributions continue to provide a deep understanding of the psychological suffering behind addictive symptoms.

Readers are encouraged to discuss and expand on these theories and further their study with additional research.

SELF-MEDICATION THEORISTS

Lance Dodes

Lance Dodes (2002) is a psychiatrist from Harvard University who has worked in the field of addiction for over 20 years. He proposes that true addiction, or the "heart of addiction," is fundamentally psychological in nature. Addiction exists when there is a psychological need to perform the addictive behavior (p. 74). Dodes straightforwardly highlights the transient nature of physical addiction, and urges us not to confuse its consequences and complications with the problem of addiction in general. He sharply suggests that "physical addiction is surprisingly incidental to the real nature of addiction" (p. 76). These symptoms are largely a medical problem attended to during the early hours of withdrawal. Most people can be safely detoxed in a matter of days or weeks. His emphasis is on addiction's psychological nature, not its physical complications (pp. 3–9).

Context of addiction: People often feel trapped in a problem or dilemma. This results in feelings of helplessness and powerlessness.

Drive behind addiction: Being and feeling trapped creates rage. The rage at feelings of helplessness is the irresistible force that drives addiction.

Purpose of addiction: Addiction is used to reverse feelings of helplessness and powerlessness. It provides a false sense of empowerment, seducing the addict into believing that he is in control of his emotional experience, as well as his life.

Addiction as a substitute action: All addiction is a substitute action because another, more direct response to one's helplessness does not seem possible or permissible.

People may feel hopeless, helpless, and thus trapped in many areas of their lives. These include:

- A lifestyle
- A relationship or marriage
- A gender
- Raising children
- Illness
- Emotional inability
- A body
- Caretaking
- Mastery of technology
- Expectations
- Work
- Financial pressures
- Depression or anxiety

Feeling trapped often results from living with a rigid or anxious perspective about any of these issues. Nicky, a patient who is actively using, tells me she has had a rough 24 hours with a recurring relationship problem. "My partner, Lisa, once again doesn't get it. She'll never get it. How many times do I have to tell her? I'm furious and all alone in raising our children." Nicky felt trapped in this perceived dilemma of overresponsibility, pain, and isolation. She felt hurt by her partner's abandonment and righteous about Lisa's perceived parental delinquency. Nicky was drawn into recalling the details of her sorrow and anger in repetitive and distressing ways. These surrounded her mind and soon immobilized her body. Nothing seemed helpful, no action comforting. She felt stuck on a wish, caught in an emotional standstill. She was breathless; no air seemed available. Agitation and frustration set in. She found a Vicodin and ingested it without thinking.

Dodes suggests that addiction is often the only action that feels available at these moments. Again, it is a substitute action in an effort to reverse the terrorizing feelings of helplessness; it provides an illusion of control in a situation that feels out of control.

The work of recovery involves helping P/SUDs reconsider their substitute response to a problem, and start to consider a healthier, more direct response. This begins by understanding and embracing the patient's sense of helplessness and gently offering a broader perspective. I encourage people to consider *TOES*—that is, to learn to *Tinker On the EdgeS* of a problem and to work with the many layers involved in human emotions, behaviors, and dilemmas. It takes time to learn that a fantasized wish is not the only solution that feels good.

Use of *TOES* released Nicky from her righteous and omnipotent rumination. "My partner doesn't get it. Nothing is going to feel better until she gets it, and she needs to get it right now." Nicky felt trapped by her thinking, lost in its repetition. She withdrew, isolated, and eventually felt worse. She panicked at their increasing distance. She felt stuck and rageful; she had taken herself down with her narrowing perspective.

I reflectively listened and heard her yearning for her partner. I recommended a couples session for the two of them. She angrily responded, seemingly convinced that their busy schedule could not accommodate it, "She has no time for a session; don't you get that?" I didn't respond. We both sat in silence. In a matter of seconds, she replied, "I never even thought of that." I could see and feel the relief in her.

Nicky's expectation for satisfaction was exclusively tied to "my partner has to get it." She was unable to imagine any other relief until a couples session was proposed. The *TOES* suggestion invited her to think on another level, to consider connecting rather than stewing.

I try to help patients feel the value of tinkering around the perimeters of a problem. *TOES* is a tool that shifts perspective and encourages an affective appreciation of these incremental shifts. Actively broadening a perspective opens up an opportunity for reflective and creative thinking, and often allows for healthier choices. Thinking is something you can build a tolerance for—that is, something you want to do more of. Over time, it feels better than taking drugs and alcohol.

Dodes's work reminds us to avoid the trap that "my fantasized solution is the only avenue of true satisfaction." This misguided hope results in a frustration and sense of helplessness that beckon the illusionary soothing capacities of a drug high.

Ed Khantzian

Ed Khantzian (1999, 2011) is the founder of the self-medication theory of addiction. His early theories in the 1970s and 1980s challenged the prevailing notion that P/SUDs were weak-willed, and thus doomed to forever capitulate to hedonistic desires. For decades, he has been moved to look at the psychological suffering of P/SUDs. One of his earliest theories looked at the relationship between an individual's emotional suffering and his choice of drugs (Khantzian, 1999, pp. 69, 117–119).

Motivation to use: Not self-destruction, sociopathy, or euphoria; rather, it is to turn uncontrolled or passive suffering into controlled or active suffering.

P/SUDs: They are sitting on an affective storm of chaotic emotions. People live with the sense that something is wrong but are at a loss for how to explore it. This is passive suffering.

Choice of drugs is not random: People choose a specific drug because it predictably and reliably works on their internal storm. It quiets or animates the storm. Returning to this relief again and again results in addiction. This is active suffering.

Most P/SUDs did not get a good emotional education while growing up. As a result, they live with a limited number of words for feelings. In this condition, emotions feel both big and small, intense or absent, and often collide together. The individual's psychic capacity is compromised; this is a handicap to problem-solving. Something feels off and wrong, but one lives with a sense that this discomfort and frustration are just a part of life. This causes a tremendous amount of suffering. P/SUDs don't know how or whom to ask for help. AOD relieves this passive sense of suffering.

The choice of drugs or alcohol is important here (Khantzian, 1999, p. 59). Random experimentation quickly loses its appeal as soon as the P/SUD discovers that something works, that a specific mind-altering substance changes this feeling of passive suffering. The drug of choice quiets, dulls, deadens, silences, or conversely enlivens, animates, or excites one's chaotic emotional storm. The sufferer finally feels a solution to his pain. Returning to this experience again and again becomes a way of life. The result is addiction.

This feeling of passive suffering is replaced by the active suffering of the addictive process. One hasn't always known or understood one's emotions or feelings; but one now knows what it is to be an individual living with an addiction. It brings unwanted attention from family and friends, but it feels better than living with a chaotic and confusing emotional storm inside one's psyche. Actively suffering with addiction and its consequences feels better than passively suffering with an unknowable internal world (Khantzian, 1999, pp. 117–119). "True addicts don't use to escape life; rather, they use to find a place in life" (Zoja, 2000, p. 15). The rituals of addiction give the passive sufferer's life a purpose. "I can do life with my addiction." Sadly, many, many people live in this compromised solution.

The recovery work here includes expanding one's emotional vocabulary, helping people locate the place and name of feelings in their body, heart, and spirit. A user who is "upset" feels frustrated inside and frustrates those around him. Global feelings need deeper exploration. The process of working through upsetting emotional states is a painstaking task. It takes time, patience, endurance, and tenacity. Recovering individual users can develop the capacity to explore emotions at greater depths. This ultimately turns passive and active suffering into active thinking, problem-solving, soothing, and living.

A woman in her 50s is going through a divorce and has also just begun a very exciting and satisfying relationship. She was emotionally and physically abused by her father. Her pattern has been to abandon herself and her feelings in the face of male demands. Her drug of choice was alcohol. She's in her first year of sobriety.

Her soon-to-be ex-husband is demanding and threatening. She also doesn't want to disappoint her new boyfriend. Her extended family sees her as a trouble-maker, and her children are withdrawn. Pressure is mounting, and life is heating up. She walks into my office short of breath, holding back tears—and, I quickly see, feeling emotionally numb. She confirms the passive sense of suffering that accompanies being numb. She is willing to do some work, and we pull out a feeling chart. She circles 32 words in her chaotic, undifferentiated emotional storm and is shocked by "all that was going on." She agrees to redesign her day and make room for some journaling, and calls me later in a much more comfortable spot: "I now know what I feel certain about, and I now know what I am not sure of." Alcohol would have quieted and dulled her emotionally anxious storm. She might have temporarily relaxed, but drinking would have prevented her from learning from this experience. She would not have gained an understanding of her distress.

Ed Khantzian With John Mack

A hallmark contribution of Ed Khantzian with John Mack (Khantzian, 1999, pp. 335–356) is the discovery that individuals with addiction self-medicate because they are unable to self-care. Self-care functions are ego functions developed through the process of internalization. Responding to a child's needs and fostering healthy dependency over time build his ego capacities and skills. These are necessary to live well. Self-care ego functions serve to warn, guide, and protect individuals from hazardous or dangerous involvements and behaviors, including SUDs and addiction, unhealthy and violent relationships, impulsive choices, and destructive situations. Khantzian looks at self-care deficiencies as a way to explain a range of troubled human behaviors (Khantzian, 1999, pp. 335–355).

Addiction is about two things: These are problems of control and psychological suffering in four areas (described below).

Problems of control: Addictions are troubled and destructive behaviors. People have lost choice and lost control. P/SUDs are unable, and thus unwilling, to make healthier choices.

Psychological Suffering in Four Areas:

1   A chaotic affect from the experience of qualities and quantities of feelings that are either too intense or too vague, nameless, or confusing

2   A pained sense of self with little or no confidence

3   A wish to make contact and have relationships with others, but it is a wish filled with a sense of hazard and impossibility

4   An inability to experience the desire for self-care

Self-care functions: Early and responsive caregiving results in self-care functions that produce:

- An energized sense of one's value and worth. A feeling that one is worthy of care and protection either from self or others.
- An ability to listen to anxiety that says some kind of trouble is approaching, with the desire and ability to anticipate, as well as attend to, the danger.
- An ability to control impulses and renounce pleasures whose consequences are harmful.
- An enjoyment of appropriate levels of risk, in which dangers are realistically measured.
- An accurate and real knowledge about the outside world and oneself sufficient for survival.
- The ability to be self-assertive or aggressive in order to care for and protect oneself.
- Important relationship skills, especially the ability to choose friends and loved ones who ideally enhance one's sense of value and worth and encourage one's self-care and protection. The ability to rebuff and avoid people who interfere with and jeopardize one's sense of value, self-care, and protection.

Human nurturing comes with limitations, and thus many of us did not get enough of these ego functions. We all can make poor choices without them. Not all of us choose AOD to compensate for their absence. P/SUDs do so as a result of marked deficiencies in their nurturing experience. They lack a sense of value and feel unworthy of protection. They are unable to say no to everyday dangers. They self-medicate with drugs and alcohol without these ego functions of protection and care.

The good news is that these deficiencies can be repaired. As soon as a patient sits down in my office, I vest him with my libidinal or life-force energy of interest, curiosity, and wonder of his life. My clinical intention and hope is that my energy of interest will be taken in by him and, over time, will transform into his own vitalized sense of self-interest, worth, and value. All good caretaking is about the transfer of this investment energy, as any clinician, teacher, or parent knows. An energized interest in one's experience of self is a key ingredient for living a full life. Drugs and alcohol feel necessary without this sense of vitality.

Patients in ongoing psychotherapy gradually internalize these ego functions of self-care. The recovering individual starts to feel consistently more valuable and worthy, and thinks in terms of his own care and protection. He asserts and risks, and he chooses friends who encourage more of the same. Self-care vitality starts to expand his sense of possibilities. His world starts to feel more pleasurable, and also more rewarding, than AOD ever did.

Ego functions of self-care are valuable for everyday psychological management. Students and patients like working with these functions. P/SUDs really like it. All their lives they have been called selfish. To learn that valuing and protecting oneself is not selfish, but rather an act of self-care, is a most exciting notion and a welcome relief for those suffering with addictions. I often warn patients and clinicians alike that we will never execute these capacities perfectly. These guidelines help us catch a failure or deficiency sooner rather than later.

Donald Rinsley

Donald Rinsley, a psychiatrist who wrote in the 1970s, focused on what is missing in the psychological structure of people with a borderline personality disorder. He was struck by their inability to self-soothe. P/SUDs lack the same capacity (Rinsley, 1988).

Soothing introject: An element of psychological structure that allows one to identify, monitor, and modulate the emotional shifts that occur throughout a day. It is missing in P/SUDs. They are unable to soothe feelings of frustration and helplessness without the use of substances.

Reason individuals use drugs: To self-medicate as a coping mechanism for this deficit in psychological structure.

Infants and children are dependent on caregivers for food and care, as well as the development of emotional capacity. Rinsley focuses on one's ability to self-soothe. His work suggests that P/SUDs are unable to internally soothe themselves, and thus they look externally for this function in AOD (Rinsley, 1988, p. 3).

One internalizes a soothing introject in several ways. Some opportunities can occur during the preverbal periods in a child's life. Often, he is carried around by a caretaker or parent who is doing double duty. She (or he) is both attending to the child and also attempting to identify, figure out, and calm her own upset about other life events. The parent patiently works through nameless emotional states in an effort to calm her distress.

The child in her arms takes in and learns from her effort to self-soothe. Hopefully, he internalizes her success. He learns that mom can feel bad, clammy, and cold when anxious. He learns that soothing takes time, and that eventually we are able to quiet ourselves. He senses that frustration can be modified, either through emotionally clear thinking or support from other people. The mom's ability to self-soothe is taken in and becomes a part of the child's psychic structure. During this introjective process, he is developing a capacity to eventually soothe himself.

Another opportunity for internalizing a soothing introjection occurs when a child expresses concern or fear to the caretaker—for example, about going to the dentist. The child is soothed if the mom stops what she is doing, listens to his concerns, and engages in a conversation addressing his worries. The child takes in her skills.

In both of these healthy examples, the external function performed by the caregiver is likely to become an internal function of the child's. Repeated external soothing develops internal calming capacities. The adolescent, and then later the adult, will then be poised to draw on himself in times of stress or discomfort, rather than reach outside for soothing in the form of AOD or other compulsive behaviors. Self-soothing capacities take time to develop and more time to trust. Eventually, they become the instinctive go-to tool. These skills greatly enhance self-confidence. Repeatedly using these capacities is gratifying—eventually much more so than taking drugs or alcohol.

Therapists and Alcoholics Anonymous (AA) sponsors do a lot of soothing during the very early days of sobriety. These needed functions are then internalized. They are essential for long-term recovery.

Karen Walant

Karen Walant (1995) is a social worker from Katonah, New York. For decades, she has been interested in attachment and addiction. Walant suggests that a denial and devaluation of merger moments throughout the life cycle have increased the likelihood of addiction. She proposes that premature autonomy and independence have been encouraged at the expense of attachment needs. She applied this interest to her own version of the theory of self-medication and addiction (p. 2).

Merger moments: Transformative experiences between a parent and dependent child that result in the child developing a cohesive sense of self.

Normative abuse: When parents and caretakers do not honor a child's healthy dependency needs, but instead honor the cultural norm of independence and separation.

Normative abuse results in: A child, adolescent, and then later adult who is disconnected from his needs and desires, and thus lacks a cohesive sense of self.

At the heart of addiction is: A detached, alienated person looking for pseudomerger with AOD.

Walant suggests that merger moments are necessary experiences for the child, as shown in the diagram (see Figure 8.1). A fearful child with a healthy dependency need is represented by X1. Let's say the child is concerned about going to a birthday party with children he doesn't know. He approaches his caretaker, and if she is responsive, they merge together in an intimate relationship characterized by healthy dependency, talking, and problem-solving, represented by XX2. When this moment is over, the child is transformed (Walant, 1995, p. 112). His anxiety is now soothed. This is represented by X3.

The child figured out his response to the birthday party dilemma. Healthy dependency and merger increased his confidence. The child learned three things from this experience of transformation. He learned that dependency is good, that it's okay to ask for what you need, and that it is possible the universe might provide it. He senses there is a solution to his fears. This feels good, and life feels doable (Walant, 1995).

Walant also postulates that, particularly in America, there is a tendency to deny or become fatigued with a young child's repeated dependency needs. When this happens, we often urge him to be a big boy and remind him that "Johnny down the street doesn't have a problem with birthday parties."

Figure 8.1 The Flow of a Merger Moment

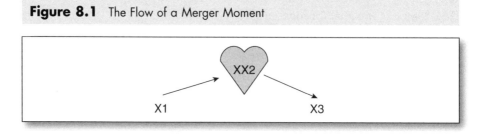

Walant suggests that the loss of these merger moments produces a child who is detached and alienated from himself and his needs, and thus at a loss for how to respond to them. He is in a dilemma when problems arise. The child is then poised to look for pseudotransformation in unhealthy merger experiences with his thumb, his navel, his twirling hair, his bottle, his fetishes, or his other secret solutions. The child, adolescent, and then later adult continues this pseudomerger with drugs and alcohol. He then becomes dependent on these ungratifying compromises to soothe life's distresses. They create a temporary sense of feeling better, but provide little or no opportunity to learn from experience. Nonetheless, they become a way to deal with life.

In very early recovery, the sensation of merger with another person or therapist is often a new and profound experience. If repeated often enough, there develops a growing expectancy that merging with people is safe and desirable, that healthy dependency needs should not be ignored and dismissed, and that drowning them in AOD is undesirable and unsatisfying. Recovering individuals start to feel more connected to who they are and what they need, and look for healthy ways for the universe to respond to them—relationships, hobbies, teaching, and writing. A sense of self-cohesion and self-order is reborn.

Heinz Kohut in Jerome Levin

Jerome Levin is a major contributor to the field of addiction theory and treatment. His seminal work, *Therapeutic Strategies for Treating Addiction* (2001), includes Heinz Kohut's psychoanalytic theory of self psychology. Kohut sees narcissistic (or self) disturbances as central to the psychopathology of the addict. Internally, the addict feels empty, fragmented, and unorganized. Alcoholic drinking is the pathological compromise that attempts to make up for this depleted sense of self.

Therapeutic relationships that foster a sense of self-cohesion are essential in recovery. Addiction doesn't inhabit individuals with a sense of self-cohesion and life purpose (Kohut, cited in Levin, 2001, pp. 71–97).

Selfobjects: Important others in the life of a child who are experienced as part of the self or in the service of the self.

Selfobject needs: Specific, empathic responses that the child needs in the areas of grandiosity, idealization, and likeness.

Selfobject experiences: Occur when parents provide needed responses to the child. These parental responses assist in the building of his self-structure. We seek similar experiences throughout our lifetime.

Transmuting internalization: Occurs when needed aspects of important selfobjects are internalized. Functions of the parents are taken in and transmuted into the child's sense of self and self-worth.

The experience of the addict: An inner emptiness felt as a result of an absence of an internal self-structure. This is experienced as a void that addicts try to fill with AOD. It cannot be done. This effort is "futilitarian."

Motivation to use: Striving toward health no matter how disturbing the behavior. Use of AOD is an attempt to preserve and protect a fragile and fragmented sense of self.

The need during recovery: A relationship with a person or persons that can build and replace deficient and missing selfobject capacities in the areas of tension regulation, self-soothing, and self-esteem regulation.

Kohut (in Levin, 2001, pp. 71–97) sees the self as present at birth. Hopefully, parents feel it and respond to an infant's initiations, assertions, and joys. These empathic responses provide early selfobject experiences for the infant.

According to self psychological theory, the self of the child has needs that must be responded to in certain ways for healthy self-development. These responses provide necessary functions for the child. Self-structure is then internalized from these selfobject experiences.

Kohut identifies three sets of needs or three poles of self-structure. The first set of needs pertains to the grandiose sector of the self-structure. The child needs to receive confirming and mirroring responses from others regarding his greatness, specialness, and importance. If all goes well, this sense of greatness translates into healthy ambitions and goals.

The second set of needs pertains to the idealizing sector of the self-structure. The child needs to extensively idealize selfobjects in his world. This idealized merger allows for vicarious participation in the perceived strength and calmness of the other during anxious or fearful times. A child eventually translates this borrowed capacity into his own; he can self-soothe.

The third set of needs pertains to the twinship sector of the self-structure. The young child needs selfobject relationships with others that create a sense of essential sameness. These experiences provide a sense of "My needs are okay, and I am like other people." This translates into a sense of belonging and self-confidence.

The child internalizes early empathic responses to these three sets of needs. They become a part of the child's sense of self. A cohesive self-structure is formed that is filled with a sense of vitality, tension regulation capacities, self-control, and self-confidence.

Gross empathic failures to these three sets of needs result in deficits in the child's self-structure. These result in a sense of self that lacks vitality and cohesiveness, that feels fragmented, empty, and enfeebled. This failure of inter-nalization, with its feelings of being lost, can lead to addiction.

Kohut sees this disturbance of self as central to addiction. Addicts' core difficulty is the absence of internal structure. Again, this results in deficits in the self's capacity for tension regulation, self-soothing, and self-esteem regulation. These missing parts of the self are experienced as a void. It's an inner emptiness that addicts try to fill with drugs and alcohol, food, or other substances. Addiction is a desperate attempt to compensate for missing parts of the self. It cannot be done. Whatever is compulsively taken in goes right through, like pouring water into a sieve. It is a "futilitarian" effort. What is missing can only come from other people, from a certain kind of relationship that can be internalized.

For many recovering addicts, a therapeutic relationship is a very good start. The work of recovery and repair takes time and involves the use of transferences to reverse lifelong empathic failures in relationship experi-ences. Therapeutic skill is required to reawaken the addict's desire for people, long replaced by drugs and alcohol. This first flourishes in the form of a selfobject transference to the therapist. The therapist's essential skill here is not to interfere with the development of this need. Once the selfobject trans-ference is in sway, the patient, by psychic necessity, will ask the therapist to function as part or parts of the patient's missing self-structures (Baker & Baker, 1987).

The functions the recovering addict looks to the therapist to provide through this transference experience will most likely be related to one or more of the three major selfobject states from Kohut's theory of self-development:

- The grandiose self—the recovering addict needs to experience his essence as interesting, valuable, and worthy of others' attention.
- The idealized parent imago—the recovering addict needs to merge with the calm, strength, wisdom, and greatness of the therapist in order to join in his perceived strength and calmness.
- The alter-ego twinship—the recovering addict needs to feel that he is like another, to develop a comforting sense of his essential sameness and belonging.

An important task of the therapist is to discern which type of selfobject response the patient needs at which point in treatment. When the right selfob-ject transferences have formed, the patient is ready to resume the develop-ment of the self, fueled by what Kohut calls the Zeigarnik phenomenon

(Kohut, cited in Chessick, 1992, p. 152). This is the wonderful, delightful human tendency to complete interrupted tasks of development if given a chance to do so. Over time, and by transmuting internalization, psychic structure is built. The therapist serves as a selfobject that provides needed functions. These then become internalized and self-structure is rehabilitated to new levels of health, strength, and maturity. The recovering addict is then able to seek out important selfobject experiences and relationships with other people in his own life. He begins to learn that drugs and alcohol actually interfere with the richness of these experiences.

Wilfred Bion

Wilfred Bion, a British psychoanalyst who wrote in the mid-20th century, made a major contribution to our understanding of how we as people learn how to think.

Bion (1967) considers tolerance of frustration an innate factor of our personality (pp. 110–119). In other words, we can face frustration if our mother (caretaker) helps us. When she accepts, contains, and modifies these overwhelming and upsetting feelings, she turns them into what Bion calls our apparatus for thinking thoughts. She acts as a soothing container for difficult emotions. We learn, from her, how to face life's upsets. We learn the pleasures of thinking, and thus don't need the gratuitous satisfaction that comes from AOD (Fetting, 2009, p. 7).

Deficiency in the P/SUD: The apparatus of thinking thoughts.

Causes of deficiency: Lack of reverie from his childhood caretaker. Reverie is maternal containment of a child's frustrations, transforming painful sensations into tolerable states of being by her thinking and soothing functions.

Motivation to use: To avoid dealing with frustration. Frustration is repeatedly felt as an overwhelming emotion that needs to be evacuated at all costs. This frustration and upset are discharged during repetitive addictive behaviors, which can only bring temporary satisfaction.

P/SUD's need: A relationship with someone who has the capacity for reverie (see below). The recovering addict can then internalize this person's capacity to think through and soothe frustrations. He is then less likely to act them out in addictions.

An infant is frustrated and cries; mom responds and enters a mental state that Bion calls reverie. Reverie is emotional availability, fueled by fierce maternal instincts. A mother takes in and takes on the baby's frustrations. In the process, she tolerates them and tries to figure them out. Her instincts keep her focused until she determines his relief. After the baby is held and if all goes well, sensations are transformed—frustration is now satisfaction, emptiness is now fullness, pain is now pleasure, isolation is now company, anxiety is now calm, and dread is now hope (Fetting, 2009, p. 7).

The baby starts to sense, via the mother's capacity for reverie, that he can handle these upsetting feelings. He begins to internalize her capacity to think through and soothe his frustrations. It gradually becomes his capacity. His instinct is to face frustration, not avoid it. Thinking feels better than acting it out. It brings better results.

Without these repeated experiences of reverie, a child, adolescent, and then later adult is left unequipped and uninterested in facing life's everyday frustrations in healthy ways. The individual is left with one solution, and that is to avoid them. Addiction becomes a reliable avoidance strategy, and a way to discharge the tensions of frustration. While one feels temporarily relieved, the path of addiction usually results in the degradation of one's life and relationships. Lack of capacity to think through frustration moves one toward addiction, and lack of capacity to think through the tragic and harmful consequences keeps one in addiction.

A major part of recovery is in the development of the capacity to think, to learn how to take in and take on one's frustrations, worries, and fears and to reflect on them. Reverie is a learned state. Thinking brings its own pleasures. People gain confidence in thinking things through rather than impulsively acting them out.

Christopher Bollas

Christopher Bollas is a British psychoanalyst and writer. He has written on many topics, including free association and unconscious communication. He also has drawn on the classical notions of fate and destiny, as well as on D. W. Winnicott's ideas about the true self and the false self. Together, these notions are very helpful in understanding some of the deeper self-medicative purposes behind addiction (Bollas, 1989, p. 8).

P/SUD's vulnerability: The P/SUD's object world (parents, caretakers) did not provide the right conditions for the child to evolve and articulate his idiom. This person feels tragically fated and unable to experience life as conducive to the fulfillment of his destiny.

Purpose of addiction: To remove the suffering that comes from living the fated and reactive life of a false self; to self-medicate the suffering that comes from feeling unable to achieve one's true destiny.

The need during recovery: A relationship with a person who hears the faint murmurs of a true self with its desire to express its idiom through its destiny.

Idiom: The unique nucleus or defining essence of each individual.

Sense of fate: A person who feels fated has not experienced reality as conducive to the fulfillment of his inner idiom. Such a person is frustrated at the very core of his being. A false self and its expressions become his guide through life.

Sense of destiny: Refers to the urge within each person to articulate and elaborate his idiom, a form of a life instinct in which the person seeks to come into his own true being through "an experiencing" that releases his potential.

Bollas (1989) helps us comprehend why some people seem destined to live a life of meaning and fulfilment and others seem fated to live a life of endurance and survival. It goes back to the days of infancy, childhood, and adolescence.

If all goes well, an infant, child, and later adolescent experiences his mother as reliable. She enables him to come into contact with and experience his true self or his inherited potential. The child establishes his personality and feels real, alive, and capable of fulfilling his inner idiom, or his defining essence. He is then poised to select objects in his school, peer, and cultural world that facilitate the development of his unique destiny. People of destiny are passionate about what they are doing in life and how they relate to others. They feel strong about what they want. This does not necessarily mean that they are selfish or self-centered, but rather that they are in touch with their idiomatic desires (Bollas, 1989, pp. 7–47).

If all does not go so well, an infant, child, and then later adolescent lives in a world of commandments. These are experienced as drastic demands dictated by his caretaker. These commands most often have nothing to do with the child's true self or inner essence. He feels required to adopt a certain way of thinking, choose certain friends, attend certain schools, and dress in certain ways. These declarations feel topsy-turvy to the child's sense of self, but he feels fated to follow them. The child is alienated from the experience of his true self and his idiomatic desires. He is then poised to feel despair and hopelessness about the world. He loses all interest in the search for objects that will help him experience his true self and unique destiny. A sense of emptiness shadows his life. He feels fated to live a life that he is not really connected to. Without this connection, he is unable to steer for himself. A false sense of self serves as his guide. He despairingly moves forward. He knows no other way (Bollas, 1989, p. 45).

Drugs and alcohol provide much comfort for the fated individual. He ruthlessly selects them as a reliable source of soothing and reprieve for these feelings of nameless dread (Bion, 1967, p. 116). AOD seems the perfect complement to a fated life with no imaginable future: "I can live in this rudderless world if I'm protected with Vicodin or alcohol." Henry David Thoreau said that so many individuals in our culture live lives of quiet desperation. They also live with addictions.

During recovery, the work is both directive and psychoanalytic in spirit. P/SUDs in their early days of moderation or abstinence need direction, guidance, and support. They also need attentive listening by important others. Their true self is searching for a connection who hears their essence and their destiny desires. If that listening occurs, a formerly fated P/SUD can soon begin to live an unimaginable life of his future. It requires the fortune of staying drug-free, as well as focused determination and a long, steady road of very difficult work with some healthy assertion and aggression to get what he needs.

Lisa Director

Lisa Director looks at omnipotence in the psychoanalysis of substance users. Living in a state of omnipotence suggests that one desires a sense of complete control or influence over the self, an object, or others in the outside world. Director (2005) describes elements of omnipotence that are present in drug use. These include a dominant wish, a focused drive with an insistence on pleasure (pp. 567–587).

P/SUD's vulnerability: Individuals live with a pervasive and disturbing sense that one's needs cannot be met by the self or others. This results in an aggressive and destructive search to meet them through AOD.

Instrument of omnipotence: Drugs, alcohol, and the world of ritualized addiction provide the addict with a sense of omnipotent control. The use of drugs and alcohol promises that needs will always be met.

The need during recovery: A relationship with a person who has the capacity to hold and contain the P/SUD's defensive feelings of omnipotence. The function of this state of mind can then be more easily explored and discussed.

An infant regularly fed and attended to develops a sense of healthy omnipotence. With this comes a sense of trust that the universe and the people in it can satisfy basic needs. D. W. Winnicott calls this a "moment of illusion." This experience provides an infant, child, adolescent, and then later adult with a faith that other people can provide support during overwhelming times (Winnicott, cited in Director, 2005, p. 575).

P/SUDs seem to live a very pained life without this internalized sense of illusion. Many have been dramatically and repeatedly disappointed in childhood, adolescence, and later, adulthood. They live in a state of frustrated need without a clear sense of what to do or how to help themselves. Director and others suggest that addicts aggressively and rather exclusively seek out drugs and alcohol to satisfy these frustrations. They discover that they work, and over time, AOD becomes the central organizing principle in their lives.

P/SUDs develop a love affair with this omnipotent provider. The sense of ever-present provisions brings with it tremendous feelings of security and safety. While it is akin to the moment of illusion of the early infant when breastfed, it is a miscarriage of reality based on a perverted relationship with a dangerous object. This relationship provides neither a healthy relational back-and-forth nor lasting satiation. Its pleasure lies exclusively in its control (Director, 2005, p. 575).

Director (2005) goes on to highlight the frustrations experienced by persons in the life of the P/SUD. When the P/SUD is ruthlessly devoted to control of the drug experience, he pushes people to the periphery with aggression and hostility. Family members, loved ones, and even therapists know too well the experience of feeling devalued and unimportant to the P/SUD—even hated, particularly if his using feels threatened. Unconsciously, the P/SUD pushes others away as ruthlessly as his needs were pushed away as an infant. The P/SUD's omnipotence belies his terror; feelings of uselessness bring much suffering to his loved ones (pp. 567–587).

Certainly it is critical for a therapist to contain this omnipotence if it should reappear in early recovery. It requires much tact and patience to listen to a P/SUD's overbearing enthusiasm and sense of certainty about his plans in his early days of sobriety. This certainty has a brittle protectiveness to it. Many times, it prevents real contact with therapists or loved ones, and many times relapse occurs. It is not uncommon to feel as irrelevant to a newly sober person as one did during his days of using.

Omnipotence needs to be addressed, and the deeper reasons behind pushing people away understood. This is very delicate; it takes time and patience. Adam Phillips (1994) says it best for the plight of the recovering omnipotent addict: "Hell is not other people, but one's need for other people" (p. 45). Learning to trust others without the use of omnipotence is a daunting undertaking.

CHAPTER SUMMARY AND REFLECTIONS

Summary

This chapter presented a self-selected collection of addiction and psychoanalytic theories that shed light on the etiology and psychological suffering behind addiction. A concise synopsis of selected aspects of these theories was presented using discipline, imagination, and creativity. These nine unique, yet overlapping theories proposed that untreated human psychological suffering drives some people to self-medicate their pain with alcohol and other drugs. Each theory presented provides the reader with an insightful and useful perspective on what might cause this suffering. These theorized essentials were followed by discussion ideas, brief clinical vignettes, and suggestions for their use in recovery treatment.

Reflections

Consider the following questions in a classroom discussion or paper:

- How is this theoretical material useful for your clinical work?
- Which self-medication theory feels most clinically and intuitively appropriate for your style?
- What are some of the overlapping themes in these self-medication theories?
- How are you able to combine the use of the self-medication hypothesis with other theories and interventions, including cognitive, evidence-based, harm reduction, and other approaches?

CHAPTER 9

THE SYMPOSIUM APPROACH: USE, PREVENTION, EDUCATION, AND TREATMENT

INTRODUCTION

For over 80 years now, the addiction field has been steadily developing single-focused and multifocused models of treatment that identify a range of etiological assumptions and a range of spiritual, dynamic, and cognitive-behavioral interventions. These have included moral, learning, disease, self-medication, dual diagnosis, and biopsychosocial models, to name a few. In the United States, the disease model has been heralded as the primary lens to view excess use, and the medical and treatment communities have developed inpatient, outpatient, and pharmacological treatments based on abstinence. Support groups such as AA and Self-Management and Recovery Training (SMART), as well as interventions such as motivational interviewing, cognitive-behavioral strategies, and evidence-based protocols, have turned many people's lives around, including many I have treated professionally and many I have known personally. These models will continue to occupy treatment space in the United States for some time. Please refer to a survey text for an overview and likely more in-depth study of these helpful treatment models and interventions.

This chapter presents a symposium approach that joins ancient ideas about prevention and education with the modern treatment approaches of harm reduction and self-medication, as well as the use of some contemporary psychoanalytic concepts. The symposium approach was constructed with exploration in mind, not pathology. It evolved in my mind from many contemporary forces, including the introduction of the DSM-5 SUDs spectrum model for diagnosis, growing fatigue with the disease approach and its insistence on abstinence, decades of successful professional experience with the use of individual clinical sketches for assessment, and the increasing number of clinics and in- and outpatient facilities using harm reduction and self-medication to treat the high percentage of problem drinkers in the United States who are not alcoholics (Parker-Pope, 2014).

This approach embraces the following ideas: The natural desire for intoxication is considered the *fourth drive*; each person has a unique relationship with AOD; some people will naturally struggle with impulse control while enjoying something so pleasurable; excessive use of AOD is a form of psychological-social adaption; people will willingly seek help if given the chance and a choice to reverse self-defeating behaviors; certain types of drinkers will intuitively choose "gentle drinking" or moderation, and other individuals will end up choosing abstinence as their best approach.

The symposium approach was inspired by the ancient Greek gymnasiums that provided the *philopotes*, lovers of drinking, a range of helpful options to consider while learning to drink better. These symposiums embraced the notion that wine was a universal human pleasure, as well as a human right. This chapter's new conceptualization of use, prevention, education, and treatment is developed from the ancient philosophers who felt that wine was a gift to humanity, and with it came an ethical responsibility to learn to "tipple wisely" under the supervision of assigned philosophers in the symposium. Alcohol or drugs provided the individual with a variety of experiences, some of them to one's apparent advantage, some to one's obvious detriment. Every Greek adult male was faced with the challenge to get alcohol to work for him rather than against him (Allhoff, 2007, pp. 16, 22). According to Hippocrates, "Should a patient be suffering from an overpowering heaviness of the brain [mind], then 'there must be total abstinence from wine'" (Gately, 2008, p. 13).

The philosophy behind this symposium approach is based on the notion that most of us want to find a way to enjoy our ancient love affair with the elixirs, to more responsibly identify our current relationship with AOD, and to consider healthier options for any distressing AOD habits. This approach feels particularly well suited for our times. The 2013 DSM-5 revisions have dropped the diagnostic terms *abuse* and *dependence* and presented a spectrum of categories instead, ranging from nonproblematic use to severe use and addiction. This spectrum design encourages problem users and more severe users to seek either a path to moderation or a path to abstinence.

This use, prevention, education, and treatment approach is composed of two phases, each phase to be used independently or in conjunction with the other phase, depending on the needs of the individual. For example, one person may only need exploration, prevention, and education in Phase 1; most will benefit from both phases; and, of course, severe cases need immediate medical treatment.

The first phase asks individuals to embrace and explore the nature and nuances of their own relationship with their fourth drive, and then discover their unique relationship with AOD with the help of the DSM-5 spectrum and clinical sketches (see Chapter 6). The second phase encourages clinicians to use a harm reduction approach to reverse any self-recognized destructive behaviors and also use self-medication theories and psychoanalytic concepts to treat the underlying psychological wounds and traumas. It is a simple model, driven by an appreciation of our natural desires and the reversible, and sometimes irreversible, troubles that result.

The philosophical and clinical approach that *Perspectives* proposes for consideration is diagrammed below:

Table 9.1 The Symposium Approach: Use, Prevention, Education, and Treatment

Phase 1	
Use	*Prevention and Education*
Fourth drive, healthy	Explore and assess • DSM-5 spectrum • 15 clinical sketches
Phase 2	
Unhealthy Use	*Treatment*
Fourth drive, unhealthy—problematic and addiction	• Harm reduction—addresses problems with behavioral controls/cognitive distortions • Self-medication/psychoanalytic—addresses problems with psychological suffering

FOUR GUIDING PRINCIPLES OF THE SYMPOSIUM APPROACH

The symposium approach invites all people to become more conscious of their relationship with the fourth drive. This approach is exploratory-based, not pathology-based; its focus is philosophical, not scientific; it is preventative, not reactive; it is educational, but not formulaic; it encourages individual discovery, not predetermined solutions; it leads to well-being, not necessarily to abstinence.

The symposium approach is supported by the following complementary four pillars that respect our human desire for intoxication and our innate desire for health and well-being, and suggest clinical approaches and skills to achieve these ends.

1. The Unstoppable Fourth Drive

This section of this chapter presents some of the highlights of Ron Siegel's school of ideas that are well presented in his spirited and well-researched book *In Intoxication* (2005). For starters, history shows that we have always used AOD. In every age, in every part of this planet, people have pursued intoxication with plants, drugs, alcohol, and other mind-altering substances. This pursuit has so much force and persistence that it functions just like our other drives of hunger, thirst, and sex. This fourth drive is a natural part of our biology, and is seen as an ordinary part of the human experience—a healthy drive and a right belonging to each individual. The pursuit of intoxication is no more abnormal than the pursuit of love, social attachments, thrills, power, or any number of other acquired motives (p. 208).

The fourth drive approach assumes that the ancient pursuit of intoxication is benign not sinister, inevitable, and unstoppable. The fourth drive is not just motivating people to feel good, better, or bad; it is primarily a desire to feel different, to achieve a rapid change in our state of mind. We have found a way to ingest AOD and transform uncomfortable states of mind into more tolerable or more lively ones. There is a pattern of drug-seeking and drug-taking behavior that has been consistent across time, a natural force in us that searches for the pursuit of pleasure. Again, a war on drugs is a war on ourselves, a denial of our nature.

Over time, unfortunately, moralistic philosophies have prevented us from considering that these pleasurable changes in the body or mind are actually fulfilling healthy needs for many individuals (p. 309). As a matter of course, most of us are likely to resist the notion that the use of intoxicants has a beneficial or medical purpose, or that we need intoxicants. We need these substances of pleasure, not in the sense that an addict needs a fix, but because we need the benefits of the intoxicants as treatments for the human condition. Siegel suggests that escaping or expanding our consciousness with AOD can be considered a wonderful way to lighten our lives with chemical glimpses into a more appealing world. The need is natural, yes, even healthy. Again, this assertion is far from the prevailing and contemporary view that considers the use of most intoxicating drugs as fraught with potential peril, inherently troublesome, and immoral, if not evil and beastly as well (pp. 206–251). It seems, as hard as we try, that we cannot eliminate this ancient desire for pleasure, relief, and escape.

That being said, during specific periods in history, we have also seen this physical and psychological drive "run amok" (p. 1). Individuals tend to overuse this drive during periods of cultural stress, cultural hedonism, or both. These are times when we notice that master passions and excess are ever-present and on the rise. *Perspectives* suggests that along with embracing the pleasures of our fourth drive nature, we also accept individual responsibility for staying consciously connected to our fluctuating patterns with AOD. *Perspectives* anticipates that a deep acceptance of our natural drive will allow us to better appreciate, understand, and manage these pleasures when they turn to excess.

During decades of clinical work and teaching, I have developed 15 clinical sketches for working with clients who use or struggle with AOD (see Chapter 6). These are guidelines to assist you to freely explore your relationship with AOD, not defensively protect it. These are sketches designed to help you discover the meanings behind these entrenched healthy or unhealthy habits. *Perspectives* proposes that more empathic and responsible care will occur when we move away from the "diseasing" of our desire to get high and see this *fourth drive* for intoxication as a universal and natural phenomenon.

2. Registering Impacts

A sentence in Mike Eigen's *Psychic Deadness* (1996) caught my attention the moment I read it: "A core ingredient in the kind of work I have in mind is the *impact* of the patient on the therapist" (p. 143). Registering impacts has become a core clinical ingredient in my work in the substance use disorder field. It nurtures a "here and now" alive contact between the therapist and patient. As a result of feeling so deeply heard and contained, the patient soon feels "allowed" to initiate and investigate his own path of transformation from destructive choices to healthier ones. This provides a radically different experience for the P/SUD in treatment. He is usually prepared to be *caught, controlled,* and *directed* by a family member or even a therapist.

Waiting on impact contrasts sharply with the panicked sense of urgency that has dominated the SUDs field. "All we have to do is listen" and wait out impact until we have something useful to say to the patient. "I play for time" and wait for the relationship to become a trusted container for the patient, allowing him to reveal his passionate, obsessive attachments to alcohol and other drugs (MEigen Workshop, 2013).

Impact as core—what does this mean, and how can it be used clinically? The quotes below are mostly Eigen originals, some combination of Eigen originals, or some combination of Eigen and Fetting. I hope these register with the reader:

- The most private, intimate fact of a meeting between two people is impact. Keep dipping into the impact someone is having on you, the sensations, feelings, imaginings, and thoughts that grow from mute impact. If we are lucky, we give the other's impact time, we wait until the reality at hand finds voice, and then we might have something helpful to say to a patient or loved one. We let the other's impact play on us; we feel it, dream it, think about it, and let it give rise to creative musings (Eigen, 1996, p. 195).
- Impact is the primary raw datum. It occurs instantaneously, but needs the therapist's faith, time, and loyalty in order to take root and grow. Let it unfold, better not to put it into words and share it too soon (Eigen, 1996, p. 143).
- One must make inner sacrifices and adjustments to hear another person or really feel heard. This requires a mutual resonance, speaking, listening, feeling, and working imaginatively with the impact of each other's being (Eigen, 1996, p. 210).
- If you are preoccupied with an intervention, you might miss the session, miss the patient's impact, and miss the response the patient needs in order for something more to happen (Eigen, 2011b, p. 17).
- Most often impacts are shocks, the shock of one personality impacting on another. Sometimes the impact is pleasant, sometimes not; often it is mixed and usually mute. A monolithic shock soon becomes variegated, having many different forms. As one lives with the shock, one comes to know different parts of it. One becomes more familiar with its colors, tonalities, textures, and tensions. There are blue, red, white, and black shocks, and sometimes we see stars or hear ringing or voices or music (Eigen, 1996, p. 144).
- One's personality may contract or constrict itself around the shock of the other, the point of impact. If the shock is great, stiffening may be widespread. One goes blank and waits. The mind may race to get its bearings. If the shock is unpleasant the mind may freeze. It takes moments to realize that the danger is psychic, not physical, so that the primary process may come out of hiding and work (Eigen, 1996, p. 144).
- If the shock is wonderful, even the shock of joy, one cannot open enough, sound carries. If the shock is horrible one cannot close fast enough, sound flattens. Sometimes the shock comes through, sometimes one wades through layers of numbness to get the taste (Eigen, 1996, p. 144).

- If distracted in any way during the clinical encounter, remember: always return to impact (Eigen, 2011b, p. 17).
- Much depends on the therapist's ability to sustain the buildup of the patient's impact until the realities at hand find voice. An inability to achieve this buildup may murder the experience of the patient's psychic death (the painful surrender to vulnerability, weakness, or need) and perhaps the possibility of life as well. An interpretation may kill or support the growth of experience, including the experience of surrendering to the ego (Eigen, 1996, pp. 145, 147).
- The therapist's processing of the patient's impact provides new psychic experiences:

  o It gives the patient a sense of being taken seriously: "I must be of value."
  o The patient experiences the therapist's metabolizing catastrophic bits of affect that the patient could not due to lack of psychic equipment (thus starts the process of building his missing psychic equipment).
  o The patient learns by the therapist's acceptance that he is not disgusting, not extremely indigestible, nor entirely digestible. He eventually starts to feel less of a menace to others.
  o Feeling this registering from the therapist allows the patient to begin to link up with himself.
  o "The therapist allows the patient's empty depression to wash over him, no matter how confusing and difficult to experience. Empty depression reflects the relative emptiness of self, paucity of psychic structure and lack of good internal objects" (Kohut in Fetting, 2012, p. 103). The patient is relieved; "someone can be with my feelings of nothingness. Someone wants to hear, support, and process my experience(s) and inner struggles."

My clinical practice, teaching, and writing in the SUDs field have been highly influenced by Eigen and psychoanalysis, as you will see in Chapters 10 through 14. A psychoanalytic attitude listens and waits. It adds merit to a field that tends to be overzealous, overcontrolling, possessive, too directive, and prematurely reassuring. Eigen challenges, "There are those [SUDs] patients who respond to the faith that underlies the analytic attitude. There are those wishing to open to the moment, with all its uncertainty, rather than foreclose on a chance for more experiencing [with the use of a didactic behavioral directive]. There are those that begin to view life more truthfully and are finally able to extend the horizon towards all possible solutions. And then there are those who fall back on the status quo [relapse] and try to remain inured to the call of the more or another" (Eigen, 1999, p. 190).

Eigen reminds us that faith is the open attitude that allows impacts to register. Listening with faith allows the treatment provider to stay true to impact, and helpful responses may follow. "Faith plays an important role in transformational processes in therapy. Faith supports experiential exploration, imaginative conjecture, experiential probing" (Eigen, 2011a, p. vii). Eigen and Bion suggest that we meet absolute destruction (of SUDs) with faith and openness, faith in the radical openness of the moment. Bion suggests this attitude for psychoanalytic treatment, and I strongly suggest its incorporation into the treatment of substance use disorders.

This attitude encourages us to wait with the patient. *Bion suggests that the transformational process (in SUD recovery) may not happen without risking, waiting in faith.* When Eigen is asked about how transformations happen he answers, "I have no idea, except that creating an atmosphere where people [with SUDs] can just hear themselves sometimes does strange and marvelous things" (Eigen, 1999, p. 221).

What is suggested for readers of *Perspectives* is that the clinician spend less time trying to possess a patient's mind and conquer and control his behavior, but instead take in his impact, dream it, feel it, and imagine it. Let these impacts wash over you and see where they take you. Listen, hold, wait, and back off. Allow the patient to have the experience of being seen and heard. Avoid the imperative toward urgency and the histrionic warning, "They will die if we do not do something now."

3. Harm Reduction

Andrew Tatarsky is a pioneer. He intuitively embraced the concept of harm reduction early in his career, with the encouragement of the renowned Alan Marlatt (1998), who called this approach "compassionate pragmatism." Tatarsky delivered his ideas to the United States and the addiction field in his book *Harm Reduction Psychotherapy* (2002). As harm reduction rejects the presumption that abstinence is the best or only acceptable goal for all problem alcohol and drug users, you may understand why its acceptance and adaption in our disease model culture is very slow going. It is important to keep in mind that harm reduction is not at odds with abstinence, but includes it as one possible goal (2002, p. 21).

The goal of harm reduction is to engage clients in a relationship that will support them in clarifying the problematic aspects of their substance use and work toward addressing these problems with goals and strategies that are consistent with who they are as individuals. Harm reduction values engaging clients around their own initial goals as the starting point. Harm reduction places respect for the client's strength and capacity as the starting point for developing egalitarian relationships. This is a departure from the paternalistic model associated with more traditional substance use treatment (p. 2). The ideal outcome of Tatarsky's approach is to support the user in reducing the harmfulness of substance use to the point where it has minimal negative impact on other areas of one's life (pp. 25–26). Moderation in the form of mindful use, watchful use, or discontinued use depends on what emerges out of treatment discussions (see Chapter 6, pp. 60, 69, 74).

Perspectives has embraced harm reduction as a clinical approach essential to effective treatment of substance use, disorders, and addiction. Says Tatarsky: "The practice of harm reduction is a needed correction to the limitations of our current professional and public policy response to drug use problems in this country. I have developed an effective, integrative approach that blends dynamic, cognitive, behavioral, and biological strategies" (2002, pp. 3–10). Harm reduction's psychotherapy is rooted in the basic principles of good psychotherapy practice and is consistent with psychodynamic and cognitive behavioral models of substance misuse.

Bruce Alexander suggests that harm reduction may be the most effective paradigm to restore the individual's psychosocial integration when it is threatened by the disruptive aspects of our globalized world. He sees addictions of all types as adaptions to these social disruptions. Alexander writes, "The essence of harm reduction is establishing ongoing respectful relationships between addicted people and caring service providers, which increases the likelihood of 'addicted' people finding a more socially acceptable and productive way of living. The harm reduction movement may be expected to play a much fuller and more vital role when understood in terms of globalization and dislocation theory" (Alexander, 2014, p. 27).

Ed Khantzian supports harm reduction as well: "My training then and now persuaded me to adopt a perspective that a reliance on alcohol and other drugs serves an adaptive purpose in the lives of such individuals. Rather than stress abstinence or sobriety, I immediately attempt to ascertain the amount and pattern of drinking, and I ask patients respectfully and empathically to share with me their own reasons for drinking, especially what the drinking does for them. I also ask patients as tactfully as I can to reflect on how much danger and harm they have caused themselves as a result of their drinking" (Khantzian,1999, p. 246).

My teaching, clinical work, creation of clinical sketches, and writing naturally aligned with harm reduction's approach. Harm reduction accepts substance use on a continuum of harmful consequences to the user and the community, very much in line with the clinical sketches identified in Chapter 6. In doing so, harm reduction accepts small, incremental steps in the direction of reduced harm, with the goal being to facilitate the greatest reduction in harm for a person at a given point in time (Tatarsky, 2002, p. 2).

In closing this section, consider the following insightful observations from Tatarsky's 2002 book, likely to be useful in your clinical work: "For many clients whose substance use continues to *serve some positive function*, the question of whether they can moderate their use must be answered before they can consider stopping. The psychodynamic assumption that drug use holds important personal meanings suggests why some drug users may not be able to give up or modify drug use until other alternative ways of expressing these needs are found." Another thoughtful suggestion: "I take my lead from what is most pressing to the client, and for some, what is pressing is how AOD is a positive adaption in their lives, and its healthier continuation needs to be explored." And finally, these insightful words in *Harm Reduction Psychotherapy* (2002): "We strive to find the ideal pattern that the client envisions for himself. And then the delightful and rewarding day when drinking or drugging is no longer an active issue" (pp. 1–49).

4. Self-Medication

Ed Khantzian (1999, 2008) has truly gifted the SUDs field of addiction with vision, creativity, courage, focus, tenacity, and kindness. In 1985 he proposed the Self-Medication Hypothesis (SMH), and he is recognized as the founder of the self-medication model of treatment for addiction. His hypothesis is rooted in the inner experience of those who psychologically suffer and endure it (Khantzian & Albanese, 2008, p. 118). Khantzian has always favored psychodynamic therapy for the treatment of SUDs: "I am drawn more to process and narrative data than to data of an empirical nature" (1999, p. 5). He continues, "The treatment relationship is a rich source of data" (1999, p. 2).

Khantzian encourages us to directly address problems of AOD control and begin to look at the psychological suffering driving the need to self-medicate, all in the first session. The SMH, from its inception, addressed important emotional and psychological dimensions of the addictions that had been dismissed, neglected, or inadequately considered in previous scientific and clinical investigations. "I found it necessary to adopt a more over-arching view of substance dependence problems as a self-regulation disorder" (1999, p. 246). "Addicts and alcoholics share in common general problems in self-regulation involving difficulties in affect life, self-esteem, relationships, and self-care. These self-regulation problems combine to make people more desperate, driven, isolated, and impulsive, and more likely to assume the risks of drug- or alcohol-seeking or using behavior" (1999, p. 197).

Khantzian first starts out reminding us that, under ordinary circumstances, alcohol is used widely as a means to relax and serves as a social lubricant for enjoying the company of others. For the more tense and anxious, alcohol and drugs such as the benzodiazepines become more necessary and eventually excessive, and may lead to addiction. Khantzian has found that extreme discomfort and defensiveness about matters of emotional closeness and dependency drive the need to self-medicate (2008, p. 45.) While under the influence, many of us are able to achieve a neurotic feeling of closeness.

Khantzian, like Bruce Alexander, Ron Siegel, and Andrew Tatarsky, has also adopted a perspective that states that reliance on alcohol and other drugs serves an adaptive purpose in the lives of some individuals. Each of these theorists focuses on how the patients' use of substances fits into their overall adaption, as well as their perceived treatment needs and goals (1999, pp. 98, 246).

Khantzian has found in his decades of clinical practice and research that without the capacity to self-regulate in the four areas identified below, patients self-medicate instead. What follows is a very brief overview of these four areas.

Affect

Painful, inaccessible, and confusing affects are at the core of addictive suffering. Alcoholics and addicts experience their emotions in the extreme. They seem overwhelmed with distress, or they seem unable to feel their feelings at all (Khantzian, 1999, p. 657).

Many addicts seem chronically "disaffected" (McDougall, 1984) or "alexithymic" with their own feelings (Krystal, 1982/1983). They are unable to name their feelings and are thus unable to use them while navigating through life. Some seem beside themselves with intense affects such as rage, shame, loneliness, and depression, and yet others "flip-flop" between these extremes of experiencing too much or too little.

When individuals feel a need to repeatedly resort to AOD, it is usually a sign that they suffer from overwhelming emotion and developmental handicaps, and therefore need drug-alcohol effects to achieve and maintain states of feeling that they cannot achieve on their own (Khantzian, 1999, p. 187).

Well-Being and Self-Esteem

Basic states of well-being and positive self-regard derive from the early stages of development. Addicts and alcoholics suffer with developmental deficits from the failure to internalize the comforting, soothing, validating, and mobilizing aspects of their parenting or caregiver environment (1999, p. 188).

A sense of inner well-being is the bedrock for an evolving sense of self, and ultimately the capacity for self-respect and self-love. When people do not feel good about themselves, it permeates their relationships with others and makes satisfying or satisfactory relationships unlikely or more difficult. Alcohol softens overdrawn, self-sufficient, and rigid defenses that are often adapted to cover a shaky self-esteem or a sense of feeling cut off and empty (1999, p. 659).

Relationships

Relating to and depending on others is a precarious, if not annihilating, experience for P/SUDs. As much as they need others to know how they feel, they often fear and distrust their dependency, disavow their need for others, and act in counterdependent ways. Their defense of self-sufficiency leaves them feeling isolated and cut off, and they disguise from themselves and others their need for nurturance and validation (1999, p. 189).

"As much as we are social creatures, we can also be avoidant of relationships, even when we most need them. Some of us are better than others at relationships" (Khantzian & Albanese, 2008, p. 17). Addicts seem less able to connect to others, and life often feels dreary, lonely, and depressing to them. "Unfortunately, if the capacity to relate to others gets derailed early in life, addictions can be substituted for the comfort and well-being that relationships can provide" (Khantzian & Albanese, 2008, pp. 17–18).

Self-Care

Addicted behavior is governed less by self-destructive motives and more by developmental failures and deficits in ego functions that leave certain individuals unable to possess an energized sense of self-value and self-worth; to care for and protect themselves from danger; to renounce pleasures whose consequences are harmful; to enjoy an appropriate level of risk; to navigate the outside world with accurate and real knowledge; to assert themselves as individuals; and to choose people who enhance their value, worth, and protection, not jeopardize it. Self-care deficits are on a continuum, and in the more extreme cases it is necessary to actively intervene to help patients who have a blind spot when it comes to anticipating danger (1999, pp. 189–190, 660–661).

Patients have a limited capacity to effectively use these ego functions of self-care. They self-medicate instead. Effective treatment for these deficiencies must be based on a more precise and empathic identification of the disturbances in these ego functions of self-care.

READING THE CASE STUDIES

Case studies are presented in the next five chapters that apply the four guiding principles of the symposium approach to my clinical work with patients during their individual paths to moderation, abstinence, and well-being. All have given permission to be written about in *Perspectives*.

Readers are encouraged to review the content of the seven philosophical unifying themes of *Perspectives* identified in Chapter 1. These are also used in guiding my clinical attitude and treatment decisions.

The case studies are presented within the framework of the new DSM-5 diagnostic spectrum and are coupled with the 15 clinical sketches. These sketches provide an individual clinical picture for the broad diagnostic categories used in DSM-5. A DSM-5 diagnosis along with a descriptive picture will help you and your patient arrive at the most responsive treatment approach (see Table 9.2 below).

Readers are advised to answer the reflection questions at the end of this chapter, as well as review Chapters 6 and 8 before reading the case studies.

Table 9.2   DSM Spectrum Categories and Corresponding Clinical Sketches

DSM Spectrum	Clinical Sketches
Nonpathological	Use, voluntary nonuse, experimental use, take-it-or-leave-it use, social use, misuse, mindful use, watchful use, and discontinued use
Mild Substance Use Disorder	Experimental use and misuse
Moderate Substance Use Disorder	Experimental use, regular misuse, problematic use at a problematic time, problem use, and shadow use
Severe Substance Use Disorder	Experimental use, problematic use at a problematic time, problem use, shadow use, and psychological reliance not yet physical
Addiction*	Addiction

* DSM-5 allows for individual discretion about adoption of this term.

CHAPTER SUMMARY AND REFLECTIONS

Summary

This chapter introduced the reader to a symposium approach that underscores our natural desires for intoxication and appreciates various responses to excess use and addiction. Four guiding principles of the symposium approach were presented: the unstoppable fourth drive, registering impacts, harm reduction, and self-medication. Case studies presented in the next five chapters will demonstrate the application of these principles.

Reflections

Consider the following questions in a classroom discussion or paper:

- What is your understanding of the symposium approach?
- What are your likes and dislikes?
- What are some of the differences between a symposium approach and the contemporary inventions and practices used today?
- How might you adopt this approach in your personal and professional lives?
- George Vaillant (1983) asked a question: "Is treatment really necessary, or will people mature out of destructive habits with the help of natural healing forces?"

CHAPTER 10

NONPROBLEMATIC USE

INTRODUCTION

This chapter, a short one for obvious reasons, includes examples and four case studies that reflect nonproblematic use.

CLINICAL CASES

Ashley: Nonproblematic Use

Ashley grew up in a family that enjoyed nightly cocktails before dinner and wine during the meal. Like Socrates, her family believed alcohol is part of the good life (Allhoff, 2007, p. 22). Her parents invited her to join them during their nightly cocktails and wine when she returned on home visits while in college. Her mother knew to tipple wisely, but her father did not possess this gift and drank very heavily, if not alcoholically, during most of his life. He stopped in the last 5 years of his life due to "health reasons."

Ashley is married, with four grown children. She and her husband consider alcohol, cocktails, and partying with their friends "as a part of our lifestyle. It's been that way since we were married, raised and married off our four children, and now as grandparents of five children. It is a regular part of our everyday life." Ashley and her husband, Michael, admit that he has a tendency to drink too much on many occasions. He is a shadow user. He lives a successful, proud, and robust life that indeed includes overindulgence of alcohol. He has had periods of discontinued use for a year or two, but has always returned. At 66 years of age, he is determined to moderate his daily drinking habits and continue with alcohol use as a very important part of his life.

Ashley, on the other hand, does not appear to have a "drinking problem." She acknowledges that she enjoys alcohol and misuses on occasion. "But I seem to have an internal monitor that says, 'I have had enough. I don't want to go overboard, nor do I want to feel sick. It's time to start putting ice in my wine, drinking water with my wine, or stop drinking altogether.'"

Ashley is like many healthy individuals around the world who love the place of AOD in their lives; have internal breaks; and if they overdo it, are desirous and able to learn from experience and drink with moderation the next time and most times thereafter. Many individuals are intuitively gifted with the Socratic philosophy on drinking: Rather than succumb to drink, control the drink (Allhoff, 2007, p. 28).

Donya: Nonproblematic Use

Donya, a southern European woman, has been married for 40 years and has two grown children. She has been a homemaker and caretaker for her family and her husband. She sometimes has regrets: "I wish I had developed more of an independent identity, had created a career of my own. However, in my day, our culture strongly encouraged marriage and children for the woman."

Donya has "a wonderful life. While it has been difficult at times—for example, I wish my husband talked more, let me in on what he is thinking—over the years I have adapted to his quiet ways, and we have a good life within our home and with our friends."

Donya makes time for her close friends and their husbands. She makes sure to keep the connections going and regularly organizes dinner parties, trips, and family vacations with other couples, often including everyone's children as well.

Donya, her husband, and friends enjoy drinking wine, beer, and Italian spirits when together at a dinner party or on a trip. "None of my friends are big drinkers. Everyone stops at a certain point during the brunch, dinner, or celebration. I have developed this habit over the last 20 years. I always put water in my wine as a way to make sure I don't end up feeling intoxicated." Like the ancient Greeks, Donya and her friends enjoy wine, but they are also discriminating drinkers who found mixing water with wine "was far more pleasant and far less inflammatory" (Gately, 2008, p. 14).

Dr. Rebecca Simon: Nonproblematic Use

Dr. Simon is an academician and a professor at an Ivy League school. She is 74 years old, well established in her field, and has maintained a rigorous and reputable professional life. She is highly respected for her political skills, her personal and professional integrity, and her academic contributions to the literature in her specialized area of expertise.

She has two grown children and maintains close contact with them, enjoying holidays, vacations, and just spending time together. "I feel blessed." She divorced their father over 20 years ago and has had sporadic relationships since then. "I have kind of given up on a relationship and am so grateful for my academic affiliation and my close colleagues in my department—they are my other family. I want to be a part of my faculty as long as I can. I need them, and I'm grateful to have them."

Dr. Simon really looks forward to and enjoys the place of alcohol in her life. As you recall, the Greek word for drinker is *philopotes*, meaning a lover of drinking and a lover of drinking sessions. Being a *philopotes* bore no stigma (Gately, 2008, p. 15). She occasionally enjoys a glass of wine at the faculty club while lunching with other faculty members. "I will occasionally drink alone at night. I'd rather have fun with my friends, but at this point in my life, I am not at all worried about my solitary drinking." Dr. Simon and her friends will get tipsy when traveling together, at dinner parties, or at academic celebrations. She is a hearty social user, looks forward to a night with wine and friends, and loves to reminisce about the good times and antics the day after. Ancient Greek philosophy reminds us that it is understandable that people would want to indulge in the pleasures of drinking as much as possible.

She relishes her enjoyment with alcohol, even her periods of excess, but "I'm not the kind of person that is going to let things get out of control." To the ancient Greeks, being an *apeles,* a careless and carefree drinker, bore no disgrace, but rather at times only mild criticism (Gately, 2008, p. 15).

Joanne: Nonproblematic Use

Joanne is a 28-year-old clinical social worker. She has earned her stripes, including an MSW from a well-respected school, and sat for her California license. She wears her ambitions well, is thriving in her private practice, and is a joy to have as a member in one of my supervision groups. She is a clinician who is deeply devoted to the development of her emotional life and clinical mind.

Joanne relies on a solid group of friends, struggles with her relationships with men, has courageously individuated herself from "overbearing parents," and loves her two "sons"—her Labrador Retriever dogs.

Joanne enjoys alcohol and marijuana; as a matter of fact, she has done both since she was 16 years old. "I've certainly done both to excess, particularly in my late teens and early 20s, but these episodes never developed into a pattern.

I feel blessed." Joanne adds, "My bigger problem is that my last four boyfriends all had big problems with pot or bigger ones with alcohol." She continues, "I always begin a relationship with the hopes that both of us will be able to enjoy both drugs and both of us will know when to stop. That hasn't happened yet, although I am reestablishing a relationship with someone who likes both in hopes that we can enjoy them together."

Joanne sees both alcohol and pot in her future. She embraces her fourth drive, refuses to be pathologized, and is determined and able to maintain a level of intoxication that is acceptable to her. She considers herself a social user with occasional misuse. "My parents enjoyed pot and alcohol as well, but I rarely, maybe once or twice, saw them overdo it. That was a useful gift for me from them."

CHAPTER SUMMARY AND REFLECTIONS

Summary

This chapter explored four case studies of nonpathological use. It utilized the four guiding principles of the symposium approach, as well as the seven philosophical and clinical ideas identified in Chapter 1.

Reflections

Consider the following questions in a classroom discussion or paper:

- Do you agree with the DSM-5 spectrum category given to the four case studies in this chapter? Why or why not?
- What other spectrum categories might you consider?
- What are the difficulties you might encounter as you consider a person with a non-problematic relationship with substances?

CHAPTER 11

MILD SUBSTANCE USE DISORDER

INTRODUCTION

This chapter, also a short one, includes two case studies of individuals who were concerned about their recent drinking patterns. Both had solid ego functions of self-care and developed more satisfying habits in less than a year.

CLINICAL CASES

Karen: Problematic Use at a Problematic Time to Social Use

Karen was a 42-year-old woman in psychotherapeutic treatment with me for 5 months. She had recently earned a master's degree in clinical psychology, found a clinical therapy job at an outpatient clinic shortly thereafter, and was very well regarded by its director. As usual, I found myself instinctively registering her impact and quickly felt the energy of her strong ego functions of self-care.

She was eager to learn more about herself and was quite attentive to her emotional well-being. She entered therapy because she had an increasing concern about the "fit" between herself and her husband. "He is a very successful sound engineer for private clients in Hollywood. He is kind, good, and caring, but he is not able to engage with me at a level of depth that feels safe and satisfying. I'm scared and worried. I feel distant from him, and he has reacted to my distance with more distance, and even coldness." Karen continued, "He feels nervous and anxious around me and is unable to put his anxiety into words. I don't want to be his therapist or mother. I am tired and turned off, and I'm drinking every night of the week. That's new and very different for me, and I am here to discuss all this and stop this recent pattern of nightly drinking."

Karen had a mild SUD that fell into the clinical sketch of problematic use at a problematic time. It is not often over the years that I have treated a mild SUD that also falls into this category. These individuals, as you may recall from the case study in Chapter 6 (see pp. 61–62), are not discounters of their issues, recognize their self-medication habits, and also have a strong desire to grow in a therapeutic environment.

We talked weekly for 6 months. Karen utilized every moment of the session for her growth, but what most influenced Karen's growth was the incredible amount of thinking with feeling and dreaming she undertook between sessions. She was in therapy to learn how to live with and love her husband, figure out how to work with their differences, as well as to change a drinking pattern that created too much regret. "I know the drinking every night is not helping me. I know that my worry and discomfort is quieted when I drink my wine. I also know I don't want to self-medicate." Her energized ability to self-care, anticipate danger, and renounce pleasures whose consequences were harmful was apparent (see Chapter 8, pp. 118–120).

Karen was internally motivated, and within 4 months, using a harm-reduction approach of adhering to nightly agreements, reduced her evening drinking to her regular pleasure of occasional weekend wine at dinner with her husband (Miller & Rollnick, 2002).

Karen is an example of the kind of individual we may see more often in treatment since the release of DSM-5 in 2013. People may be encouraged to seek out more short-term support for mild problems with AOD, without the fear that abstinence will be imposed on them during the first session. I hope this is the case as we continue to accept and embrace our ancient drive for escape through the use of AOD, and in the process search for help to learn to "tipple wisely."

Euripides, in *The Bacchae*, brilliantly discussed the potency of wine. He suggested that wine should never be something to be thrown out or dismissed unthinkingly because of its dangers, but rather something to be used for the better, like any other power. Using anything for the better requires expertise, both a general grasp of social ethics and a more technical expertise relating to the thing being used (Allhoff, 2007, p. 28).

Peter: Problematic Use at a Problematic Time to Social Use

Peter was a 50-year-old clinical social worker who entered treatment for his depression, pressure, and anxiety that had overwhelmed him during the last 6 months. "I've never skipped a beat as a husband, father, or social worker, but the sense of dread and quicksand surrounding me is becoming unbearable. My wife and two children are seeing it creep in more and more around me." At first

Peter felt that they were too sensitive about some understandable mood shifts due to his administrative responsibilities supervising the digitizing of clinical case records in his outpatient facility, as well as the pressure he felt with some physical and psychological problems with his two boys. Eventually, Peter told me, "Now I agree something is going on with me."

Peter was mild-mannered, sensitive, and hard-working. I registered an impact of an overly self-sacrificing individual, one who was not overly assertive and all too easily carried the burdens of others. I wondered how he expressed his moods to himself, his wife and family, his friends, and his colleagues at work. He seemed resigned to carrying the weight of the world on his shoulders. I asked him if that was what he felt too. He responded, "That's exactly how I feel. The digitizing of our records has been hell. We are on our third go-around, and I see no relief in sight. My wife, while strong-willed, is not self-assured, and I worry about her free-floating anxiety and self-medicating habits with marijuana and sleeping pills at night. But mostly now, I'm worried about me."

Peter continued, "Both of my parents drank too much and for too long, and so I'm a very controlled drinker. I do not drink during the week and allow myself one beer or glass of wine on Friday, Saturday, or Sunday nights. But the problem is I've increased that to two or three drinks in the last 6 months, and I know I'm self-medicating for something. I can't have it go on."

His energized sense of value, worth, and care, his ability to anticipate danger and assert his need for help demonstrated the strength of his ego functions. These ego functions greatly help an individual figure out better ways to self-care rather than self-medicate (see Chapter 8, pp. 118–120). Lance Dodes asserts that all addiction is a substitute action because another, more direct response to one's helplessness does not seem possible or permissible (see Chapter 8, pp. 114–116). Peter could not see a possible solution to his distress, so he turned to alcohol for comfort instead.

Intuitively, I decided to sit back in my chair for the 4 months of our work together and allow Peter's impact to take root and grow on and in me (see Chapter 9, p. 138). I wanted to give him time to unfold his inner being in his own manner.

Some elaboration questions by me opened up his perspective, and rather quickly he felt less trapped. During my listening, supporting, and depathologizing his mild and short-lived problematic use at a problematic time, he began reporting that he had recently returned to one glass of beer or wine on his weekend nights.

Mike Eigen, when asked about how transformation in therapy works, said, "I have no idea, except when creating an atmosphere where people [with SUDs] can just hear themselves sometimes does strange and marvelous things" (Eigen, 1999, p. 221).

CHAPTER SUMMARY AND REFLECTIONS

Summary

This chapter explored two case studies of mild substance use disorders, utilizing the four guiding principles of the symposium approach, as well as the seven philosophical and clinical ideas identified in Chapter 1.

Reflections

Consider the following questions in a classroom discussion or paper:

- Do you agree with the DSM-5 spectrum category given to the two case studies in this chapter? Why or why not?
- Do you agree that Karen and Peter are examples of the kind of individual we may see in treatment more often since the release of DSM-5 in 2013, because these individuals may no longer fear that abstinence will be imposed on their mild substance use disorder during the first session?
- How do you imagine Karen and Peter will fare with their drinking habits in the future?

CHAPTER 12

MODERATE SUBSTANCE USE DISORDER

INTRODUCTION

This chapter includes two case studies of individuals who have moderate substance use disorders. Both women look forward to drinking wine at the end of the day and acknowledge drinking too much and too often. Each one struggled and arrived at a different solution to her concerns.

CLINICAL CASES

Samantha: Shadow Use to Watchful Use

This is a case study of a heavy shadow user who acknowledged that she had problems with alcohol but wanted to include the pleasures of drinking in her life. Samantha struggled to discover her own relationship with alcohol, rather than accept the label imposed on her by our culture.

A 49-year-old blonde Californian, fit, competitive cyclist, watercolor painter, wife, and mother of two adult children sat down across from me in my office. She had lived with her husband and raised her children in a beach city in California. She told me, "In the last year, I've been more and more unhappy in my 26-year marriage. I rented a small apartment in Venice and have lived, painted, and cycled during my weeks alone. My husband has joined me on weekends—I like my time alone much better than my weekends with him. I have begun thinking for the first time in my life that it's time to talk to a therapist."

I registered her impact, took in the sensations sounding from her body—a steely wall protecting her confusion and fear, but a determined fighter as well. She poured her words of distress and concern into my body:

I am not really sure what is going on. I just know I need to get away from my husband. Alan is a wonderful man, but I now feel that I have been controlled by him more than I ever allowed myself to acknowledge and admit. He's so quiet, so methodical, so organized, and so planned. I feel stifled, very down, very confused and lost around him. I just need to be here in town. I've discovered cycling, the cycling community, and I have a great young male mentor who is coaching me. At 49, I am a competitive senior citizen. It feels so good. I feel so alive!

Samantha's body felt bursting with joy and also burdened by despair. After several sessions of sharing her new and vibrant lifestyle, and with a pained reluctance, she began breaking into tears more often. My image during this time of our work is of her sobbing in the corner of the couch. Her stiffness suggested that she had rarely allowed herself to connect with these moments of disorganization. She fearfully asked, "What is wrong with me? I have every-thing—why do I feel so sad, so very sad?" I could feel her try to avoid her feelings; she seemed so averse to inhabiting a sense of helpless confusion. I yearned to contain her terrified body, tense with her worries and fears.

With trepidation, Samantha began to talk more about feelings that "have been buried for decades." Samantha continued, "My job was to be a perfect wife, homemaker, artist, volunteer for the needy, and most importantly, a dedicated mother to my two children. I did all that well, too well. I've exhausted myself in the process."

Too Much Drinking

I then felt an intuitive need to ask her about her drinking or likely self-medicating patterns. "How have you been coping with so much expectation and demand?" She replied, "I just did, and it's my job. Alan brings in the money, and I take care of the rest." She hesitated as if she were uncomfortable with her thoughts but then revealed, "My husband and I drink a bottle and a half of wine every night, and we drink socially as well." I asked her if this was a pattern of drinking that was okay with her. She replied, "We're functioning people, so it feels okay." It seemed that she was not curious about the deeper meanings of these daily habits.

Over the next year and a half, Samantha came twice a week to therapy. She was hesitant to engage in an eyes-wide-open look at her marriage. She told me that she felt that getting married was the ticket out of an alcoholic and physically abusive childhood home. She described her father as a "bully, tyrant, an evil man who cruelly took advantage of my mother, myself, and my siblings." Her father was a corporate bureaucrat, apparently under a lot of stress, and seemed to repeatedly discharge a lot of his tension through attacking, criticizing, and undermining everyone in her family. "My mother did nothing to protect us, she was so afraid. My family life was hell—I hated it. I took up swimming, was a good student, hard worker, and always felt scared when I was at home. My family life still haunts me today. I just wanted to get out of my house as soon as I could." Her good-girl nature got her by, and then buried her alive (Phillips, 2013).

As her children grew older, Samantha became more and more discouraged with Alan. He began criticizing her, calling her a selfish troublemaker, and gossiping about her "desire to throw me and my family away for a more exciting life in Venice Beach." She felt devastated by his attacks and helpless in the face of his smear campaign. She lived with a sense of both desire and failure. Samantha also lived with a social and personal sense of disgrace as she acknowledged that her marriage was moving in the direction of divorce. She increasingly felt ostracized and isolated.

Following her legal separation, she began a romantic relationship with a cyclist friend, Steve, with whom she had been flirting for months. They began living a "joyfully" active and simpatico lifestyle together; he supported her divorce weariness and struggles, as he had been through one recently himself. She acquired a new home and invited him to live with her. The divorce "dragged" to a rapid close by today's standards.

Reflections on Alcohol

In our work together, Samantha gradually grew more comfortable talking about her drinking patterns during her 26 years of marriage, her family's AOD history, and her drinking habits with her friends "who were all heavy drinkers." We explored the destructive behaviors in her family of origin. We talked often about her sister, who was "lost to alcohol," and her sister's son, who was in the care of Samantha's mother. Samantha sensed that her soon-to-be daughter-in-law was most likely "an alcoholic," and Samantha admitted that she herself had ended up in an inebriated state of excess on too many evenings.

Samantha's fear of being an "alcoholic" overshadowed her curiosity about her patterns. As a high-functioning mother, athlete, active citizen, and caring person, she did not want to believe her two to three glasses of wine every night, oftentimes to blackout, were of an "alcoholic nature." Samantha was a "successful and well-accomplished" shadow user.

Motivated to Change

Samantha painfully recalled the self-medicative aspects of her drinking habits during her previous marriage—two to three glasses every night, day-drinking at noon on vacations, and always during social events and celebrations—"all to keep the reality of my life hidden." She naturally compared these drinking habits to the choices of her new partner. Steve told Samantha that he had a lot of alcoholism in his family, no one worked it through, it was an unhealthy habit, and "I knew it would not land in a good place for me." Since his mid-50s, he has been dedicated to a vegan diet, regular exercise, meditation, and a life of kindness. She noticed he attended a weekly early-morning men's meeting.

Over time, with both trepidation and tenderness on his part, Steve asked her at dinner one night, "Is it okay if I talk to you about something?" He went on to say that while it is his choice in life not to drink and that he is okay with her drinking, he continued,

> But I have noticed whether it is just with us or with friends, after two glasses of wine you seem very disconnected from who you are, and I have a hard time feeling a sense of togetherness with you when I see the alcohol saturating your feelings and saturating your mind. Everything about you during these times is more amped up, and at a certain point you stop making any sense. I feel at these times that you are not as interested in being with me as you are with being buzzed. I'm trying to be okay with your drinking, Samantha, and with my not drinking, and us being a couple. I'm worried about your drinking, but I don't want to take away one of your pleasures in life.

Samantha was listening and her spirits were sinking as well. Her first sensation was that she was a bad girl doing something wrong and probably needed to "buck up" and face the need for lifelong abstinence as Steve had decided. She utilized many of her learned therapy skills, and at that moment just registered his impact and let his concerns and ideas wash over her. He asked her how she was. She responded, "I'm taking it in." And then she told me later in a session that she rather quickly shifted from being apologetic, people-pleasing, and focusing on solutions to "I'm pissed; that's *your* decision to stop drinking, and I'm going to make up *my* own mind. I love you, but this is a tough one. I cowed to my former husband's wishes, without even considering or thinking about my own desires. I did anything to prevent him from being mad. I just disconnected from my body, did anything to avoid a fight."

Steve and Samantha raised voices that night and decided to give "the conversation a rest." She feared he was going to dominate her and take away one of her pleasures in living; he feared her drinking pattern would spiral out of control. He felt she was being defensive and protective and would not be able to hear his genuine concerns; she felt he was imposing his history on her lifestyle.

Drinking Struggle in a Relationship

Samantha wanted to drink. She currently had lots of "pockets of meaning" in her life that she was invested in, nurtured, and wanted to protect. Samantha's first marriage turned out to be an empty pocket; there was nothing there that she genuinely cherished. She was scared, felt trapped in obligation, and only wanted to survive in the mechanical space that she lived in and called home. She would drink, withdraw, sit, and simmer.

Samantha, after 2 years of intense work with me and one of my women's groups, felt like she had "me back, the little girl I haven't seen since my childhood swimming days. I have made it through a draining divorce, a rupture and then a reunion with my children, the beginnings of a vibrant relationship with a loving man that is interested in me, wants to tend to my needs, and offer his love." Samantha was invested in offering him the same. Samantha had matured into an emotionally self-contained individual. She felt good and terminated our work "with an open door."

Samantha's Return

It was a pleasure to hear about Samantha's progress about a year later. She confidently, yet humbly, reported a deepening relationship with Steve and a continued union with her children. During her call, she questioned her evening wine and her desire for relaxation. She worried about the quality of her connection with Steve over dinner. "What is my need all about?"

Samantha had recently read Chapter 4 in my 2012 text. It featured 12 clinical sketches (now 15) for patient consideration (see Chapter 6). "I'd like to come in and talk to you about this chapter and my drinking habits and patterns, my relationship with alcohol. I am pretty sure that I am a problem shadow user. Maybe I should come in with Steve?" After some discussion, we decided it would be best to start this work alone.

Our work during that month was designed to be goal-driven and short-term. There was a specific problem to be directly addressed and sorted out. She wanted to explore her sometimes healthy, sometimes destructive relationship with AOD.

Samantha's greatest sense of relief came from her understanding and appreciation of the fourth drive and of the clinical sketches. She felt a well of possibility and hope. She struggled and eventually, with my support, confidently disentangled herself from a prevailing notion in the SUDs field "that if a person has some impulse control issues with alcohol, then they are surely on the path to alcoholism." She felt "set free" as she explored her relationship with alcohol; she no longer felt that she had to defend her drinking habits. Rather, she felt free to explore her sometimes healthy and sometimes destructive shadow use relationship with alcohol.

Samantha designed a drinking agreement with herself, and shared it with Steve. She decided she would drink one glass of wine at dinner, and maybe two on social occasions. She called me 8 months later and reported with enthusiasm, "I am keeping my agreements!" While writing the second edition of this book, I decided to call Samantha for an update.

Surprising Resolution

It had been about 2 years since Samantha and I worked together in my office. When I called her on the phone, she said she would be happy to talk with me. We scheduled a phone session. She told me that she was living a life that felt blessed and was "as good it gets." She was still with Steve and soon to be married. I asked her again if she would be willing to talk about her relationship with the fourth drive and share with me how she's been relating to alcohol and her drinking patterns.

"My recall is that you still wanted to continue to drink, but that you were going to take to heart Steve's loving desire to relate to you without a big buzz and that you had created some drinking agreements with yourself. Is that right?"

Samantha began,

You know, Margy, I really think that I've changed over the last year. I've thought lots about my real relationship with alcohol, why I seek out more after I have a good buzz and am really successfully working my drinking habits out, and Steve and I are in pretty good shape about this. Yes, I do want to drink and I want to respect Steve's sobriety. Although now, as we talk, I realize that Steve and I haven't openly discussed my drinking since the day we agreed to my moderation agreements. So I think it would be a good idea for me to check in with him. We'll maybe have that conversation in the next day or two.

The most powerful thing for me is that I've lost interest in being out of control with alcohol! I just don't want to drink to a point where I forget what I'm saying and I'm not really relating to Steve or others. It seems I've found a way to have drinking be a part of my relational experiences, not just a solitary experience. I know you remember those depressing afternoons where I would start drinking at 4 o'clock just for the sake of drinking. I'm not inclined to want to do that, nor have I done that since I was in your office. My relationship with Steve feels so supportive. We talk and hear each other. He is a comfort to me and me to him. Our communication is joyous at times; I don't want to get away from this connection, I want to enjoy him with a clear head.

I asked her about her specific drinking habits in the last two years. She responded,

I like wine, I look forward to wine, and I want good wine. I came to a point rather quickly after meeting in your office then that one and a half glasses of wine is the perfect amount for me. Beyond that, it doesn't feel as if I am present in my skin. As a matter of fact, what's different since we've worked together is that I *want* to be present. Before, I just wanted to get high, get intoxicated, and go into oblivion. Now, I really don't want to miss anything that is going on during our dinners, evening walks, or at parties.

I continued to gently probe about her harm reduction efforts, "Do you drink 7 nights out of the week?" She seemed startled. "Well, I probably drink 5 nights out of the week . . . maybe sometimes 3 . . . maybe even 7. But it shifts all the time. But the difference is that I'm not drinking to check out. I'm drinking because I like the taste of wine; I look forward to it as a pleasure, and for relaxation." I asked, "For relaxation?" "Well, that's a fine point," Samantha said. "Between drinking for relaxation, being relaxed, and then being too relaxed." She continued, "I guess you could say that I still have a conflict there."

I wondered aloud, "If my memory serves me well, your friends are heavy drinkers. How is that going?" She responded, "Actually, most of our friends now don't drink. For example, on the Fourth of July, we went to a party with eight couples, and there was just one bottle of wine. I had a small glass, and I was also very conscious of who was drinking and who wasn't. Probably because of my history, I'm still very aware of who drinks and who doesn't. The good news, Margy, is that since we've talked, I've never been that person who drinks too much at a party and regrets waking up the morning after. That's a big change and a big relief for me."

Samantha continued by saying that she also has more respect for her use of time. I reveried about her energized sense of value and worth and her ego functions of self-care as she told me, "I've become a big reader. I'm teaching cooking classes. I love my walks with Steve after dinner every night. Drinking would, in my opinion, ruin any of those experiences. I also would never consider drinking at lunch or early afternoon—why would I want to ruin the rest of my day?"

She wondered, "Maybe it's just a habit, and as I'm reducing my coffee habit now, maybe I'll think about reducing this habit too. But I don't feel pressured to, because at this point in my life, I want to enjoy drinking." I questioned her evolution from a daily moderate shadow user to the clinical sketch of a watchful user and asked, "How do you think this has happened?"

She said,

> You know, when I was drinking every night with my husband in an unhappy 26-year marriage, I didn't think there were any other options. I couldn't identify the nature of my pain, but the drinking quieted all that. My husband and I greeted each other over a bottle of wine at dinner every night. Today, though, I feel more balanced. Every day I work with the Ed Khantzian handout you gave me on self-care functions. "I protect myself from danger and say no to pleasures that bring negative consequences" [see Chapter 8, pp. 118–120]. I don't cycle, diet, exercise with obsession; I don't do anything with obsession anymore. So, for example, Steve and I probably need to lose 10 pounds; if it happens, it happens. Most importantly, we're healthy, we enjoy, we exercise, we feel good about our lives, and we are both now in our early 60s. To follow up on your question, what else has allowed these unhealthy drinking habits to fade away, is that I have a strong meditation practice, and again, I live a well-balanced life.

Samantha asked me a question: "Did you see the *60 Minutes* special on the survey of 1,900 Leisure Village 90-year-olds, referred to as 'the oldest old'?" I said I did not, and she told me about it. She went on to say that the *60 Minutes* correspondent asked these nonagenarians, "How is it that you live so long?" The majority responded that they do not take supplements, do not worry about their health, drink coffee, are active, know that it is not healthy to be thin, enjoy sex and affection, are social, and drink one to two glasses of alcohol every night. This reminded me of Ron Siegel's comment that the desire for intoxication is "not only a drive, it is natural, and even a right" (Siegel, 2005, p. 208).

Lindsay: Shadow Use to Discontinued Use

This case study is of a 44-year-old wife and mother of two children who is "pissed off" that her moderation efforts during 3 years of therapy have failed.

"I cannot drink, and I know it. I'm really angry I cannot fool myself and you guys in this group anymore." The reader should notice that I introduce and use many psychoanalytic concepts for a deeper understanding of Lindsay's suffering and her choice to self-medicate with alcohol.

I was recommended to Lindsay by a former student who said to her, "You seem tense and overwhelmed." Lindsay's initial impact felt child-like—confused, but determined to figure things out, determined to know. She told me, "I am frightened and frustrated by one of my children, my husband, and worry about the overwhelming demands of my daily life." I felt her sense of catastrophe in living; she was overwhelmed by her own psychic indigestion. Bion and Eigen capture this best: "There is a catastrophe in progress, life is a catastrophe, and I am a catastrophe. Help me! Help me!" (Eigen, 2011b, p. 47). Lindsay self-medicated with alcohol. Lance Dodes suggests that "all addiction is a substitute action because another more direct response to one's helplessness [feeling trapped] does not feel possible or permissible" (see Chapter 8, pp. 114–116).

Lindsay drinks too much wine every night, sometimes she says too much, and often remembers too little. She wakes up alcohol-foggy, but is determined to attend to her maternal and familial tasks. Lindsay looks forward to and counts on her glasses of wine every night. She starts salivating at 5 p.m. and promises herself a "better drinking night." Lindsay drinks two to three glasses to recover from the persecution of the "daily shoulds" similar to the ones she experienced in her childhood. "My father felt perfect, meticulous. I just wanted his approval. I still do. My mother made the most beautiful homes, nothing looked out of place. I just wanted her approval. I still do." Eigen (1996) captures Lindsay's childhood in this description: "There was a history of neglect, a mixture of over- and under-stimulation, the usual story of emotional poverty in a luxurious setting" (p. 3).

Over time, I proposed some traditional supports: group meetings, talking to a friend, talking to her husband. "Why should I have to go to meetings for my alcohol? I have my shit together." She bashfully shares her drinking worries with her husband as she prepares dinner. He says, "You don't have a problem," as he opens a bottle of wine for the two of them. Her friends drink every night too. A few friends also acknowledge to themselves, "My drinking is problematic." Most need alcohol to "work through" mismatched marriages, social pressures, envy, jealousy, and the stresses to keep it all together. Alcohol helps Lindsay and her friends feel a sense of imaginary intactness (Eigen, 1999, p. 222). My sense with Lindsay is that she keeps on the move, lags behind registering her impacts, lets experiences pile up on one another, is overwhelmed and in over her psychic head with most things, and lives in a state of psychic indigestion (MEigen Workshop, 2013).

Traditionally, addiction thinkers believe that if Lindsay's drinking is not arrested now, she will progress into the disease of addiction. Directives about AA meetings, sponsors, steps, and motivational protocols are the standard of care in addiction treatment. These are so helpful for many, yet increasingly more protest the "one size fits all" approach.

I have learned from Eigen that "if the [addict] needs you to say something, then you say it. You can say it as a supportive thing, a challenging thing, a stimulating thing, and an interpretation, whatever is needed." Eigen has wisely offered (to addiction clinicians), "You do what you need to play for time, so that links can be formed over time in therapy" (Eigen, 2011b, p. 8).

When I register and reverie Lindsay's youth, I dream of a child who lived in a stupor or dull state. No one helped her or taught her how to process and emotionally digest what was happening around her. Lindsay didn't get the chance to explore or elaborate on the impact of her parents, her sibling, her friends, or her everyday experiences. No one waited with Lindsay in faith until she felt comfortable in the face of what seemed overwhelming to her psyche. Eigen captures the addict's early plight: "One gives up noticing emotional realities if one is unable to achieve anything fruitful by noticing them. Yet these realities exert pressure" (1999, p. 147).

After years of living in a thumb-sucking and eating-disordered trance, Lindsay found alcohol in her 20s. Alcohol provided relief for her lack of capacity to live in an experience, register experience, let experience build, and learn from it. She missed out on "getting a little better at working over impacts and letting impacts work on [her] so that [she] could get something more out of living" (Eigen, 2004, p. 142).

Lindsay lived with a manic sense of self-sufficiency that convinced her that the impacts of self and others could be avoided. She found a way to escape impact, push it aside, and compulsively discharge the tension of this emptiness with AOD. Adam Phillips captures a key struggle for SUDs patients very accurately: "Hell is not other people but one's need for other people" (1994, p. 45). The therapist's challenge is to nurture an interest in accepting this need for others—a need that brought devastation and psychic retreating beginning in infancy and early childhood (Steiner, 1993).

It took about 13 months for Lindsay to feel safe enough in our relationship to not want to self-disappear. "When we make ourselves disappear, try to make pain disappear, we enter a state of madness" (Eigen, 2011b, p. 72). Over time, we created a capacity to be alone together with her madness.

"Addiction is a substitute for those who cannot wait for time's unfolding" (Bion, 1992, p. 299). Over time, Lindsay created some capacity for stillness. She soon began more deeply exploring and reflecting on her relationship with her neurotic processes, her relationship with alcohol, and what happened in her family that drove her to repeatedly search for relief with alcohol.

Containing Catastrophe, Alpha, and Partial Lies

Parents, and later the therapist, ideally act as containers able to think through the undigested catastrophic experiences of the infant-child that Bion names "beta elements." Bits of nameless, formless, catastrophic "beta buzz" (Fetting in MEigen Workshop, 2013) are reworked by maternal alpha functions and turned into moods, images, narrative in dreams and myths, and reveries (Eigen, 1996, p. 142). Turning this nameless dread into thinking or dreaming is a developmental triumph. "One of the best kept secrets about thinking is how ecstatic it is" (Eigen, 1998, p. 24).

Eigen intrigues us, "Sometimes alpha lying or lying-truthing [half lying and half truth-telling] works to suppress or rein in beta impacts and helps make more space for processing. One might even regard beta elements and their buzz as a purer truth that can only be partially processed with the help of partial lies" (MEigen Workshop, 2013). Many people can live and even thrive with these partial truths and partial lies.

Contrary to popular belief, problem users and individuals with addiction are not good liars. Khantzian has been impressed by the extreme sensitivities of SUDs patients (Khantzian & Albanese, 2008). Without their capacity to buffer life with alpha lying, living feels unbearable, and AOD creates a pseudoconfidence that life is indeed doable. Lindsay relied on this confidence for decades.

False Self Horn

Eigen, in his book *The Psychoanalytic Mystic* (1998), elaborates on our understanding of a false self. He describes an inauthentic expression of self that has two horns. One horn has toughness to its edge; another horn is driven by a compulsion to please. It seems that an individual's false self expression can rely on one horn or a blend of both (p. 55). Lindsay relied on both.

Lindsay's disposition developed compliance as a way to respond to the pressures she felt to falsify her inner essence. Pleasing people and getting along with others ensured her everyday survival. When compliant, Lindsay discovers that being "easy" for others brought peace to her world. This false self silently screams, "I please, and I placate!" (pp. 56–57). Lindsay's compliant self found safety and security in not being a burden to her mother. She learned to be loyal to her mother's wishes at the expense of her own. Her school peers, friends, teachers, and neighbors took advantage of this willingness to cater to others.

She married to serve her partner. She parents to satisfy her children's every wish. Her sense of sacrificial nobility muffles the intensity of her inner despair. Eventually, her compliant expression fatigues and fades out. Lindsay searches for alcohol or resorts to using her other horn.

Lindsay's disposition also developed a toughness to handle the horror of so much parental misunderstanding. This toughness ensured everyday survival and brought her feelings of temporary triumph. Her false self screamed, "I can, and I will!" (p. 55). This sense of bravado persuaded her true self to retreat in silence. It was seduced into protective submission. This shelter permitted a manner of functioning. Eigen reminds us that toughness can be counted on to maintain a sense of aliveness (p. 56). Careers are chosen, marriages are entered, and children are born from this deceptively determined, yet wayward, self. These solutions bring moments of aliveness that can go on for years and decades. Sadly, they are based on self-fraudulence and conformity to social expectations.

Lindsay's true self despaired in exile, and eventually her horn of toughness also grew weary of its job. She began to live with an empty heart and with frustration at the very core. What was accomplished in work and love could no longer be sustained. In these situations, the fatigue cannot be avoided and, more often than not, one's entire being fades out and goes under (p. 57).

During these times when Lindsay's false self horns grew weary and could no longer support her, her self-medication with alcohol provided much comfort. She ruthlessly and repeatedly selected alcohol as a reliable source of soothing and reprieve. It reversed ongoing feelings of false self fraudulence and quieted her longings for true self expression in her life. AOD seemed the perfect complement for her painful, prescribed way of living. The possibility of an alternative future was beyond her grasp: "I can live in this world if I am fortified with alcohol." A fated childhood, adolescence, and adulthood are now fated by addictive consumption (Bollas in Fetting, 2012, p. 249).

Lindsay lives the words of one of Eigen's patients:

> My contact with what people call reality is monitored. I'm not really in the experience. I've committed to a life of caring behavior. I believe people are connected by love, the most precious thing we know about in the universe, but I don't partake of it. I'm excruciatingly sensitive, but I don't feel for another person. I look like I'm feeling and feel that I'm feeling; in the feeling I'm not feeling. It is the most painful of all to not care in the caring, to not feel in the feeling. (Eigen, 2004, p. 106)

Deficits in psychological equipment can be experienced as emptiness (Eigen, 1996, p. 145). Lindsay drinks to avoid feeling this emptiness, and to avoid telling somebody about it.

Impacts in the Room

Lindsay and I have a session. She sighs and says, "I'm so frustrated with collecting a few sober days and then losing them. This whole business about my drinking just feels like a 'should.' I know that my drinking is problematic, I know it is interfering with my sense of peace, my parenting, and my marriage; and I know I should stop."

I dream her frustrations and then respectfully ask her if she wants to keep on drinking. Does she need it now just to get through life? She does not respond yes, but instead says, "I know I should stop. I just want to let the effort go and see where it ends up." I open to her impact of fatigue, weariness, and hesitancy. As a result of this, I decide not to impose my "memory" of her unsuccessful attempts at "letting it go." Lindsay feels me registering her impact, rather than offering a "helpful" suggestion. Lindsay begins to slow down. I sense her softening and wondering.

Eigen urges us to give the addict's impact time to build and unfold (1996, p. 210). We offer the psychoanalytic attitude when we dream and wait, and in the process become a feeling person more deeply attuned to the patient's incapacity and overreliance on AOD. This feeling therapist is now felt by the patient, and a connection begins or deepens (Coltart, 2000, pp. 154–157).

The session turns away from solutions and resolutions. Lindsay easily opens up about all her pressures, her tendency to placate her husband, always please her parents, and tolerate her trying daughter. I just listen and follow and don't mention drinking. I just hear and hold, hear and hold, register her impact. No memory or desire. I become a feeling therapist at that moment. Lindsay moves to me and I to her. We feel connected. She now has hope, and I renew my faith.

When I listen from this open and receptive attitude, the therapy relationship feels like a space for Lindsay to "let down" in (Eigen, 1999, p. 49). I am then able to feel Lindsay who lives in a chaotic and chronic state of paralyzing absence within a psyche that cannot process its own psychic indigestion.

Without this internal equipment, Lindsay is naturally oriented toward external objects (AOD) for soothing and survival (1999, p. 138). Eigen provides wisdom: "The grim paradox is that insofar as [the SUDs patient] lacks the capacity to tolerate the sense of catastrophe that saturates [his] psychic reality, [the SUDs patient] may heighten external catastrophe [addiction] as a way of objectifying himself. He may finally 'know' himself through this dramatization [addiction]" (1999, p. 138). A clinician that can reverie the patient's objectification processes will soon feel the patient's sense of lack, confusion, fear, and desperation.

Eigen encourages therapists to respect the patients' absolute otherness. They are on their own search. He suggests that we register and follow the patients' instructions of living rather than our own. He dares us to give them space to do their best—or their worst (Eigen, 2008, personal communications).

Every week, Lindsay returns to therapy not understanding how this seemingly "unsolvable problem is happening to me." Lindsay is frustrated at the core, but she continues to adhere to her struggle. Eigen reminds us, "no faith . . . no path" (MEigen Workshop, 2013). I continue to wait in faith as Lindsay searches for her path.

A Year Later

Lindsay and I explored and waited. She scared herself when she browned out at a family party and drove home drunk. "I remember very little and could have done some real damage." Shortly after she decided with two of her friends, "Let's just stop for a year. We all know we're not able to manage our nightly wine. We always intend to drink just one glass of wine, and most nights we drink between three and four."

Lindsay has remained alcohol-free with two exceptions. There was a night of an impulsive drink at dinner in month 4, and 8 nights of planned-for holiday drinking in month 11. The latter drinking period followed immediately after her mother's brain cancer surgery, an ongoing tedious divorce process, and the beginning of the Thanksgiving and Christmas holiday season.

After 8 nights of binge drinking, she told the group in our first meeting in 2015, "I'm really pissed. I mean, I'm really pissed that it is now so clear to me that I cannot drink. I'm really pissed that I told myself that I would only have one glass of wine, and I can tell you all as we sit here now that I could not stop at one. After all I've learned this year, I could not even pace myself. I'm pissed I cannot handle my wine, I'm pissed I know I have to stop, and maybe for a lifetime." Carol, one of the other group members, also approaching a year sober, started to cry and sobbed, "I know that this is true for me too." Later I reminded the group of the prescient and cautious words of Hippocrates, who suggested, "Should a patient be suffering from an overpowering heaviness of the brain [mind], then there must be total abstinence from wine" (Gately, 2008, p. 13)

Both Lindsay and Carol signed up for another year of no drinking, and the third group member, Penny, 2.5 years sober from opioid pills, committed to "sobriety" in her relationship with sugar and food. All members of the group nodded their heads when I suggested with kindness, "Right now, I think we have a group of heavy-minded individuals in this room."

CHAPTER SUMMARY AND REFLECTIONS

Summary

This chapter explored two case studies of moderate substance use disorder, utilizing the four guiding principles of the symposium approach, as well as the seven philosophical and clinical ideas identified in Chapter 1.

Reflections

Consider the following questions in a classroom discussion or paper:

- Do you agree with the DSM-5 spectrum category given to the two case studies in this chapter? Why or why not?
- What were some of your major learnings from Samantha's case?
- What were some of your major learnings from Lindsay's case?
- Will this be a difficult spectrum category for you to utilize and work with? Why or why not?

CHAPTER 13

SEVERE SUBSTANCE USE DISORDER

INTRODUCTION

This chapter includes three case studies of individuals with severe substance use disorders. We struggled as a therapeutic team, and each individual was satisfied with his progress.

CLINICAL CASES

Jon: Shadow Use to Termination of Therapy

This is a case study about a long-term marijuana user who started using at age 13. When he was 36 we terminated our 4-year therapy relationship, recognizing that Jon did not want to stop his shadow using habit at this time in his life.

A former student of mine called with a feverish tone in her voice and asked if I was accepting referrals. She conveyed a sense of immediacy as she told me about her friend who was being "bullied, pressured, and cornered" by his family and also by a well-known treatment center. She continued, "I feel bad that he is in this battle all alone. I told him about my class experience with you, and he said that he was very interested in meeting with you."

Jon, age 32, was introduced to marijuana at age 13 by friends and became a daily smoker at age 18. He is now married and the father of two young boys. During the previous year, he had been periodically and uncontrollably physically and verbally abusive to his wife while under the influence. Lori, his wife, called the police in terror one night. Shortly afterward, she informed Jon's parents of both his ongoing daily marijuana use and his tendency to lose all impulse control while under the influence. His first-generation Asian parents immediately sought out "the best and most reputable" treatment center in America.

Jon's parents, brother, sister-in-law, sister, and Lori enrolled in a family treatment week at a center in Palm Springs, California. As is common in Asian culture, this family fully embraced the "ultimate authority" of this renowned international treatment center. The message they took away from their week of family education was to set firm and non-negotiable boundaries with Jon and insist that he attend 90-day inpatient treatment at the center. The family, as advised, adopted a strong, authoritarian stance toward Jon. "Addicts deceive and manipulate; strong boundaries are the best and most caring thing you can do as a family." Understandably, Jon felt targeted, isolated, judged, and alienated from his family. As Anne Fletcher quotes in her recent book *Inside Rehab* (2013), after 4 years of researching and visiting hundreds of treatment facilities in the United States, "The system leads families of addicted loved ones to think that they can't do much of anything else aside from orchestrate sit-down interventions and learn about 'the disease' in psychoeducational family weeks, when research studies show that other approaches are far more effective" (p. 379).

Feeling pressure to accommodate, with also a desire to remain connected to his family, Jon volunteered to participate in a treatment facility at a location physically closer to his home. He acknowledged his need for treatment, but wanted to continue to work and provide for his family, repair his marriage, and coparent his children. He attended a cognitive-behavioral therapy (CBT) program and completed 6 weeks of outpatient, individual, and group therapy.

The family did not agree with his choice; it was not the recommendation of the treatment center. They felt on the side of right and compelled to follow the center's advice. They admonished Jon for his choice to seek a different form of care and ended all contact with him. They promised reunification if he decided to attend the 90-day program in Palm Springs. "We stand by what the best in the world recommended, Jon. We love you so much and just want you to be truthful with us and get the help you need. We are doing this for your own good."

Jon began weekly psychotherapeutic treatment with me in 2010, declaring 60 days of sobriety. I immediately registered his frustration, anger, and hurt. I imagined that he might be feeling confused, ashamed, and humiliated about the situation as well. He conveyed a willingness to continue his sobriety with marijuana and an honest desire to repair his relationship with his wife. He was committed to being a professional breadwinner and an active after-work and weekend father to his young boys. As I allowed his impact to wash over me, I felt a well-worn use of evasiveness in him, but I wanted to give our work time to determine if this was part of a personality character evasion or SUDs evasion.

As we began work, I grew to understand more about Jon's preferences. He did not feel the need or want to attend 90 days of inpatient treatment, nor mandatorily attend AA meetings. He affirmed, "I have completed a treatment program, and I am sober, and I need to work to support my family now." He believed his sobriety would add clarity to his exploration of the family violence and childhood suffering that led to his severe SUD. He expressed a desire to understand. He felt deeply rejected and excluded from his family. "I don't get this, I don't get this," he painfully repeated. He courageously muttered a hope that at some time in the future, family therapy may become an option. Jon was tearful and acknowledged to me, "Right now, I'm too scared to be in a room with any of them."

Jon earned an MBA from an Ivy League school. He was cognitively and strategically savvy. He was one of those patients I have seen over the years who knows a lot about how to strategically survive in life despite navigating with a restricted range of emotionally felt vocabulary. He appeared to have a cognitive grasp of the ideas that we talked about, but this grasp felt devoid of his own emotional pulse. His was a confusing, if not cunning, combination of obsequiousness and a desire to be a good boy, with a determined refusal to be known. I gingerly brought attention to these contradictions. He initially rejected my impressions, then sat back on the couch and rather quickly struggled to be still and feel through my interpretation. I saw that Jon was trying to understand and also reflect on the use of his protective defenses.

Jon was raised in a family that communicated with global emotional feeling states such as anger, upset, or ridicule. He lived in an environment of judgment, commandments, injunctions, cynicism, and sarcasm. The sought-after positions were to win, not lose; get over it, not be too sensitive; hide feelings, not share them. If he chose to get over it and hide his feelings, he was considered a good boy and rewarded with membership in the family unit with the sense of belonging it gave him. If he brooded over confusing feelings, he was treated like a bad boy, and felt excluded from a sense of belonging. Jon was sensitive, frightened, feelingful—a lonely and bad boy in the eyes of his family. No wonder he discovered and began dabbling with marijuana at age 13. He only knew, "It made me feel good and relaxed, and I wanted to do it as often as I could get it." More and more, getting high became his default option, the easiest path to follow when his subjective internal pressures wore him down. He wanted a change in his state of mind.

We talked more about his early years. He lived with a sense of domestic and global disorientation, feeling excluded from his immediate family, feeling alienated from his birth country, and feeling marginalized in the United States. He said he was "a goofball, taking nothing seriously, always joking around." He loved confusing people and catching them off-guard. He seemed to love mischief, and the disorientation and bewilderment it put on the faces of others.

He reported a lot of fighting in the family. His parents argued and were physically violent frequently, and he and his brother got into fistfights, and he and his sister verbally quarreled. Liz Karter reminds us that the key to understanding excess with problematic using is all hidden in our relationships (2013, p. 31). If we grow up in relational environments that do not tolerate spontaneous expression of our feelings, we slowly withdraw, retreat, and lose trust "in the necessary and ruthless use of others" to act as containers, allowing us to express, understand, turn over, and turn around our feelings (Bollas in Fetting, 2012).

Without this relational support, Jon was left in an intolerably vulnerable state—needing someone to help him, but with nowhere to turn for help with feelings of humiliation and shame about his need. Jon's early choice of marijuana was not random. He engaged in daily smoking of marijuana as he discovered that it reliably and repeatedly soothed a chaotic, affective storm of undifferentiated feelings of alienation, loneliness, shame, anger, and fear (Khantzian, 1999, pp. 117–119). He had company and connection with his "ruthless use" of pot.

Individual Treatment

In our first year of work together, Jon maintained abstinence from marijuana. He was regularly drug tested and it always came back negative. During this time, we talked about his desire for and use of alcohol on occasion. He maintained it was not in the "same league as marijuana use." He drank several times that first year, seemingly without incident or rekindling the desire to use marijuana. He just wanted some temporary relief in his life. I periodically checked in with him about the frequency of his alcohol use. I sensed he might be using more than he wanted to share.

More often than not, it was difficult to make real contact with Jon. Protection was more important to him than connection. I was continually struck by his first sentence after sitting down in my office: "Things are going great. Things are going really good." We explored what that really meant, and often used a feeling chart to help him deglobalize his feelings. He teared up and looked down in embarrassment any time he allowed himself to connect with his feelings and abandon his well-cultivated strategic and cognitive view of the world.

After a year of sobriety, Jon began to mourn the loss of any contact with his family. We began to explore the possibility of family therapy. After much back and forth between his wishes and feelings of threat, Jon decided he wanted to begin therapy with his family. Jon asked me to initiate a discussion with the Palm Springs staff and see if they would talk to his family and ask them about the possibility of meeting in my office to reconnect and then, if all agreed, move on to family therapy with an addiction family therapist. Jon longed for the chance to reunite: "My kids need to know their grandparents." He always teared up when he said the following: "It's so sad, it's so sad to me. I just don't understand."

During this year of treatment in 2012, I also engaged in phone and e-mail communication with the physician who was the director of treatment at the Palm Springs facility about possible family reunification with therapy. The team understood that Jon was sober with a 1-day marijuana relapse and in weekly treatment with me, that he was periodically urine tested, and that he chose not to attend MA (Marijuana Anonymous) regularly. The doctor and his team wanted to reevaluate Jon to determine if, indeed, his year away from the facility had been successful by their standards. The full battery of testing would involve 2 days and a fee of $2,500. The treatment physician was very skeptical that the facility staff would be willing to endorse Jon's year-and-a-half-long recovery approach or his progress. They did reiterate, however, "We always encourage family reunification." They stipulated that his marijuana addiction recovery, to be ultimately successful, should begin again with a 90-day treatment stay and include AA and MA meetings daily or several times a week.

I appreciated the facility staff's willingness to engage in periodic discussions with me in an effort to reunite the family. I also felt like an annoying gnat on their back, condescended to as a result of a different approach to problems with a substance, and only politely and formally tolerated. They seemed frustrated by my efforts to communicate with them and spoke to me in a tone that suggested a skeptical dismissal of my approach and work with Jon. The facility was on top of the mountain and seemed adamantly certain about its treatment design. As Mike Eigen says, "We seem addicted to feeling right, as if this gives us the right to assert our position of supremacy over others who are less right or even wrong" (personal communications). This captured many of my feelings about the dominance of the disease model of abstinence.

We launched the family reunification therapy process in my office. All family members were present, Jon's parents on the phone from South Korea. The meeting was understandably tense, and in spite of stern differences in treatment choices, as well as underlying intensities impacting everyone in the room, the family agreed to go forward with the family therapist, Dr. Java.

Reportedly, the first meeting with Dr. Java deteriorated into defensive and aggressive arguing rather quickly. The tensions between the apparent group-think of the facility treatment plan and Jon's desire for his family to embrace his year of sobriety and individual treatment with me escalated to unmanageable levels. Three quarters into the session with the family therapist, a violent fistfight erupted between the two brothers.

Dr. Java reported to me that Jon was evasive about one point during the recollection of a shared historical event among them, and the family felt this was another piece of evidence of Jon's pattern of lying. One too many sarcastic statements followed another, and the brothers jabbed fists into each other's bodies, threw vases, and pushed each other around. Surprisingly, they stopped by themselves. The meeting was terminated shortly afterward.

I volunteered to attend the next meeting with Jon, to be both supportive of this lone individual and provide a sense of containment for him. A letter from the psychologist sent to me prior to the session strongly suggested that Jon had purposefully misled the group about an important detail, and that the group would not be able to continue without the "truth." The minds and hearts of the five family members seemed closed, and they insisted on conveying to me that it was almost impossible to trust Jon. Jon felt helpless, and then shut down.

Jon wrote back to the group trying to explain his point of view and appealed to possibly meeting with smaller groups within the family, suggesting his desire to continue somehow. There was no response. Jon was devastated, dejected. We spent months processing and grieving the short-lived family therapy experience. Despite this disheartening setback, Jon said he was determined to remain sober.

Travel and Therapy

Shortly after this, I began living half the year abroad. The majority of my patients eventually decided to discontinue therapy with me. I helped them find referrals. Some other patients like Jon, after much discussion, decided to continue our work over the phone. Jon had already started missing sessions or cancelling sessions at the last moment when we decided to commence our work on the phone.

As I look back, I believe that I too easily accepted sporadic phone sessions without more in-depth exploration of what was occurring in our relationship. I believe now that we were in a therapeutic stalemate with each other resulting from the unmetabolized and overwhelming frustration, humiliation, and despair we continually experienced at the hands of the Palm Springs facility and his family. The family's rigid adherence to the facility's policy left us feeling dismissed and demoralized. The abusive nature of this part of the addiction treatment world was a frightening and discouraging experience. I feel certain that these emotions coupled with sporadic phone sessions rendered me unable to properly contain Jon or contain our relationship.

Jon then cancelled two sessions, and sadly, we began to let go of our therapeutic expectations of each other. We drifted apart and blamed it on time zone scheduling difficulties. Despite our ambivalence, we did not quit each other. Jon called me again in November 2013, and with a faint voice said, "I am back into it again."

He told me that the previous spring he was attending a conference away from home, alone, and felt "bored." He found a dealer, began smoking occasionally, and soon every night beginning between 4 and 5 p.m., as well as on the days and evenings of the weekend. Jon said, "It was summer, my schedule was looser, I thought it was okay, and I'll address this after the summer. Well, the summer ended 2 months ago, and I haven't been able to stop." His tone baffled me—despite the meaningful words. He spoke in the breezy tone of a man who was not inhabiting his body or acknowledging the importance of what he was saying. His unconscious and conscious use of sarcasm, hesitancy, obsequiousness, and mockery conveyed to me a feeling that he didn't think he would be listened to.

Around this time, I returned to California. We began meeting weekly in my office in Santa Monica. He was disturbed by his return to using and how it had overtaken his life again. He was drinking more during social and work occasions, he felt it was too much, yet he felt trapped and terrified of not being able to stop.

We spent several months together, making inconsistent and uneven progress with the part of him that believed he should stop. "I'm better off when I don't smoke." He continued to see his regular prostitute more often, and then planned a Las Vegas weekend trip with two young women. I called Jon and left a message: "I've been thinking about you, and I'm worried about your reckless behavior." He later called me and said he cancelled the trip, and he thanked me for reaching out to him.

The ambivalence toward our connection was apparent. Jon either showed up to our session, or he didn't. He began a curious pattern of texting me the night before our appointments to see if we were still on. He was deeply conflicted about what he wanted to do with marijuana, his marriage, his relationship with his prostitute, and his relationship with me. Facing it all felt too overwhelming. "My immediate family is the only family I have. I have to stay. I have nowhere else to go."

He was jarred and jolted one morning. His wife aggressively confronted him about separating. She sighed, "I'm tired of your smoking, I'm tired of your anger, I'm tired of your withdrawal, and I'm tired of feeling trapped, and I want to do more of my own thing." He reported a back-and-forth conversation between them that ended with both agreeing to seek couples therapy. He asked me for a recommendation, and she searched for one as well.

Her confrontation caught his attention; he was frightened. He reminded me, "We are not close—we sleep in separate bedrooms, and bicker and fight more often than not. But I don't want a divorce. I like having a family." He needed a family, his family. He decided to start being nicer and more polite to Lori, and she did in return. They chose not to seek out therapy, but have remained in a less argumentative environment to this day.

Jon sarcastically asked me about his relationship with marijuana: "What do you think, doc? Do you think I'm an addict who's lazy, or just a bum who can't stop? I'm bad, huh?" I repeated again, "You have a long history of problematic use of marijuana, and our work is just trying to help you figure out if it has a place in your life, to see if you can find a space of using that causes you less stress, or if you want to stop." He was confused, baffled by my response. He didn't seem to believe me. He had been so used to being badgered by his family and other "reputable" treatment providers. He didn't believe that all I wanted to do was help him develop some kind of ego conviction and peace of mind about his relationship with marijuana.

At this time, I also began to explore some of his ambivalence with our relationship. Jon continued to miss appointments and continued to text me to confirm the night before a session. I conferred with a therapist colleague about Jon's ambivalence and hesitancy in general. I waited for the right time and interpreted to him his lifelong pattern of being half-heartedly involved with almost everything in his life—his marriage, his parenting, his exercise maintenance program, his recovery, his professional work, his relationship with his prostitute, and now his relationship with our work. His initial response was tangential, and then he returned to it: "Yeah, I'm kind of one-foot-in and one-foot-out of almost everything in my life." I was struck by his honest and courageous admission here.

I wondered out loud to Jon, "You seem to be having difficulty using our relationship for change. I wonder lately if you really want to change at this time in your life. You've told me on several occasions, 'I need to remain in the marriage, daily marijuana use feels like a part of a necessary compromise for me.'" I sensed he interpreted my recommendation as a suggestion to begin to try to figure out what he wanted to do with his marijuana use and our treatment. "Let's explore if you are able to manage your marijuana in a moderate and guilt-free way. If not, let's accept that this is what you want to be doing at this time in your life."

Jon considered this and said, "I want to set a limit, and I want to figure something out. Here's my program: I'm not going to use Monday through Friday, and I'll 'scratch the itch' late Saturday and Sunday nights. I feel good. I like the weekday rule. I have to be sober during the work week. I can't be zonked out anymore."

He said several times in that session, "I am now having relationships with people without smoking. It feels so much richer. A neighbor asked last week if our family wanted to have a spontaneous supper in a couple of hours. I said 'Sure,' but a few weeks ago I would've said, 'I'm too busy,' and gone off to smoke alone. We had a great time as a family."

Jon broke his agreement and picked up smoking again 3 weeks later. He begrudgingly came to a recognition and acceptance that a predominantly love-less and cruel marriage coupled with the loss of his Asian roots and the disown-ment of his family of origin had him in a painful bind.

Dislocation theory suggests that addiction provides many dislocated peo-ple with some much-needed relief and compensation for their bleak existence. Socrates stresses that if people like Jon lack a sense of belonging, they are likely to be overcome by master passions. Dislocation theory considers addiction to be a narrowly focused lifestyle that functions as a meager substitute for people who desperately lack a sense of psychosocial cohesion. Dislocated individuals struggle valiantly to establish or restore psychosocial peace of mind—to carve out a life for themselves (see Chapter 3, p. 12).

Jon freely asserts, "I know I'm self-medicating with daily marijuana use, sometimes in the night, sometimes during the weekend days and nights." He con-tinues, "I also strongly believe that my wife and I are likely mismatched and have developed a contempt for each other over the years." Jon loves his children and cannot bear divorcing and being without "the only family that will have me."

Our therapeutic history had included intensive outpatient treatment, group therapy, and individual therapy over a period of 5 years. He is a severe shadow user (see Chapter 6, pp. 67–69), and after a year of fits and starts of abstinence and attempts to remain sober, he came to a realization that daily marijuana use is a compromise that he can live with for now. We have discussed the "adap-tive," not ideal, nature of his SUD. Khantzian, Siegel, Alexander, and Tatarsky have all adopted a perspective that states that reliance on alcohol and other drugs serves an adaptive purpose in the lives of some individuals. All four exam-ine how the patient's use of a substance fits into his overall adaption. The adap-tive function of AOD is a primary consideration during the development of treatment needs and goals.

At age 36, with two young boys and a wife to support, Jon's daily use reflects his thinking that "there is no way out." His conflicts about his use and his secrecy from his wife are something "I can learn to live with, accept that is not ideal, but feel is necessary for me to keep our family together."

Jon, like many with severe SUDs, dismisses the impact of his suffering at home because he feels shamed by his sense of weakness, failure, and inability to create a meaningful partnership with his wife and meaningful relationships with his children. Jon has internalized the adaptive function of his addiction.

Our frank discussions about the nature of Jon's compromises led to a reevaluation of our therapeutic relationship. It was neither a battleground for fighting his "denial" nor a deep working relationship used to address the underlying forces driving his adaption. We both eventually came to see weekly therapy for growth and change was at odds with his compromises and goals, and discontinued our increasingly sporadic sessions. Jon said, "I really believe terminating our work for now is the honest and best thing for me to do, and I shouldn't be spending money on therapy under these circumstances. However, I really get something out of our conversations, and hope I can check in periodically." I replied, "Of course."

Can a lifestyle that appears harmful to many people actually be considered adaptive? Can our disease-driven culture let Jon go and allow him to find his way?

Diana: Psychological Reliance
Not Yet Physical to Discontinued Use

This is the case study of a 55-year-old woman who was a severe daily drinker who longed to keep alcohol in her life, but recognized that she was unable to pace her drinking.

Diana was an eager, self-revealing student in one of my graduate school classes. She was fiercely engaged in listening and participating, an unusual and noticeable characteristic of a student struggling with the challenges of technology in a virtual classroom. Diana called me for psychotherapy, and abided by university policy that we would start only after the semester had ended and her grades recorded, and with the agreement that she would never take a class with me during her future education at USC. She announced that first session, "It is time to get down to business, to face my relationship with alcohol—it has been far too long. Avoidance of my problems is over for me. I think your approach suits me."

Diana told me about her love affair with gin and tonics. She savored the smell and the taste in those early moments, but searched quickly for "the feeling of being buzzed." She drank to brownouts (remembers sketchy details only) on most occasions, was a day and night drinker during weekends, and felt bloated and foggy-brained most mornings. My first impressions led me to consider the clinical sketch psychological reliance not yet physical (see Chapter 6, pp. 69–70).

Her pattern of drinking did not alarm me, but her memory of her family life did. "My mother did not like me, my sister and my mother joined forces against me, and my father left me." Later I asked, "Do you remember any warm moments with your mother?" "Good question," she said as she turned her head to think, and then decisively said, "No."

Diana began working with me in 2012. My clinical work with SUDs patients was less about an agreed-upon goal of abstinence and more about creating a joint discovery to understand "the meaning and the matters" of their behavior, as well as their ideas about their path to more health and well-being, the Greek definition of happiness. In our early months of working together, Diana drank through the evening hours of 6 to 10, her weekends included day and evening drinking, and she fell asleep intoxicated and woke up hung over. During this time our role transformed from student–teacher to patient–therapist.

Diana had studied my clinical sketches in class and experienced relief. She felt "encouraged that you will help me find my own way" (see Chapter 6). Using these clinical sketches, I recognized Diana as having a psychologically reliant, not yet physical relationship with alcohol. Diana lived her life within a state of nameless dread, duty, and obligation. She changed that edgy state of mind at the end of the day with the help of her gin and tonics. Exhausting day, relieving nights; Winnicott reminds us, "Don't assume that we all live a life" (Bollas, 1989, p. 26).

Diana acknowledged her chronic worries about her desires and the frequency of her drinking; she acknowledged loss of memory, digestive and stomach problems, hangovers, and embarrassing and regretful behaviors. Diana shared her wishes: "I would like to continue to drink." She was hopeful to find a comfortable moderation behavioral pattern that was pleasurable, not full of guilt and remorse. Andrew Tatarsky's harm reduction approach allowed her to explore her wish, and at the same time challenged her to address her serious problems with actions.

A harm reduction approach that I have found successful includes the concept of agreements. Diana began designing agreements (see Chapter 6, pp. 63–64) in those early months. These began with a plan of two drinks every night, starting at 6 p.m., no chugging, and 1 night off a week. Over the next 3 to 4 months, she upped the challenge and went to 2 nights off, then 3 nights off, then 5 nights off. She was successful with her behavioral plan and accomplished her goals, yet one day she came in and announced,

Two days ago, I stopped drinking. As you know, my destructive drinking is nonexistent at this point. I've developed self-control, I can live nights without drinking, and I can tolerate time's unfolding. I am proud of myself. This is a dream I've had for years, to drink with pleasure, self-control, and moderation. However, it is not the real answer for me. I feel this deeply. I can do it, but I'm beginning to feel like it's too much work, with too much rigidity. Most importantly, I know that I really want to understand what has driven my desire to drink, as well as my desire for emotional eating.

Diana was a psychic retreater, driven into her retreat from overwhelming feelings of being hated and unloved by her mother and the world, with the shame and humiliation that this caused her. John Steiner founded the concept of psychic retreats. These are well-worn internal structures of the mind that were organized and deployed during an individual's infancy and childhood. These are the mind's way of offering shelter during overwhelming trauma and neglect. Retreats both camouflage suffering and cause suffering during adolescence and early adulthood. AOD provides ongoing relief—many retreat-prone individuals develop substance use disorders (Steiner, 1993).

Diana didn't think there was anybody to talk to and felt no option but to withdraw. When I work with a psychic retreater, I have found that group work provides a containing space for an individual emerging from a retreat and learning to tolerate the experience of seeing and being seen (Steiner, 2011). I suggested AA, and Diana was adamantly disinterested. Spirituality, powerlessness, coercion, and 12-step work were not for her. She attended SMART Recovery (Self Management and Recovery Training) for about 6 months instead. Diana gave it her all, but decided to leave her meeting composed of young men and searched instead for a mixed peer group. She soon lost interest in searching for any kind of group support.

Gradually in our individual work together, Diana's sober mind allowed repressed material to enter her consciousness. She was able to begin to relive and reintegrate experiences of rejection from her mother, her loss of her father, and being excluded from the mother-sister relationship. It was a challenge for Diana to live in the experience of the moment, and her difficulty was a challenge for me. As she struggled to feel, she often preferred to talk about gossip at work and stories about witchcraft. She was protecting such fragility.

We talked about her ability to distract herself and avoid issues during our therapy. Los Angeles psychoanalyst Linda Sobelman gave me some useful wording when distracting stories become frequent occurrences in therapy: "Let's move on to something more relevant to our work. I don't think that these types of discussions are useful for what we are doing together." Diana seemed undamaged by the directness of this comment and contained by my boundary. It took a few sessions, but to this day she begins each session with the work of our work and welcomes a respectful reminder to stay on task.

During our first year of therapy, we worked on many levels of addiction. Diana had lost 50 lbs, and she said, "I must have been physically and psychologically exhausted from carrying around so much weight for decades." Her ego functions blossomed. She developed an energized sense of self, anticipated psychological danger, and was able to renounce impulses and pleasures if the consequences were harmful. Khantzian identifies these capacities as a form of self-care that replaces the need for self-medication (Khantzian & Albanese, 2008).

Diana is without these ego functions with spending habits. She has accumulated quite a bit of debt, is a fantasy spender, frequently indulging whims: "I hope I have enough money to cover this bill or maybe somehow someone will miraculously save me from my debts." While she allows herself to spend with this fantasy in mind, she is not disassociated from the damage that this causes. She has made painful and considerable reductions to her debt and tries very hard, but has not yet developed a satisfying and tolerable range for her spending. I have been encouraging Debtors Anonymous. "A great idea, Margy"; however, Diana is not using this as a resource at this time.

Diana is now in her third year of elected sobriety, except for those very well-managed occasions when she enjoys an alcohol flavor in certain foods and desserts. I have tremendous respect for this woman, and as Ed Khantzian has said about many of the patients he's seen through a similar process, "[These] are some of the most admirable and mature individuals with whom I have worked" (Khantzian, 2014, p. 2).

My clinical approach with Diana's substance use disorder feels very successful. I have practiced the Bionian notion of no memory or no desire at the beginning of each session. I let go of all memories as I prepare for my appointments. I am open to her impact and work hard to let it build before I feel like I have something to say. I have learned to value her defenses, value her concrete thinking, and have developed deep respect for her rigid and courageous tenacity, her faith and hope in the face of so much aloneness and minimal support. The results are objectively visible and also satisfying to her. I have operated within the psychoanalytic attitude of waiting in faith through her problematic and excessive evening and weekend drinking, her decision to initiate a harm reduction approach, her increasingly challenging agreements, her ability to feel clearly that drinking was no longer about pleasure, but had become a "thing unto itself. My evenings were about drinking; the drinking was the thing for me."

Eric: Shadow Use to Watchful Use, and
Millie: Addiction to Discontinued Use

A husband and wife team came to see me for consultation recently, and we worked together for 3 months. I again was pleased to have developed my clinical thinking about the natural place of AOD in our lives, as well as developing a more flexible approach to diagnosis and assessment. Psychoanalytic literature strongly suggests that the attitude of the clinician is the most dominant force in treatment. *Perspectives* suggests that addiction counselors and clinicians reexamine their current attitudes as well.

Eric and Millie, both 42 years of age, married young and have two adult children. They both drank heavily together during their early courtship years and early days of marriage. They lovingly raised Jason and Donna, and on weeknights and weekends Eric and Millie enjoyed their alcohol. Millie expressed to me in our first session, "I took it too far too often. I ended up going into rehab for help. I had gotten to the point where I was doing too much cocaine and too much alcohol together. As a matter of fact, I went to rehab twice. Today, I am an active member in AA, attend meetings regularly, and sponsor newcomers. I am a sober girl."

Eric seemed reserved as he listened. I wondered what he was experiencing. Millie continued, "We are here because my husband's drinking is getting out of hand. I want him to take responsibility for all his excess drinking. I cannot tell him to stop, and I cannot 'do his inventory,' but it is really hard for me to see him intoxicated so many nights during a week. I notice empty wine and beer bottles in the trash too often. I do not know how to communicate with him. I think he is in trouble."

Eric by now was flush-faced. He appeared weary as he began to talk. "I know what Millie thinks. We have had this conversation for years. I really wanted to be here today; my wife says you have a nontraditional approach to recovery, that you consider patterns other than addiction, and that you don't sell abstinence as the only ticket to recovery. I'm hoping that Millie will hear me. I'm hoping we can work this out; it's a big tension between us."

Eric repeated many times, "I know I can overdo it at times, I know that. And I do hear Millie's concern, and I do love her very much. However, I'm glad to be here with a third party. Millie, you have been sober for 10 years, and I respect and support you very much. I, however—and please understand how I'm saying this—did not end up in a hospital. Yes, I have drunk to excess during our heavy drinking days, but I want to have alcohol in my life, and I have tried hard to learn from my bad experiences." Millie's initial response was, "I hear you, and I've heard you before, but I think you are really in denial." I imagined they had very different perspectives on the fourth drive and very different views on the absoluteness of abstinence.

During that conversation, I addressed Millie. "Yes, if you believe he is addicted, I can understand how you came to your conclusion. However, as you know during our discussions of the clinical sketches, Eric really identifies with the shadow use sketch. He also believes that he has grown with discipline and effort and success to become a watchful user, one who has had problems but is now watchful." Millie tentatively listened during that conversation, and over the time of our consultation work together, gradually accepted Eric's choices and, yes, occasional difficulties with alcohol. "I'm not sure I buy all this fourth drive stuff and flexibility, not sure at all, but I'm beginning to take it in." I acknowledged Millie's efforts here.

Eric and Millie stopped our work together after 3 months. I felt I provided them with a framework for thinking about SUDs and addiction and new ways to respond and address each other's concerns. My patients, students, and I have increasingly found that using the 15 clinical sketches allows for so much variability in discussions. I felt that Millie and Eric stepped out of the decades-old binary box of either you're an alcoholic or you're not.

The clinical sketches provided an individual opportunity for each person to identify their own relationship with AOD and decide the place of AOD in their lives. Both felt an increasing willingness and freedom to work through their problems. When this clinical case was terminated, I had much satisfaction and once again found useful the 1983 comment by George Valliant: "Addiction is not just defined by symptomatic using, but also defined by who is watching the user." The others watching can either be open-minded and willing to support the user's discovery process, or deliver their ideas with controlling projections.

CHAPTER SUMMARY AND REFLECTIONS

Summary

This chapter explores three case studies of severe substance use disorder, utilizing the four guiding principles of the symposium approach, as well as the seven philosophical and clinical ideas identified in Chapter 1.

Reflections

Consider the following questions in a classroom discussion or paper:

- Do you agree with the DSM-5 spectrum category (severe) given to the three case studies in this chapter? Why or why not?
- What were some of your major learnings from Jon's case?
- What were some of your major learnings from Diana's case?
- What were some of your major learnings from Eric and Millie's case?
- Will this be a difficult spectrum category for you to utilize and work with? Why or why not?

CHAPTER 14

ADDICTION

INTRODUCTION

The two cases in this chapter reflect my adoption of the use of the word *addiction* for the approximately 3% of the U.S. population who are physically and psychologically addicted (Esser et al., 2014). One individual has decided, "I'd rather die drinking." The other individual has chosen abstinence.

CLINICAL CASES

Dr. Conrad Park: Addiction

I receive an emergency call from Julie, the wife of Dr. Conrad Park. I have seen this couple infrequently and periodically during 3 years. Dr. Park is a physician and a patriarch. He drinks too much, hides it, and denies it. Together, he and his wife have battled this problem for years. Julie tells me that he is drinking a lot more than usual and has gotten more aggressive and hostile; the kids are fed up, and they want to put him in a treatment facility. I ask her if he wants to go into treatment. She says that his response is, "I'd rather die drinking." I suggest a conversation with the two of them in my office. She's not sure how to get him there but thinks their daughter may help. It all sounds very frantic, and the family feels in a panic.

The daughter, Sharon, arrives before her father. We talk, and she is anxious and terrified. She reports that her father is hiding liquor, spending $400 a week on vodka, and drinking and driving. She is not sure if he is drinking while working or drinking around the clock. I am rather sure he is doing both. I suspect physical and psychological addiction has set in, and he is drinking just enough to stave off a debilitating withdrawal, just enough to marginally keep functioning. Family members seem unable to grasp the utter lack of choice involved when physical and/or psychological addiction sets in. If one's body and mind are physically and/or psychologically addicted, one drinks—end of story.

Dr. Park shows up 15 minutes later, and I smell alcohol. This confirms my suspicion that he is drinking 24/7. He is bleary eyed, trembling, and unsteady in his gait. He is tragically and poignantly dressed in physician scrubs, reflecting his desire to hold on to a semblance of normalcy to the bitter end. He sits down and seems embarrassed, disoriented, frightened, and sullen. He clearly doesn't want to be in my office.

Sharon is in tears, begging him to go into treatment and get help. She chokingly assures him of his family's love. She gently reminds him that everybody needs help sometimes and that now it's time for him to get help. She reminds him of the times he has helped her in college. She's nervous and pleading; he is withdrawn yet tolerant. His dismissal of her words is painfully obvious.

I listen and observe this exchange for a while. I go into reverie and decide I want to address him directly. I want to intervene and interrupt the family's controlling and coercive sense of authority about what they perceive is best for him, and instead tap into Dr. Park's wishes. I purposefully decide to reverse the family trend of pleading, imposing, and begging to give Dr. Park a semblance of authority. I also decide I want to use Eigen's work on impacts to take in what he is thinking and feeling, as well as what he wants, and have both of these wash over me. I want him to register me taking him in and respecting his point of view. I want him to hear my professional recommendation. This swap of registering impacts is useful in all phases of treatment, but it felt absolutely critical here. It creates a visceral connection and an emotionally truthful bond.

I turn my chair toward Dr. Park and look him in the eye, receptively and respectfully. I ask him, "How do you think you're doing with your drinking?" The look in his eyes is softly murderous. His hateful hold reflects a combination of sentiments including "I hate you," "can't stand you," and "get out of my face." And at the very same moment there is an expression of "I hope so much you're not afraid of me, you're not bullshitting, and you can actually stick with me to help me out of this mess I'm in." He looks back at me, and I sense he sees I am taking him seriously. He seems to understand on some level that I am registering his impact, allowing his hatred and hope to wash over me as I take the experience of him into my being.

Dr. Park manages to mutter, "I am not doing so well now." I reply, "I see that." I continue, "So you're a physician; you get this dependency thing. I'm sure you know that you're not doing so well with drinking as a result of your physical and psychological addiction to alcohol. We both know you need this stuff so as not to get sick from withdrawals." He nods in agreement and seems okay with our talking. I ask him what he wants to do about this; does he want to go into a treatment facility? He says emphatically, "No," and adds, "I want go to a motel, and stop drinking over a 3-day period. I can handle this by myself. I don't need anyone to help me. I'm a physician, and I know what I'm doing." I see that he wants to take matters into his own hands, design his own detox program.

I again look Dr. Park in the eye and say to him with firm kindness,

You know, you don't have to be so mean to yourself. That's a cruel and old-fashioned way to help you get through the shakes, sweats, and nausea of physical addiction. There are hospital settings in town that provide detox with medical support. The current treatment industry offers different levels of support. There are places designed to help you through detox without trying to rope you into a 28-day stay. There are places designed to get you through this crisis period and allow you to be somewhat responsive to your own treatment decisions. There are facilities geared to accomplish what you want without the pain or the isolation of a motel room. There is a way to clean out your body and mind without the torture of a cold turkey detox.

We were both engaged in the ongoing registering of impacts; he knew I was taking him in and taking him seriously (see Chapter 9, pp. 137–140). It was tense and intense as we took each other in. He looked at me and said, "I'll think about it." I asked, "What does that mean?" He responded with a hostile tone, "I hear you and I will think about it, and now I want to leave." I felt I wanted to say something about how alone and desperate he must have felt. We met eyes again, and I said, "I'm going to say something that feels difficult. When you leave now and go down to your car, I understand that you need to drink. I understand going for that bottle of vodka on the backseat of your car. If you can, just remember our conversation now and know that you can consider another way to detox, that there is a safer and kinder way to get through this." Without a word, he got up, stumbled out of my office, and left my suite.

Sharon was very relieved, yet cautiously hopeful. I told her that I thought he was in serious trouble and that she should go get him. She said she would do that, and also called her mother and told her to wait at home. At Sharon's request, I called the hospital, set things up, and later let her know of the admission process. I gave her my "professional" recommendation: "I think it's best now to go get your dad and start driving up to Vista Del Mar, regardless of admission possibilities. I'll call and inform you of their bed availability, but for now, my suggestion is to go buy a bottle of vodka, get him, and start driving."

They did just that. Dr. Park agreed to get in the car. She drove, and he drank. His admission was only briefly delayed. He was admitted to a local

ER while his blood alcohol content dropped to levels that matched Vista Del Mar's medical capacities. After that, he furiously sulked into the facility, but he did so voluntarily. At that moment, he had finally stopped discounting. The healthy side of his ambivalence was victorious; he was ready to accept help. His wife called me at midnight, joyous about "the miracle." She thanked me profusely.

Dr. Park stayed in Vista Del Mar for 5 days of medical detox and was discharged with a recommendation for further treatment. He chose not to follow up on the aftercare directive. His wife called 2 weeks after his discharge and left a message saying that he was better but still drinking. She hoped he would call me and said, "He still needs help, and I hope you can help him again."

This is a classic example of authority clashes in families. The family authoritatively wanted him to go into treatment, and he authoritatively did not. This tension prolonged his using, as well as their distress. This man clearly wanted to continue drinking; letting go of alcohol seemed an impossibility. I respected his choice, despite the life-threatening aspects of his situation. He and I came together the moment we began registering each other's impacts in the office. We each were able to make the inner adjustments and inner sacrifices necessary to really hear each other. This involves a mutual resonance, speaking, listening, feeling, and working imaginatively with the impact of each other's being (see Chapter 9, pp. 137–140). He knew that I believed he needed medical detox. I knew he wanted to keep drinking. This mutual respect for our impacts created a connection. If we are lucky, we give the other's impact time, we wait until the reality at hand finds voice, and then we might have something useful to say to the patient (see Chapter 9, pp. 137–140). He was able to hear my recommendation, think about it, and eventually walk into a dual diagnosis treatment facility voluntarily. I consider this a life-saving intervention.

I thought about Dr. Park often. A year and a half later, I ran into him in a neighborhood deli. He carried the countenance of a sober man. I was beside myself with excitement. He volunteered some family facts. I registered his impact, and he mine.

I asked him, "So how are you doing?" He looked me in the eye and said, "Life is good. I am sober, and have been for about a year." I responded with a warm recognition, "I thought so." We do what we can, and then we wait in analytic faith.

Dr. Park's wife, Julie, called me just before I completed this book's second edition. Her voice sounded frantic once more. She came in for one session and told me, "My husband went back to drinking in 2012. He is drinking a lot of vodka 24 hours a day. His business is in real trouble, his debts are rapidly increasing, he does not tell me what he is thinking or doing. Not too long ago, my daughter and I walked in on him when he and his girlfriend were having oral sex." Julie told me she ran up to him, punched him in the face, and left. Then she said, "I think I love him, and I feel paralyzed and do not know what to do." I listened for more and then asked, "How are you doing with all this?" "Not good, just nervous, not good, just nervous . . . but I'm his wife, and I have to stay in the marriage, and I love my children."

I was overwhelmed by her abuse and batterings, and her utter inability to register his maltreatment of her. My clinical action side suggested support groups, which could provide an opportunity for her to belong, listen, and eventually identify with domestic abuse. My clinical intuition side recognized that she would not likely abandon ship for deep-seated reasons. I have seen many individuals who are willing to career from one reckless crisis to another and are very focused on bailing out the mess and are not interested in exploring the situation in more depth. Julie, for example, came in for only one session, desiring marital and family advice after this disturbing incident. She was not registering the impact of her husband's behavior or consciously aware that she might benefit from some kind of social reinforcement elsewhere. She was not consciously aware of her own individual needs, and she didn't want to be, either. I recognized this and chose not to probe her denial further.

Dr. Park is truly a heavy-minded drinker (see Glossary, p. 197), with an increasingly alcohol-compromised body and clearly suffering with an alcohol addiction. Hippocrates, the father of Western medicine, guides us here: "Should a patient be suffering from an overpowering heaviness of the brain [mind], then 'there must be total abstinence from wine'" (Gately, 2008, p. 13). Wayne Sandler, a Los Angeles psychiatrist, blessed me and my clinical addiction practice 20 years ago with this guidance as well: "Some of them, Margy, we just don't reach."

Melinda: Addiction to Discontinued Use

Melinda is a 30-year-old "floppy stoner mom." She arrives at her first therapy session under the influence and tentatively announces her desire to stop smoking marijuana "eight times throughout the day." She has a medical marijuana prescription card and has discovered that pot gets her through the pressures of mothering, the stresses and humiliations of living with a verbally abusive and domineering husband, as well as the pain of unresolved conflicts from her childhood. As we begin talking, she asks me, "Do you think I'm an addict, or do you think maybe I could learn to moderate my marijuana use?" She continues, "You know, I don't really want to be an addict; I just want to be less of a stoner mom." These are common sentiments heard during therapy sessions with a person suffering from a substance use disorder or addiction. Many people in trouble with drugs and alcohol have just as much trouble with any kind of widely used label that causes them to feel trapped in a black-and-white diagnosis.

Melinda grumbles, "I hate the term *addict*. It implies so much weakness. I think I have some control. I have just gotten myself into some bad, bad habits." Melinda is not interested in the disease model and abstinence; however, she acknowledges her problems and seems to have some willingness to explore them. I join her desires and suggest a harm reduction approach.

I explain to her that harm reduction does not immediately insist on abstinence, but rather on everyday action steps that reduce harm while using. I discuss this with Melinda: "This approach is like a research project. The data collected from your action steps will both demonstrate and help us determine if you can achieve your goals of 'stopping marijuana' in outpatient therapy, or if you might need a higher level of care, possibly intensive outpatient groups or an inpatient setting."

Melinda is enthused by the harm reduction concept, and she begins a program of reducing her marijuana intake, as well as reducing the strength of the marijuana she currently smokes. She was ready, willing, and able (Miller & Rollnick, 2002, pp. 10–11) to change and adjust. "At times, my smoking of Mary Jane causes me to really hate myself—when I smoke first thing in the morning, or when I'm with the kids, or when I am driving the kids, or when I am chasing a pot crash and the kids want to go to the park, or when I just keep doing it and doing it. These are situations I want to change, and I feel ready to change them." She is quickly able to drop from smoking eight times a day to three times a day. She and her husband drink a bottle of wine every night, "but I am staying away from the hard stuff." She feels good that she is trying, and she feels good about her reductions.

Melinda continues talking about her long-term goal of stopping marijuana altogether. Her ambivalence kicks in: "I don't really want to stop, and I don't think I can. My husband asks me to throw my stash into the ocean. I can't. If I think about stopping on my own at home, I think I would just sleep and drink to get over it." Together, we compare her painful approach with detox in an inpatient facility. The former leaves her in a hangover and a haze, and without any support. The latter has Melinda in a protected setting, medically supported, and beginning the work of recovery. She seems to get the difference. "I think I am headed toward going to the hospital. Our harm reduction is working well in many respects, but I am not stopping. I think I need a hospital, but it's so hard to go away and leave the kids. It's embarrassing. What do I say? Right now, I still want to work with harm reduction."

Melinda's goal of abstinence remained. We continued our harm reduction approach. Eventually, she acknowledged, "Therapy isn't working. I'm not able to stop. I'll call you when I am ready."

Melinda did call me 4 months later. She had remained in treatment with her psychopharmacologist. Her medical marijuana card had recently expired. She tapered off from what remained and stopped completely on her own:

> I just got sick of it, and sick of the whole thing. I am doing okay but still have the same problems with my husband and taking care of my children. I thought it would be a good idea to go to that inpatient facility we talked about. I just need to get away from my husband, my children, and my life. I felt I could stop on my own, and I did. I woke up this morning and instantly thought about Vista Del Mar. I'm grumpy, I'm worried about my marriage, I need more help and want more support. What do you think?

I thought she was a young mom who was internally and externally ready to work. Two days later she entered Vista Del Mar for 2 weeks of intensive outpatient treatment. She remains abstinent today, although it is clinically imaginable that this young woman may one day reconsider her choice of abstinence as discontinued use for a period of time, and decide to experiment with social marijuana use.

CHAPTER SUMMARY AND REFLECTIONS

Summary

This chapter explored two case studies of addiction, utilizing the four guiding principles of the symposium approach, as well as the seven philosophical and clinical ideas identified in Chapter 1.

Reflections

Consider the following questions in a classroom discussion or paper:

- Do you agree with the optional DSM-5 spectrum category given to the two case studies in this chapter? Why or why not?
- What were some of your major learnings from Dr. Park's case?

- What were some of your major learnings from Melinda's case?
- Have you decided if you will adopt the word *addiction*, the use of which DSM-5 leaves to our discretion? Or would you classify these two cases as severe substance use disorders? How so?

GLOSSARY

Addiction: A narrowly focused lifestyle that functions as a meager substitute for people who desperately lack a sense of psychosocial cohesion.

Ambivalence: The P/SUD's true response to his relationship with AOD. He loves it and hates it.

Analytic Hovering: A psychoanalytic technique. Freud recommends that the therapist or the analyst listen to her patients with a hovering and suspended attention, and rely on her unconscious to do the rest.

AOD: Alcohol and other drugs.

Authoritative Versus Authoritarian Hint: An authoritative hint gives the P/SUD room to make something of his own of it, and also gives him space to dream up something from it. An authoritarian hint is more like an order.

Authority: The sense of ownership that patients and P/SUDs have about the direction of their own lives and what they think is the best course of treatment for them.

Beta Elements: The undigested, nameless, formless, catastrophic experiences of the infant-child.

Blind Eye: Noticing something but not registering its real impact.

Clinical Sketches: Fifteen descriptive clinical pictures, including substance use, misuse, problematic use at a problematic time, shadow use, and addiction. These clinical descriptors provide a picture of the individual with a nonproblematic, mild, moderate, or severe substance use disorder and addiction, the diagnostic spectrum categories of DSM-5 (2013).

Context of Destiny: An ongoing relationship with an attentive and intuitive caretaker that allows the child to have ongoing contact with his real essence.

Context of Fate: An ongoing relationship with an inattentive caretaker. The child does not feel safe to be or safe to explore his essence and thus feels compelled to adjust to a prescribed climate of commandments.

Counseling: A form of psychotherapy that is supportive, clarifying, and encouraging. Counseling usually does not involve the in-depth working through of early trauma.

Countertransference: The analyst's or therapist's transference to the analysand, or patient. This includes the analyst's realistic reaction to the reality of the patient's life, to her own life as it may become affected by the patient, and the analyst's reaction to the transference.

Death/Rebirth Moments: When an individual says no (death) to a part of his life he has outgrown and says yes (rebirth) to an unknown future. Often experienced in developmental rites of passage.

Destiny: The urge within each person to articulate and elaborate his own idiom through the selection and use of caretakers (objects) in his environment.

Dikaiosunê: Socrates defines this as psychosocial integration, which provides a shield against domination by master passions or addiction.

Discounting: When a P/SUD discounts the existence, significance, and impact of a problem as well as the ability to do anything at all to address it.

Dislocated Individual: A person overwhelmed by the disruption of living in an increasingly globalized world, including adaption to new environments, excessive communications, and the increasing demands for technological mastery.

Dislocation: Refers to the rupture of enduring and sustaining connections between individuals and their families, friends, societies, livelihoods, rituals, traditions, nations, and deities.

Dislocation Theory of Addiction: Does not view addiction as either a medical disease or moral failure; rather, it depicts widespread addiction as a way of adapting to the increasingly dominant and onerous aspects of the modern world. This includes a barrage of communications and a demand for technological mastery.

Dream or Dreaming: To think about the patient using both conscious and unconscious thinking processes.

DSM-IV-TR: Previous edition of *Diagnostic and Statistical Manual of Mental Disorders* (APA, 2000), which used the words *dependence* and *abuse* for alcohol and other drug diagnosis.

DSM-5: Current edition of *Diagnostic and Statistical Manual of Mental Disorders,* released in May 2013, that deleted the terms *abuse* and *dependence* and presented a diagnostic spectrum for substance use disorders.

False Self: A part of the self that is unable to feel and express vulnerability or weakness, and compensates by developing around the wishes, defenses, and dictates of others; and is unable to experience life or feel real.

Fantasy: A daydream.

Fated: Can be described as the feeling the child has when his spontaneous self-expressions are rejected and he feels forced to adapt to others' commandments of living.

Fourth Drive: In every age, in every part of this planet, people have pursued intoxication with plants, drugs, alcohol, and other mind-altering substances. This pursuit has so much force and persistence that it functions just like our other drives of hunger, thirst, and sex. This fourth drive is a natural part of our biology.

Gentle Drinking: A form of temperate or balanced drinking.

Global Weightlessness: Vagueness and ambiguity experienced by the immigrant, asylum-seeker, and global citizen, a sense of floating similar to weightlessness.

Harm Reduction: An approach to the treatment of substance use, disorders, and addiction that rejects the presumption that abstinence is the best or only acceptable goal for all problem alcohol and drug users.

Heavy-Minded User: In psychoanalytic parlance, an infant (later adult) who is traumatized by experiencing aspects of existence and reality before the experience and feelings of union and appreciation of the mother. This ongoing wound will never be soothed by AOD, only tolerated over one's lifetime (Goldman, 1993, p. 95).

Hippocrates: Renowned ancient Greek doctor who gave the following advice: "Should a patient be suffering from an overpowering heaviness of the brain [mind], then 'There must be total abstinence from wine'" (Gately, 2008, p. 13).

Holding Environment: Created when the mother allows an infant's true self to develop. A therapist provides a similar space, and gives the true self another chance to emerge.

Idiom: The unique nucleus of each individual.

Master Passions: A term used by Socrates to refer to unhealthy devotions that involved ongoing and destructive use in excess. A person under the tyranny of his passions is one who is consumed with wine and its abundance.

Natural History: The rhythm and course of one's distinct using relationship with AOD, and the rhythm and course of one's distinct path of recovery.

Ordinary Passions: Refers to healthy devotions, habits, or preoccupations that take place in ordinary societies, families, or communities of people.

Philopotes: The ancient Greek term for a lover of drinking sessions; it bore no stigma.

Pockets of Meaning: Passions that are invested with importance. These are things that are valuable in a person's life, the things people pocket and protect. These may include children, family, friends, hobbies, religion, or work.

P/SUD: Person with a mild, moderate, or severe substance use disorder.

Psychic Retreats: An area of the mind where reality does not have to be faced, where fantasy and omnipotence can exist unchecked, and where growth and development are sacrificed.

Psychoanalysis: A form of psychiatric treatment that uses the analysand's (patient's) transference to the analyst (therapist) as the primary source for working through deep conflicts.

Psychoanalytic Attitude: Waiting in Faith. When an analyst or therapist receives the patient's (the P/SUD's) infantile and unmetabolized feelings and projections and, as far as possible, refrains from reacting to them. This results in enabling the P/SUD (patient) to take these feelings and projections back and integrate them into his own thinking and emotional mind.

Psychodynamic Therapy: A form of psychotherapy that considers the influence of historical traumas on one's current life, and can be supportive, be educational, or involve deeper explorations of traumas.

Psychosocial Integration: Living with a sense of belonging and significance.

Receptivity: An attitude of listening without penetrating or intruding.

Registering Impacts: Allowing the experiences of events and other personalities to wash over and through one.

Relational Home: A secure relationship that provides a safe context for the reworking of early trauma. A therapist provides a relational home for exploring one's relationship with AOD and decisions about treatment.

Reverie: Emotional availability, fueled by fierce maternal instincts. After the baby is held and all goes well, sensations are transformed—frustration is now satisfaction, emptiness is now fullness, pain is now pleasure, isolation is now company, anxiety is now calm, and dread is now hope.

Ruthless Usage: When a child of his destiny feels free to assert his needs and aggressively express his wishes. He uses members of his village of living objects for satisfaction and fulfilment of these needs and wishes. There are degrees of ruthless usage.

Self-Medication Theories: Theories that emphasize and identify the psychological suffering driving the need for destructive use of AOD. P/SUDs self-medicate because they are unable to self-care.

SUD(s): Substance use disorder(s).

Symposium: Comes from the ancient Greek word meaning "drinking together." A formal but hospitable educational gathering to learn to "tipple wisely" or abstain.

Temperance: The philosophical doctrine that Plato promoted for healthy drinking habits. It meant subordinating the desire for pleasure to the dictates of reason, using will and discipline to avoid overindulgence and indiscriminate drinking.

Therapeutic Action Moments: When treatment theories and psychoanalytic concepts are practically applied to the struggles of each stage.

"Tipple Wisely": An ancient Greek term for learning to drink with temperance.

Transference: A libidinal phenomenon. The analysand, or patient, ascribes unsatisfied libidinal impulses from infancy and childhood to the analyst or therapist. Love for the analyst provides the necessary extra force to induce the ego to give up its resistances, undo the repressions, and adopt a fresh solution to its ancient problems.

Trauma: A sudden, unexpected event that severely interrupts one's sense of a continuity of being.

True Self: Inherited potential that exists only in experiencing. The true self is able to experience life and feels real.

Village of Living Objects: People and things that will foster the elaboration of the child's creative strivings and provide the right conditions to evolve his idiom.

REFERENCES AND FURTHER READING

AddictScience.com: A sober addict's guide to the science of addiction and recovery.

Alexander, B. K. (2011). *The globalization of addiction: A study in poverty of the spirit.* Oxford, England: Oxford University Press.

Alexander, B. K. (2014, July 3). *The globalization of addiction: The rise and fall of the official view of addiction.* (Speech, Simon Fraser University, Burnaby, British Columbia).

Allhoff, F. (2007). *Wine and philosophy: A symposium on thinking and drinking.* Boston, MA: Wiley-Blackwell.

Allhoff, F., & Adams, M. P. (2011). *Whiskey and philosophy: A small batch of spirited ideas.* Hoboken, NJ: John Wiley & Sons.

American Psychiatric Association. (2000). *Diagnostic and statistical manual of mental disorders* (Rev. 4th ed.). Washington, DC: Author.

American Psychiatric Association. (2013). *Diagnostic and statistical manual of mental disorders* (Rev. 5th ed.). Washington, DC: Author.

American Society of Addiction Medicine. http://www.asam.org

Baker, H., & Baker, M. (1987). Heinz Kohut's self psychology: An overview. *American Journal of Psychiatry, 144,* 1–9.

Beck, A. T. (1979). *Cognitive therapy and the emotional disorders.* Madison, CT: International Universities Press.

Beck, A. T., Wright, F. D., Newman, C. F., & Liese, B. S. (1993). *Cognitive therapy of substance abuse.* New York, NY: Guilford Press.

Bion, W. R. (1967). *Second thoughts.* London, England: Karnac.

Bion, W. R. (1992). *Cogitations.* London, England: Karnac.

Bloch, H. A. (1949). Alcohol and American recreational life. *American Scholar, 18*(1), 54–66.

Bollas, C. (1989). *Forces of destiny: Psychoanalysis and human idiom.* London, England: Free Association Books.

Bollas, C. (2007). *The Freudian moment.* London, England: Karnac.

Bourne, E. (2000). *The anxiety and phobia workbook.* Oakland, CA: New Harbinger Publications.

Breacher, E. M., & the editors of *Consumer Reports.* (1972). *Licit and illicit drugs.* Boston, MA: Little, Brown.

Brower, K. J., Blow, F. C., & Beresford, T. P. (1989). Treatment implications of chemical dependency models: An integrative approach. *Journal of Substance Abuse Treatment, 6*(3), 147–157.

Brown, S. (1985). *Treating the alcoholic: A developmental model of recovery*. New York, NY: John Wiley.

Brown, S. (1988). *Treating adult children of alcoholics: A developmental perspective*. New York, NY: John Wiley & Sons.

Brown, S. (2004). *A place called self: Women, sobriety, and radical transformation*. Center City, MN: Hazelden.

Brown, S. (Ed.), & Yalon, I. D. (General Ed.). (1995). *Treating alcoholism*. San Francisco, CA: Jossey-Bass.

Caron Treatment Center. (2013). http://www.caron.org/current-statistics.html

Centers for Disease Control and Prevention (CDC). (2012, January). Binge drinking: Nationwide problem, local solutions. *Vitalsigns*.

Centers for Disease Control and Prevention (CDC). (2015). Smoking and tobacco use. *CDC 24/7*. Retrieved January 31, 2015.

Change4life. http://www.nhs.uk/Change4life

Chessick, R. (1992). *What constitutes the patient in psychotherapy?* London, England: Jason Aronson.

Clark, R. P. (2010). *The glamour of grammar: A guide to the magic and mystery of practical English*. New York, NY: Little, Brown.

Coltart, N. (1993). *How to survive as a psychotherapist*. London, England: Sheldon Press.

Coltart, N. (2000). *Slouching towards Bethlehem*. New York, NY: Other Press.

Costello, R. B. (Ed.). (1997). *Random House Webster's college dictionary* (2nd ed.). New York, NY: Random House.

Denzin, N. (1987). *The alcoholic self*. Newbury Park, CA: Sage.

Department of Health, United Kingdom. (2012).

Director, L. (2005). Encounters with omnipotence in the psychoanalysis of substance users. *Psychoanalytic Dialogues, 15*(4), 567–587.

Dodes, L. (2002). *The heart of addiction*. New York, NY: HarperCollins.

Dodes, L. (2011). *Breaking addiction: A 7-step handbook for ending any addiction*. New York, NY: HarperCollins.

Dodes, L., & Dodes, Z. (2014). *The sober truth: Debunking the bad science behind 12-step programs and the rehab industry*. Boston, MA: Beacon Press.

Doweiko, H. E. (2009). *Concepts of chemical dependency* (7th ed.). Belmont, CA: Brooks/Cole.

Earleywine, M. (2002). *Understanding marijuana: A new look at the scientific evidence*. Oxford, England: Oxford University Press.

Efran, J. S., Lukens, M. D., & Lukens, R. J. (1990). *Language structure and change: Frameworks of meaning in psychotherapy*. New York, NY: W. W. Norton.

Eigen, M. (1986). *Psychotic core*. Northvale, NJ: Jason Aronson.

Eigen, M. (1996). *Psychic deadness*. Northvale, NJ: Jason Aronson.

Eigen, M. (1998). *The psychoanalytic mystic*. London, England: Free Association Books.

Eigen, M. (1999). *Toxic nourishment*. London, England: Karnac.

Eigen, M. (2001). *Ecstasy*. Middletown, CT: Wesleyan University Press.

Eigen, M. (2002). *Rage*. Middletown, CT: Wesleyan University Press.

Eigen, M. (2004). *The sensitive self*. Middletown, CT: Wesleyan University Press.

Eigen, M. (2004b). *The electrified tightrope* (Adam Phillips, Ed.). London, England: Karnac.

Eigen, M. (2006). *Lust*. Middletown, CT: Wesleyan University Press.

Eigen, M. (2009). *Flames from the unconscious*. London, England: Karnac.

Eigen, M. (2010). *Eigen in Seoul: Volume 1: Madness and murder*. London, England: Karnac.

Eigen, M. (2011a). *Eigen in Seoul: Volume 2. Faith and transformation*. London, England: Karnac.

Eigen, M. (2011b). *Contact with the depths*. London, England: Karnac.

Eigen, M. (2013–2015). MEigen Workshop.

Eigen, M., & Govrin, A. (2007). *Conversations with Michael Eigen*. London, England: Karnac.

Eigan, M. (2014). *Birth of consciousness*. London, England: Karnac.

Emerson, H. (1932). *Alcohol and man*. Norwood, MA: Norwood Press Linotype.

Epstein, M. (1995). *Thoughts without a thinker: Psychotherapy from a Buddhist perspective*. New York, NY: Basic Books.

Erickson, C. K. (2007). *The science of addiction: From neurobiology to treatment*. New York, NY: W. W. Norton.

Esser, M. B., Hedden, S. L., Brewer, K. D., Gfroerer, J. C., & Naimi, T. S. (2014, November 20). Centers for Disease Control and Prevention. "Prevalence of alcohol dependence among U.S. adult drinkers, 2009–2011. *Preventing Chronic Disease, 11*.

Euripides. Dodds, E. R., translator. (1960). *Bacchae; Plays of Euripides*. Clarendon Press.

Fetting, M. (2009). Presidential reverie: An invitation to become a country of thinkers. *California Society for Clinical Social Work, 38*(7), 1–7.

Fetting, M. (2009b). Let's make it through transition: A time of fits and starts. *California Society for Clinical Social Work, 38*(10), 3.

Fetting, M. (2011a). An interview with Ed Khantzian.

Fetting, M. (2011b). An interview with Stephanie Brown.

Fetting, M. (2012a). Our national discourse on abstinence: A winning white lie. Unpublished paper.

Fetting, M. (2012b). Fresh perspectives on problem using and addiction—Part I. *California Society for Clinical Social Work, 42*(9), 1, 9–12.

Fetting, M. (2012c). Fresh perspectives on problem using and addiction—Part II. *California Society for Clinical Social Work, 42*(10), 1.

Fetting, M. (2012). *Perspectives on addiction*. Thousand Oaks, CA: Sage.

Fetting, M. (2013). Eigen in Seoul: Volume 1. Madness and murder. *Clinical Update, XLIV*(10): 11–14.

Fields, R. (2010). *Drugs in perspective* (7th ed.). New York, NY: McGraw-Hill.

Fingarette, H. (1988). *Heavy drinking: The myth of alcoholism as a disease*. London, England: University of California Press.

Fletcher, A. (2001). *Sober for good*. New York, NY: Houghton Mifflin.

Fletcher, A. (2013). *Inside rehab: The surprising truth about addiction treatment and how to get the help that works*. New York, NY: Penguin Books.

Flores, P. J. (2001). Addiction as an attachment disorder: Implications for group therapy. *International Journal of Group Psychotherapy, 51*(1), 64.

Flores, P. J. (2004). *Addiction as an attachment disorder*. Plymouth, England: Aronson.

Frank, J. D. (1963). *Persuasion and healing: A comparative study of psychotherapy*. New York, NY: Schocken Books.

Franklin, J. (1987). *Molecules of the mind*. New York, NY: Dell.

Garner, D. M., & Garfinkel, P. E. (Eds.). (1985). *Handbook of psychotherapy for anorexia nervosa and bulimia*. New York, NY: Guilford Press.

Gately, I. (2008). *Drink: A cultural history of alcohol*. New York, NY: Gotham Books.

Glaser, G. (2013). *Her best-kept secret: Why women drink and how they can regain control*. New York, NY: Simon & Schuster.

Glaser, G. (2015, April). The irrationality of Alcoholics Anonymous. *The Atlantic*.

Goldman, D. (1993). *In search of the real: The origins and originality of D. W. Winnicott*. Northvale, NJ: Jason Aronson.

Goodrich, R. E. (2015). *Smile anyway*. CreateSpace Independent Publishing Platform.

Gorski, T. T., & Miller, M. (1986). *Staying sober: A guide for relapse prevention*. Thorofare, NJ: Independence Press.

Gregson, D., & Efran, J. (2002). *The Tao of sobriety: Helping you to recover from alcohol and drug addiction*. New York, NY: Thomas Dunne Books.

Grinberg, L., Sor, D., & de Bianchedi, E. T. (1977). *Introduction to the work of Bion*. Lanham, MD: Jason Aronson.

Grotstein, J. S. (2009). *But at the same time on another level: Psychoanalytic theory and technique in the Kleinian/Bionian mode* (Vol. 1). London, England: Karnac.

Guralnik, D. B., & Friend, J. H. (Eds.). (1968). *Webster's new world dictionary of the American language* (college ed.). Cleveland: World Publishing Co.

Hanson, D. J. (1995). *Preventing alcohol abuse: Alcohol, culture, and control*. Westport, CT: Praeger.

Hanson, G. R., Venturelli, P. J., & Fleckenstein, A. E. (2009). *Drugs and society* (10th ed.). Sudbury, MA: Jones and Bartlett.

Herlihy, P. (2012). *Vodka: A global history*. London, England: Reaktion Books.

Horvath, A. T., & Velten, E. (2000). Smart recovery: Addiction recovery support from a cognitive-behavioral perspective. *Journal of Rational-Emotive & Cognitive-Behavior Therapy, 18*(3), 181–191.

Humphreys, K. (2003). A research-based analysis of the moderation management controversy. *Alcohol and Drug Abuse, 54*(5), 621–622.

Hyman, S. E. (1995). A man with alcoholism and HIV infection. *Journal of the American Medical Association, 274*(10), 837–843.

Inaba, D. S., & Cohen, W. E. (2007). *Uppers, downers, all arounders* (6th ed.). Medford, OR: CNS Publications.

Institute of Medicine. http://www.ion.edu/About-IOM.aspx

Ireland, S. & Proulx, P. J. (editors) (2004). Textualizing the immigrant experience in contemporary Quebec. Westport, CT: Praeger. Chapter 9 "Bach Mai and Ying Chen: Immigrant Identities in Quebec." By Jack A. Yeager.

Jellinek, E. M. (1960). *The disease concept of alcoholism.* New Haven, CT: Hillhouse Press.

Karter, L. (2013). *Women and problem gambling: Therapeutic insights into understanding addiction and treatment.* New York, NY: Routledge.

Khantzian, E. J. (1985). The self-medication hypothesis of addictive disorders: Focus on heroin and cocaine dependence. *American Journal of Psychiatry, 142*(11), 1259–1264.

Khantzian, E. J. (1999). *Treating addiction as a human process.* Northvale, NJ: Jason Aronson.

Khantzian, E. J. (2011). *Reflections on treating addictive disorders: A psychodynamic perspective.* Unpublished manuscript.

Khantzian, E. J. (2014). Tragic trends in the treatment of addictive illnesses. *Psychiatric Times.* http://www.psychiatrictimes.com

Khantzian, E. J., & Albanese, M. J. (2008). *Understanding addiction as self medication.* Lanham, MD: Rowman & Littlefield.

Knapp, C. (1997). *Drinking: A love story.* New York, NY: Dell.

Knapp, C. (2003). *Appetites: Why women want.* New York, NY: Counterpoint.

Kosok, A. (2006). The moderation management programme in 2004: What type of drinker seeks controlled drinking? *International Journal of Drug Policy, 17,* 295–303.

Krystal, H. (1982/1983). Alexithymia and the effectiveness of psychoanalytic treatment. *International Journal of Psychoanalytic Psychotherapy, 9,* 353–388.

Kuhn, C., Swartzwelder, S., & Wilson, W. (2008). *Buzzed: The straight facts about the most used and abused drugs from alcohol to Ecstasy* (3rd ed.). New York, NY: W. W. Norton.

Lasater, L. (1988). *Recovery from compulsive behavior: How to transcend your troubled family.* Deerfield Beach, FL: Health Communications.

Lears, T. J. (2003). *Something for nothing: Luck in America.* New York, NY: Viking Penguin.

Levin, J. (2001). *Therapeutic strategies for treating addiction.* Northvale, NJ: Jason Aronson.

Loose, R. (2002). *The subject of addiction: Psychoanalysis and the administration of enjoyment.* London, England: Karnac.

Lynch, K. (2007). More thoughts on the space of the symposium. *The British School of Athens Studies, 15,* 243–249.

Malater, E. (2013). *Review of Seoul books.* MEigen Workshop.

Marlatt, G. A. (Ed.). (1998). *Pragmatic strategies for managing high-risk behaviors.* New York, NY: Guilford Press.

Martin, S. C. (2006). From temperance to alcoholism in America. *Reviews in American History, 34*(2), 231–237.

Mate, G. (2010). *In the realm of hungry ghosts: Close encounters with addiction.* Berkeley, CA: North Atlantic Books. Lyons, CO: The Ergos Institute.

McDougall, J. (1984, July). The dis-affected reflections on affect. *Psychoanalytic Quarterly, 53*(3), 386–406.

McGoldrick, M., Giordano, J., & Garcia-Preto, N. (Eds.). (2005). *Ethnicity and family therapy* (3rd ed.). New York, NY: Guilford Press.

McWilliams, N. (2011). *Psychoanalytic diagnosis: Understanding personality structure in the clinical process.* New York, NY: Guilford Press.

Milkman, H. B., & Sunderwirth, S. G. (2009). *Craving for ecstasy and natural highs.* Thousand Oaks, CA: Sage.

Miller, M. V. (1995). *Intimate terrorism: The deterioration of erotic life.* New York, NY: W. W. Norton.

Miller, W. R., & Rollnick, S. (2002). *Motivational interviewing: Preparing people for change* (2nd ed.). New York, NY: Guilford Press.

Moderation Management. http://www.moderation.org/whatisMM.shtml

Molino, A. (Ed.). (1998). *Freely associated: Encounter in psychoanalysis with Christopher Bollas, Joyce McDougall, Michael Eigen, Adam Phillips, Nina Coltart.* London, England: Free Association Books.

Napier, A. D., et al. (2014). *The Lancet, 384* (9954), 1607–1639.

Obholzer, A., & Roberts, V. Z. (Eds.). (1994). *The unconscious at work: Individual and organizational stress in the human services.* London, England: Routledge.

Parker-Pope, T. (2014, November 20). Most heavy drinkers are not alcoholics. *New York Times.*

Peele, S. (2014). *Recover! Stop thinking like an addict and reclaim your life with the perfect program.* Boston, MA: Da Capo.

Peele, S., & Brodsky, A. (1991). *The truth about addiction and recovery.* New York, NY: Simon & Schuster.

Pelled, E. (2007). Learning from experience: Bion's concept of reverie and Buddhist meditation: A comparative study. *International Journal of Psychoanalysis, 88*(6), 1507–1526.

Perkinson, R. R., & Jongsma, A. E., Jr. (2009). *The addiction treatment planner* (4th ed.). Hoboken, NJ: John Wiley & Sons.

Phillip Z. (1991). *Skeptic's guide to the twelve steps: What to do when you don't believe.* New York, NY: HarperCollins.

Phillips, A. (1994). *On flirtation.* Cambridge, MA: Harvard University Press.

Phillips, A. (2010). *On balance.* New York, NY: Farrar, Straus & Giroux.

Phillips, A. (2013). *One way and another.* London, England: Penguin Group.

Phillips, A., & Taylor, B. (2009). *On kindness.* New York, NY: Farrar, Straus & Giroux.

Power, M. (2014). *Drugs 2.0: The web revolution that's changing how the world gets high.* London, England: Portobello Books.

Prochaska, J. O., DiClemente, C. C., & Norcross, J. C. (1993). In search of how people change: Applications to addictive behaviors. *Journal of Addictions Nursing, 5*(1), 2–16.

Ratey, J. J., & Johnson, C. (1997). *The shadow syndromes.* New York, NY: Pantheon Books.

Reilly, C., & Smith, N. (2013). The evolving definition of pathological gambling in the DSM-5. National Center for Responsible Gaming. Retrieved November 9, 2014, from http://www.ncrg.org/sites/default/files/uploads/.../ncrg_wpdsm

Richardson, J. (1979). *Memoir of a gambler*. New York, NY: Vintage.

Rickwood, D., Blaszczynski, A., Delfabbro, P., Dowling, N., Heading, K., & Giese, J. (2010). Special report: The psychology of gambling. *InPsych, 32*(6).

Rilke, R. M. (1993). *Letters to a young poet*. New York, NY: W. W. Norton.

Rinsley, D. (1988). The dipsas revisited: Comments on addiction and personality. *Journal of Substance Abuse Treatment, 5*, 1–7.

Rogers, R. (1989). Review of the psychotic core. *The Psychoanalytic Psychology, 6*(3), 367–373.

Rotskoff, L. (2002). *Love on the rocks: Men, women, and alcohol in post–World War II America*. Chapel Hill: University of North Carolina Press.

Ruden, R. (1997). *The craving brain*. New York, NY: HarperCollins.

Ruiz, P., Strain, E. C., & Langrod, J. G. (2007). *The substance abuse handbook*. Philadelphia, PA: Lippincott Williams & Wilkins.

Schaeff, A.W. (1987). *When society becomes an addict*. San Francisco, CA: Harper & Row.

Schlaadt, R. G., & Shannon, P. T. (1994). *Drugs: Use, misuse, and abuse*. Englewood Cliffs, NJ: Prentice-Hall.

Schuckit, M. A. (2010). *Drug and alcohol abuse: A clinical guide to diagnosis and treatment* (6th ed.). New York, NY: Springer.

Severns, J. R. (2004). A sociohistorical view of addiction and alcoholism. *Janus Head, 7*(1), 149–166.

Shaffer, H. J. (1987). The epistemology of "addictive disease": The Lincoln-Douglas debate. *Journal of Substance Abuse Treatment, 4*, 103–113.

Shaffer, H. J. (1999, Fall). On the nature and meaning of addiction. *National Forum, 79*(4), 9–14.

Shaffer, H. J., LaPlante, D. A., LaBrie, R. A., Kidman, R. C., Donato, A. N., & Stanton, M. V. (2004). Toward a syndrome model of addiction: Multiple expressions, common etiology. *Harvard Review of Psychiatry, 12*, 367–374.

Siegel, R. K. (2005). *In intoxication: Life in pursuit of artificial paradise*. Rochester, VT: Park Street Press.

Soanes, C., & Stevenson, A. (Eds.). (2009). *Concise Oxford English dictionary* (11th ed.). Oxford, England: Oxford University Press.

Steiner, J. (1993). *Psychic retreats*. London, England: Routledge.

Steiner, J. (2011). *Seeing and being seen: Emerging from a psychic retreat*. London, England: Routledge.

Stolorow, R. D. (2007). *Trauma and human existence*. New York, NY: Taylor & Francis.

Stolorow, R. D. (2009). Identity and resurrective ideology in an age of trauma. *Psychoanalytic Psychology, 26*, 206–209.

Street Drugs. (2005). *A drug identification guide*. Long Lake, MN: Publishers Group.

Substance Abuse and Mental Health Services Administration (SAMHSA). (2013). Behavioral health barometer: United States 2013. http://www.samhsa.gov

Szasz, T. S. (1972). Bad habits are not diseases: A refutation of the claim that alcoholism is a disease. *The Lancet, 2,* 83–84.

Szasz, T. S. (1988). A plea for the cessation of the longest war of the 20th century: The war on drugs. *The Humanistic Psychologist, 16*(2), 314–322.

Tatarsky, A. (Ed.). (2002). *Harm reduction psychotherapy: New treatment for drug and alcohol problems.* Northvale, NJ: Jason Aronson.

The Tavistock Clinic Series. (2013). *Addictive states of mind.* London, England: Karnac.

Technology Management Associates, Inc. (1998, October). *TECHMANAGE Newsletter, 1*(6), 1.

Teresi, L. (2011). *Hijacking the brain: How drug and alcohol addiction hijack our brains—The science behind twelve-step recovery.* Bloomington, IN: Author House.

Thombs, D. L. (2006). *Introduction to addictive behaviors* (3rd ed.). New York, NY: Guilford Press.

Toossi, M. (2012, January). Labor force projections to 2020: A more slowing growing workforce. *Monthly Labor Review.*

Ulman, R. B., & Paul, H. (2006). *The self psychology of addiction and its treatment.* New York, NY: Routledge.

Urbina, I. (2012). Addiction diagnosis may rise under guideline changes. *New York Times.*

Vaillant, G. E. (1983). *The natural history of alcoholism: Causes, patterns, and paths to recovery.* Cambridge, MA: Harvard University Press.

Van Wormer, K., & Davis, D. R. (2008). *Addiction treatment: A strengths perspective* (2nd ed.). Belmont, CA: Thomson Brooks/Cole.

Von Stieff, F. (2012) *Brain and balance: Understanding the genetics behind addiction and sobriety.* Tucson, AZ: Ghost River Images.

Waite, M. (2012). *Paperback Oxford English dictionary.* Oxford, England: Oxford University Press.

Walant, K. (1995). *Creating the capacity for attachment.* Northvale, NJ: Jason Aronson.

Weegmann, M. (2006). Edward Khantzian interview. *Journal of Groups in Addiction and Recovery, 1*(2), 15–32.

Weil, A. (2004). *From chocolate to morphine.* New York, NY: Houghton Mifflin.

White, W. L. (2011). *Unraveling the mystery of personal and family recovery: An interview with Stephanie Brown, PhD.* Retrieved from http://www.williamwhitepapers.com/pr/2011 Dr. Stephanie Brown.pdf

White, W. L., Boyle, M., & Loveland, D. (2002). Alcoholism/addiction as a chronic disease: From rhetoric to clinical reality. *Alcoholism Treatment Quarterly, 20*(3/4), 107–130.

Wilson, H. T. (Ed.). (2010). *Drugs, society, and behavior* (24th ed.). Boston, MA: McGraw-Hill.

Winnicott, D. W. (1958). The capacity to be alone. *International Journal of Psycho-Analysis, 39,* 416–420.

Winnicott, D. W. (1965). *The maturational processes and the facilitating environment* (pp. 140–152). New York, NY: International Universities Press, 1965.

Wolburg, J. M. (2005). How responsible are "responsible" drinking campaigns for pre-venting alcohol abuse? *The Journal of Consumer Marketing, 22*(4/5), 176–177.

Wolfe, A., & Owens, E. C. (2009). *Gambling: Mapping the American moral landscape.* Waco, TX: Baylor University Press.

Wurmser, L. (1978). *The hidden dimension: Psychodynamics in compulsive drug use.* Northvale, NJ: Jason Aronson.

Wyatt, R. C., & Yalom, V. (2007). *An interview with Stephanie Brown, PhD.* Retrieved from http://www.psychotherapy.net/interview/stephanie-brown

Yalom, I. D. (2002). *The gift of therapy.* New York, NY: HarperCollins.

Zoja, L. (2000). *Drugs, addiction and initiation: The modern search for ritual.* Boston, MA: Sigo Press.

INDEX

drinking struggle in a relationship and, 159
false self horn concept and, 127–128,
  165–166, 196
family of origin issues and, 156–157
feeling therapist felt by patient
  and, 167
"*fourth drive*" concept and, 159–160, 162
getting more out of living and, 164
harm-reduction efforts and, 161
impact time factor and, 167–168
impacts in the room and, 167–168
motivation to change and, 158–159
partial lies and, 162
patient's absolute otherness and, 167–168
"pockets of meaning" element in, 70, 72, 73,
  159, 198
psychological equipment deficits and,
  166–167
reflections regarding, 169
respect for use of time and, 161–162
self-medicating patterns and, 156–157, 166
shadow use and, 157, 159–160
shadow use to discontinued use and,
  162–168
shadow use to watchful use, 155–162
stillness capacity and, 164–165
toughness to maintain sense of aliveness
  and, 166
Moderation Management (MM), 62

Nalmefeme, SUD treatment, 90
Naltrexone, SUD treatment, 90, 94, 102
National Institute on Drug Abuse
  (NIDA), 88
Natural history
  classes of substances and, 92–110
  definition of, 197
Need for intoxication
  as "*fourth drive*," 1, 134
  See also Fourth drive; Nonproblematic
    use (NPU)
Nembutal, 102
Neuroscience
  chemical structures of drug molecules and, 83
  endocannabinoids and, 83, 84 (table), 88
  endogenous neurotransmitters and, 83–85
  how drugs and alcohol work and, 83–85,
    84 (table)
  neurotransmitters and, 83, 105

NIDA. *See* National Institute on Drug Abuse
  (NIDA)
Non-substance-related disorder
  DSM-5 diagnostic criteria and, 50–51
  See also Gambling disorder
Nonpathological use (NPU, DSM-5), 41,
  53–54, 145, 145 (table)
Nonproblematic use (NPU, DSM-5), 47,
  49, 134
  case study, Ashley, 147–148
  case study, Donya, 148
  case study, Joanne, 149–150
  case study, Dr. Rebecca Simon, 148–149
  reflections regarding, 150
Nonsteroidal anti-inflammatory drugs
  (NSAIDs), 108
Norepinephrine, 83, 84 (table), 85
NPU. *See* Contemporary concepts;
  Nonpathological use (NPU, DSM-5);
  Nonproblematic use (NPU)
NSAIDs (nonsteroidal anti-inflammatory
  drugs), 108

Obama, Barack, 87, 88
Online drug availability
  dealing in real life (IRL) *vs.,* 86
  drug substitutes and, 86
  Drugs 2.0 (Power) and, 86
  Ecstasy/MDMA and, 86, 104
  legal highs and, 88
  mephedrone, 86–87
  ring substitution and, 86
  spice synthetic marijuana and, 87–88
Opioids
  neurotransmitter systems and, 84 (table)
  reference guide to, 100–102
Ordinary passions concept, 6, 41, 76, 137, 197

P/SUD
  ambivalence and, 195
  authority and, 195
  definition of, 198
  depending on others and, 144
  discounting and, 196
  listing to, 130
  psychoanalytic attitude and, 198
  registering impacts and, 137
  self-medication theories and, 198
  term use, xxv